THE TEMPLE HAGGADAH

THE PASSOVER HAGGADAH

THE TEMPLE HAGGADAH

Israel Ariel

The Temple Institute
Carta • Cana

Co-published by:

The Temple Institute • Carta • Cana — All in Jerusalem

Copyright © 1996
Carta, The Israel Map and Publishing Company Ltd., Jerusalem

All rights reserved. No part of this book may be reprinted or reproduced or utilized in any form or by any electronic, mechanical, or other means now known or hereafter invented, including photocopying and recording, or in any information storage or retrieval system, without permission in writing from the publishers.

Translated from the Hebrew by Chaim Richman

Hebrew script: Ada Yardeni

Design: Eli Kellerman

Editor: Barbara Ball

All the drawings and photographs were prepared specially for this Haggadah by The Temple Institute.

Drawings: George Berdichevsky, Dmitry Baranovsky, Grigory Vechlis, and Michael Putilov

Artisans: Gadi Nataf and Chaim Odem (gold and silver vessels); S. Mishali "Y'dei Uman" (copper vessels); Harrari Family (musical instruments)

Photographs: Ya'acov Harlap

Color separations: Scanli, Tel Aviv

Plates: Printone, Jerusalem

ISBN 965 – 220 – 340 – 8

Printed in Israel

PREFACE

Of all the highlights on the Jewish calendar, it is certainly the holiday of Passover with which people are the most familiar. It is recalled as a joyous family holiday, with several generations gathered together around the Seder table for the recitation of the *Haggadah*—the story of the ancient Israelites' Exodus from Egypt. The holiday requirement of the eating of matzah, the unleavened bread which alludes to the Jews' affliction under Egyptian bondage, is a well-known cultural motif, as is the bitter herb and the posing of the "four questions" by the young children. Surely, of all the sacred seasons of the Lord which the Jewish people are instructed to observe in the pages of the Bible, even those who are not well-versed in Scripture have some recognition of the character and spirit of Passover.

But many would indeed be surprised to learn that the Passover celebrated today by Jews the world over bears little resemblance to the Passover Festival which was observed during the golden age of Jewish scholarship—the era of Jerusalem's Second Temple. This was the time when the Holy City served as the spiritual center for a vast segment of mankind, Gentiles as well as Jews; the very name "Jerusalem" shone forth like a beacon to a world seeking spiritual meaning.

It is this difference which we seek to address through this work, by recovering some of the "lost" details, and hopefully some of the spirit and meaning, of the Passover which was so scrupulously—and joyously—observed by the men and women, great and small, who peopled the Jewish nation during the first century.

This work is designed to be something of an explanation of the Passover *Haggadah*, which has been the central theme of the Seder night in every Jewish home since the nation's very inception. But as we shall see, it is more than an instrument of explanation and commentary; it is a tool of discovery. For just as the holiday of Passover which is celebrated in our time veritably pales by comparison to that of Temple times, so too, the holiday's main vehicle of communication, the *Haggadah*, cannot possibly be appreciated unless it is understood within the framework of its original context and setting—the vast spiritual world which was Jerusalem's glorious Second Temple.

Some have the impression that the *Haggadah* is some type of prayerbook, or the written record of a proscribed ritual. The truth is far from this, for the very word "*haggadah*" comes from the Hebrew "to tell"—just as it is used in Scripture in the form of "And you shall tell your children." This reveals to us the true nature and character of the *Haggadah*—it was designed to be used by the participants who made the pilgrimage to Jerusalem to offer the Passover sacrifice in the Holy Temple, as required by God.

But with the destruction of the Second Temple by Rome in the year 70 CE, much of the *Haggadah*'s distinct and original flavor and character—let alone its inner meaning—has been lost. Indeed, the Seder night, which has been observed by every subsequent generation, is sorely lacking the evening's most important details: gone is the joyous holiday assemblage of pilgrims in Jerusalem; the eating of the holiday and Passover sacrifices; and many other unique customs which were kept in the time of Jerusalem's glory—when the Holy Temple stood.

It is the vacuum created by the Temple's destruction that this *Haggadah* humbly seeks to illuminate. Its goal, through description and illustration, is an attempt at filling the gap of missing "Temple consciousness" so sorely lacking in our time.

We shall see that the central theme of the Passover in Temple times was the Passover sacrifice. Through story and picture, we have tried to recreate something of this experience, the atmosphere of joy and the feeling of true freedom which those festive pilgrims experienced in Jerusalem during the magnificent era of the Second Temple.

THE PASSOVER HAGGADAH

and Its Symbolism

Reminders of Slavery in Egypt

Broken matzah—a recollection of the hardships of Egyptian bondage.

Bitter herbs—to remind us that "they embittered their lives with hard labor."

Haroseth mixture—to recall the cement and bricks.

Distribution of nuts.

8

The contents of the plate can be seen as consisting of two categories:

Reminders of the Holy Temple

The Seder Plate

Shankbone—a reminder of the Passover sacrifice.

Hard-boiled egg—to recall the *hagigah* festival sacrifice.

The Plate is Arranged According to the Custom of the ARI, Rabbi Isaac Luria.

***Afikoman*—a reminder of both sacrifices.**

Dipping the green herbs.

There are several unusual customs whose purpose is to keep the young children awake and interested, by keeping them in a state of constant wonderment—such as the distribution of nuts, and dipping the green herbs before eating.

9

קַדֵּשׁ · וּרְחַץ · כַּרְפַּס · יַחַץ
מַגִּיד · רָחְצָה · מוֹצִיא · מַצָּה
מָרוֹר · כּוֹרֵךְ · שֻׁלְחָן עוֹרֵךְ
צָפוּן · בָּרֵךְ · הַלֵּל · נִרְצָה

קַדֵּשׁ

מוזגין לו כוס ראשון ומקדש עליו. המצות מכוסות

הנני מוכן ומזומן לקיים מצוות כוס ראשון של ארבעה כוסות, כנגד לשון ראשון של ארבעה לשונות גאולה, שנאמר: והוצאתי אתכם מתחת סבלות מצרים.

בשבת מתחיל כאן

וַיְהִי־עֶרֶב וַיְהִי־בֹקֶר

יוֹם הַשִּׁשִּׁי: וַיְכֻלּוּ הַשָּׁמַיִם וְהָאָרֶץ וְכָל־צְבָאָם:
וַיְכַל אֱלֹהִים בַּיּוֹם הַשְּׁבִיעִי מְלַאכְתּוֹ אֲשֶׁר עָשָׂה
וַיִּשְׁבֹּת בַּיּוֹם הַשְּׁבִיעִי מִכָּל־מְלַאכְתּוֹ אֲשֶׁר עָשָׂה:
וַיְבָרֶךְ אֱלֹהִים אֶת־יוֹם הַשְּׁבִיעִי וַיְקַדֵּשׁ אֹתוֹ כִּי בוֹ
שָׁבַת מִכָּל־מְלַאכְתּוֹ אֲשֶׁר־בָּרָא אֱלֹהִים לַעֲשׂוֹת:

בָּרוּךְ אַתָּה יְיָ אֱלֹהֵינוּ
מֶלֶךְ הָעוֹלָם
בּוֹרֵא
פְּרִי
הַגָּפֶן

בָּרוּךְ אַתָּה יְיָ אֱלֹהֵינוּ מֶלֶךְ הָעוֹלָם אֲשֶׁר בָּחַר
בָּנוּ מִכָּל עָם וְרוֹמְמָנוּ מִכָּל לָשׁוֹן וְקִדְּשָׁנוּ בְּמִצְוֹתָיו
וַתִּתֶּן לָנוּ יְיָ אֱלֹהֵינוּ בְּאַהֲבָה שַׁבָּתוֹת לִמְנוּחָה וּמוֹעֲדִים
לְשִׂמְחָה חַגִּים וּזְמַנִּים לְשָׂשׂוֹן אֶת יוֹם הַשַּׁבָּת הַזֶּה וְאֶת
יוֹם חַג הַמַּצּוֹת הַזֶּה זְמַן חֵרוּתֵנוּ בְּאַהֲבָה מִקְרָא קֹדֶשׁ
זֵכֶר לִיצִיאַת מִצְרָיִם כִּי בָנוּ בָחַרְתָּ וְאוֹתָנוּ
קִדַּשְׁתָּ מִכָּל הָעַמִּים וְשַׁבָּת וּמוֹעֲדֵי קָדְשֶׁךָ בְּאַהֲבָה וּבְרָצוֹן
בְּשִׂמְחָה וּבְשָׂשׂוֹן הִנְחַלְתָּנוּ
בָּרוּךְ אַתָּה יְיָ מְקַדֵּשׁ הַשַּׁבָּת וְיִשְׂרָאֵל וְהַזְּמַנִּים

במוצאי שבת יאמר הבדלה לפני ברכת 'שהחיינו'

בָּרוּךְ אַתָּה יְיָ אֱלֹהֵינוּ מֶלֶךְ הָעוֹלָם
שֶׁהֶחֱיָנוּ וְקִיְּמָנוּ וְהִגִּיעָנוּ לַזְּמַן הַזֶּה

המסובים שותים את כל היין שבכוס בהסיבת שמאל, ומי שקשה עליו השתייה ישתה רוב 'רביעית' (כארבעים וחמישה סמ"ק, כשליש עד חצי כוס תה ממוצעת).

הבדלה למוצאי שבת

בָּרוּךְ אַתָּה יְיָ אֱלֹהֵינוּ מֶלֶךְ הָעוֹלָם
בּוֹרֵא מְאוֹרֵי הָאֵשׁ

בָּרוּךְ אַתָּה יְיָ אֱלֹהֵינוּ מֶלֶךְ הָעוֹלָם
הַמַּבְדִּיל בֵּין קֹדֶשׁ לְחֹל בֵּין אוֹר לְחֹשֶׁךְ
בֵּין יִשְׂרָאֵל לָעַמִּים
בֵּין יוֹם הַשְּׁבִיעִי לְשֵׁשֶׁת יְמֵי הַמַּעֲשֶׂה
בֵּין קְדֻשַּׁת שַׁבָּת לִקְדֻשַּׁת יוֹם טוֹב הִבְדַּלְתָּ
וְאֶת יוֹם הַשְּׁבִיעִי מִשֵּׁשֶׁת יְמֵי הַמַּעֲשֶׂה קִדַּשְׁתָּ
הִבְדַּלְתָּ וְקִדַּשְׁתָּ אֶת עַמְּךָ יִשְׂרָאֵל בִּקְדֻשָּׁתֶךָ
בָּרוּךְ אַתָּה יְיָ הַמַּבְדִּיל בֵּין קֹדֶשׁ לְקֹדֶשׁ

וּרְחַץ

נוטל ידיים בלא ברכה.

כַּרְפַּס

נוטל כרפס פחות מ'כזית' (כעשרים ושבעה גרם) לאיש לטיבול ראשון, ומטבל במי מלח או בחומץ ומברכים:

בָּרוּךְ אַתָּה יְיָ אֱלֹהֵינוּ מֶלֶךְ הָעוֹלָם בּוֹרֵא פְּרִי הָאֲדָמָה

(ומכוון לפטור בברכה זו גם את המרור)

יַחַץ

בוצע את המצה האמצעית לשנים. את החלק הגדול מצניע לסוף הסעודה, לאכלו כזכר לקרבן פסח וכזכר לקרבן חגיגה הבא עמו. את החלק הקטן משאיר במקומו כ'לחם עוני' לברכת 'אכילת מצה'.

The Order of the Seder

KADESH—The *Kiddush* is recited over wine.

U-REHATS—The hands are washed in preparation for eating the herbs.

KARPAS—Eating the green herbs.

YAHATS—Breaking the middle matzah.

MAGGID—Reciting the *Haggadah*.

RAHTSAH—The hands are washed and a blessing is recited, before eating the matzah.

MOTSI—The blessing is said over the matzah.

MATZAH—The special blessing for the commandment of eating matzah, then the maztah is eaten.

MAROR—Eating the bitter herbs.

KOREKH—Eating a sandwich of matzah and bitter herbs combined.

SHULHAN OREKH—The meal.

TSAFUN—The *afikoman* is eaten.

BAREKH—Reciting the Grace after Meals.

HALLEL—The remaining psalms of the *Hallel* prayer are recited.

NIRTSAH—The Seder is concluded.

KADESH — Sanctification

(The first cup of wine is filled and the Kiddush is recited over it. At this time, the matzot should be covered.)

On Sabbath, begin here:

And it was evening and it was morning, the sixth day. And the heavens and earth, and all their components, were completed. And on the seventh day, God finished all the work that He had done; He ceased on the seventh day from all the work that He had been doing. And God blessed the seventh day and declared it to be holy, for it was on this day that God rested from all His work which God created and made *(Genesis 2:1–3).*

On a weekday, begin here:

**Blessed are You, O Lord our God,
King of the universe,
who created the fruit
of the vine.**

Blessed are You, O Lord our God, King of the universe, who has chosen us from all peoples, and exalted us above all languages, and sanctified us by His commandments. With love, You have given us, O Lord our God, *(on Sabbath say, Sabbaths for rest and)* days for joy, festivals and seasons for gladness; *(on Sabbath, this day of rest and)* this day of the feast of *matzot*, the season of our freedom—a holy convocation, *(on Sabbath, in love)* a remembrance of the Exodus from Egypt. For You have chosen us and sanctified us above all peoples, and with *(on Sabbath, love and favor,)* joy and gladness, You have given us Your *(Sabbath and)* holy festivals as an inheritance. Blessed are You, O Lord, who sanctifies *(the Sabbath,)* Israel and the festive seasons.

If the festival falls at the end of the Sabbath, Havdalah is said before the She-Heheyanu blessing, which is as follows:

**Blessed are You, O Lord our God, King of the universe,
who has kept us alive, and sustained us,
and brought us to this season.**

All of those assembled should drink all the wine in the cup, while reclining on the left side. If one finds it difficult to drink the entire cup, he should drink a "rivi'it" (approximately 1/3 to 1/2 the contents of the average teacup) as the minimum requirement.

Havdalah for Saturday night:

Blessed are You, O Lord our God, King of the universe, who created the lights of fire.

Blessed are You, O Lord our God, King of the universe, who distinguishes between holy and profane, between light and darkness, between Israel and the nations, and between the seventh day and the six days of toil. You have also made a difference between the holiness of the Sabbath and the holiness of the festivals, sanctified the seventh day above the six days of labor, and separated and sanctified Your people Israel with Your holiness. Blessed are You, O Lord our God, who differentiates between holy and holy.

U-REHATS — First Washing of the Hands

The host performs the ritual handwashing, but without the usual blessing.

KARPAS — Greens

The host dips the greens in salt water or vinegar and distributes small portions to everyone (each portion should be less than a k'zayit—about 27 grams). Everyone then recites the following blessing, with the intention that it should also include the maror, the bitter herbs, which will soon be eaten:

**Blessed are You, O Lord our God, King of the universe,
who created the fruit of the earth.**

YAHATS — Breaking the Middle Matzah

The host breaks the middle matzah into two pieces, hiding the larger half for the afikoman, which will be eaten at the end of the meal as a remembrance for the Passover sacrifice and the festival sacrifice which was offered with it. He returns the smaller half to its place as the "bread of affliction," upon which the blessing will be recited "for eating matzah."

MAGGID — Reciting the Haggadah

The host removes the cover to reveal the matzot, and raises the plate. He then begins the story of the Exodus. He should have the intention in mind of fulfilling the Torah's positive commandment of "And you shall tell your son. . . ."

THIS IS THE BREAD OF AFFLICTION

which our fathers ate
in the land of Egypt.
Let all who are hungry enter and eat,
and all who are needy come
and celebrate the Passover!
This year we are here,
next year in the Land of Israel!
This year we are slaves,
next year free men!

דִּי אֲכָלוּ אַבְהָתָנָא
בְּאַרְעָא דְמִצְרָיִם
כָּל־דִּכְפִין יֵיתֵי וְיֵכֹל
כָּל־דִּצְרִיךְ יֵיתֵי וְיִפְסַח
הָשַׁתָּא הָכָא
לְשָׁנָה הַבָּאָה בְּאַרְעָא דְיִשְׂרָאֵל
הָשַׁתָּא עַבְדֵי
לְשָׁנָה הַבָּאָה בְּנֵי חוֹרִין

---

children; he would not be fulfilling his obligation properly in this manner. Rather, he is commanded to bring joy to the poor and unfortunate as well, as it is written: 'And the Levite, and the stranger, and the orphan and the widow' should also be given food and drink according to his means. Therefore, he must invite Levites to his table, to lift their spirits" (Laws of Hagigah, 2:14).

Obviously, on the 14th of Nisan, when the *hagigah* festival offering is brought to the Temple together with the Passover sacrifice, the Levite, the stranger, the orphan and the widow are invited to eat as well, and in fulfillment of the all-important *mitzvah* to be charitable, the poor are included in the Passover, and given a hearty welcome: "Let all who are hungry, enter and eat, and all who are needy come and celebrate the Passover!"

Next Year—Free Men

The Holy Temple Precedes the Messiah

Upon considering these words of the *Haggadah*, one gets the impression that this sentence is out of context—for it does not appear logical. We would certainly think that it would make more sense to begin with "Next year, may we be free men" and then, "Next year in the Land of Israel." For what is the chronological order of events? Firstly, we would need to "throw off the yoke of our servitude to the nations" and leave the lands of the exile, as free men; and only afterwards would it be possible to "go up" to the Land of Israel, for is this not what transpired in the generation of the Exodus? First the Holy One removed from them the yoke of bondage, as it is stated by the rabbis (BT Rosh HaShanah 11:A): "On Rosh HaShanah, our forefathers' bondage in Egypt ceased." In so doing, Israel was transformed into a free people, celebrating their freedom within Egypt itself—and only afterwards, in the month of Nisan, they left Egypt en route to the Land of Israel.

While this is so, and the Egyptian redemption occurred precisely as mentioned above, there is still nothing to prevent the Final Redemption from occurring in the opposite order, namely: first the Jewish people will come home to the Land of Israel and Jerusalem, even while still in a state of "servitude to the nations," and afterwards they will gain their freedom.

Indeed, it is exactly along these lines that the famed Gaon of Vilna explains the words of the prophet Isaiah (1:27): "*Zion* shall be redeemed with judgment, and *those that return to her*, with righteousness"; initially, the Redemption will come to Jerusalem, and only afterwards, to all of Israel.

The Abudarham commentary explains these opening lines of the *Haggadah* in a similar vein. He explains that first the Jewish people will return to the Land of Israel, but the aspect of "free men" will only take effect with the arrival of the Messiah, and that in turn will occur only once Israel is in her land.

This is the opinion expressed by the sages in the Jerusalem Talmud (Ma'aser Sheni 5:2), where they emphasize that "In the future, the Holy Temple will be rebuilt before the Davidic kingdom is renewed"—in other words, the Temple will be rebuilt before the coming of the Messiah. Actually we find that the Babylonian Talmud also records that this will be the chronological order of events, in Tractate Megillah. There, the rabbis relate that this is the very reason for the order in which the topics

of the *Amidah* prayer of eighteen blessings are arranged. For the blessing of "Who rebuilds Jerusalem" precedes that of "the offspring of David"—because this order reflects the order of Redemption. First Jerusalem and the Holy Temple will be rebuilt, and only afterwards the messianic son of David will arrive. The Talmud's wording is most emphatic: "Since the Temple is rebuilt—David will arrive." Rashi writes that "after Israel returns to the Holy Temple, there to beseech . . . their king, David." The Zohar also says that "the Holy Temple will precede the ingathering of the exiles."

This is the thought behind the *Haggadah*'s opening, "Next year in the Land of Israel." Even if we will be there while yet in a state of servitude, we will celebrate Passover in the Temple, but the main thing is to be there! Only afterwards can we say that "next year we shall be free men"—free from the "yoke of the nations"—and then we will merit for the Final Redemption to occur.

"Tonight, We Eat Only Roasted Meat"

The "Four Questions" in the Time of the Temple, and in Exile

The questions that the *Haggadah* phrased for the son to ask his father during the days in which the Holy Temple stood differ from those which appear in the *Haggadah* after the destruction. For in the era of the Temple, the family that reclined together around the Seder table saw a different sight: two sacrifices were laid out before them, from which they would eat. One was the *hagigah* festival offering, which had been brought to the Temple on the 14th of Nisan; the other was the Passover sacrifice which had been offered afterwards. Therefore, quite naturally, the son would ask: "Father, please explain to me the reason for these two sacrifices, which we eat tonight!"

The boy's question is a good one. In the beginning of the feast, the *hagigah* is served; the Passover sacrifice is partaken of at the conclusion of the meal. Both are served roasted—exclusively—this despite the fact that as opposed to the opinion of Ben Teimah (BT Pesahim 70:A), who maintained that the *hagigah* must only be roasted, it was permissible to cook it, as we discussed in our historical overview. In practical terms, though, the *hagigah* was roasted like the Passover sacrifice, since cooking would require much more preparation, such as salting, firewood, and pots for all the multitudes of pilgrims. Additionally, it takes much longer than roasting to prepare. These are the circumstances which give rise to this "Temple-era question" as quoted in the Mishnah (Pesahim 10:4): "On all other nights we eat meat either roasted, boiled or cooked; why tonight only roasted?" His intention is simply, why do we eat from the meat of two sacrifices this evening, and why must they both be roasted? His curiosity can also be appreciated in light of the fact that at this festive meal, there are many *mitzvot* to fulfill which relate to eating: it is a *mitzvah* to eat matzah, *maror*, and the *hagigah* and Passover sacrifices. In relation to the opportunity for fulfilling commandments during the course of an ordinary evening meal, this is most unusual.

Besides all this, the son sees the appetizer of greens for dipping, which only fuels his curiosity—why are we eating so much tonight? What is the nature of all these courses?

מוזגין כוס שני. אחד המסובים נוטל את הקערה מן השולחן, כדי לעורר את התינוקות שישאלו. עורך הסדר מחלק לילדים קליות ואגוזים כדי לעוררם לשאלה:

מַה נִּשְׁתַּנָּה הַלַּיְלָה הַזֶּה מִכָּל הַלֵּילוֹת

שֶׁבְּכָל־הַלֵּילוֹת אָנוּ אוֹכְלִין חָמֵץ וּמַצָּה
הַלַּיְלָה הַזֶּה כֻּלּוֹ מַצָּה
שֶׁבְּכָל־הַלֵּילוֹת אָנוּ אוֹכְלִין שְׁאָר יְרָקוֹת
הַלַּיְלָה הַזֶּה מָרוֹר
שֶׁבְּכָל־הַלֵּילוֹת אֵין אָנוּ מַטְבִּילִין אֲפִלּוּ פַּעַם אֶחָת
הַלַּיְלָה הַזֶּה שְׁתֵּי פְעָמִים
שֶׁבְּכָל־הַלֵּילוֹת אָנוּ אוֹכְלִין בֵּין יוֹשְׁבִין וּבֵין מְסֻבִּין
הַלַּיְלָה הַזֶּה כֻּלָּנוּ מְסֻבִּין

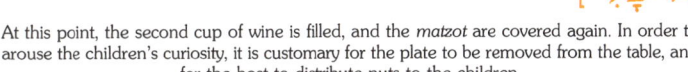

[בזמן המקדש: שֶׁבְּכָל־הַלֵּילוֹת אָנוּ אוֹכְלִין בָּשָׂר צָלִי שָׁלוּק וּמְבֻשָּׁל
הַלַּיְלָה הַזֶּה כֻּלּוֹ צָלִי]

At this point, the second cup of wine is filled, and the *matzot* are covered again. In order to arouse the children's curiosity, it is customary for the plate to be removed from the table, and for the host to distribute nuts to the children.

It is customary for the youngest child who is capable of reciting the questions to ask them, but even if no child is present, the youngest person does so. In some communities, all the children ask the questions, either together or one after the other:

WHY IS THIS NIGHT DIFFERENT FROM ALL OTHER NIGHTS?

On all other nights we eat either *hametz* or matzah,
but on this night only matzah.

On all other nights we eat all kinds of herbs,
but on this night only bitter herbs.

On all other nights we do not dip even once,
but on this night twice.

On all other nights we can eat either sitting or reclining,
but on this night we all recline.

[*In the time of the Holy Temple:* On all other nights we eat meat either roasted, boiled or cooked, but tonight only roasted.]

Let All Who Are Hungry Enter and Eat, and All Who Are Needy Come and Celebrate the Passover!

The Needy Participate in the Passover "Bands"

Because the attribute of "lovingkindness," charitable behavior, is a quality which is emphasized so much in Jewish law and life, it comes as no surprise to us that the poor are invited by the groups of Passover celebrants to join them. Indeed, this type of behavior, so necessary for society to function, is not only praiseworthy, it is a *mitzvah*, the fulfillment of an obligation to be sensitive to the needs of those less fortunate, and to provide for all their needs.

However, this invitation is much more specific—for the Hebrew word *yifsach*, which we have translated as "come and celebrate the Passover," actually has a very specific connotation: it is an invitation to come and partake of the meat of the Passover sacrifice. Now contrary to our initial assumption, this invitation is strange and most out of place indeed—for it seems contrary to *halakhah*, since only those members of each "band" who were appointed over each sacrifice at its outset are allowed to eat from it. How can individuals attach themselves to a group after the fact, when we know that each group accompanied its pre-designated sacrifice on the morning of the eve of the festival, well before the sacrifice is offered! This invitation is being extended to the general public, at night, when everyone is already sitting down to eat! Since the time for its offering has passed, how can members join a group retroactively?

Various explanations are given which attempt to solve this predicament, and it becomes clear that the true answer is based on a *halakhah* which is quoted in the Tosefta. This is quoted in several works, amongst them the *Haggadah Shleimah* by Rabbi M. M. Kasher. It conveys the idea that a certain segment of those participating in each sacrifice are the needy who are supported by public charity.

When we realize just how concerned the elders of Jerusalem were with providing for the needy, we can understand the basis for this *halakhah*. For on Passover eve in Jerusalem, it was customary for the court to purchase a number of reserved places amongst the sacrifices in advance, so that the poor of Israel who otherwise could not join a group would receive a portion of the sacrifice. Thus these places amongst the Passover groups were like a sort of "advance booking" made on behalf of the needy by the court. The court would thus behave like guardians of the poor. That evening, as each "band" assembles to conduct their respective Seder and partake of the Passover offering, at the sound of the declaration "Let all who are hungry enter and eat, and all who are needy come and celebrate the Passover," those individuals would come and join in, claiming those portions which had been provided for them in advance of the sacrifice. Thus they had actually been numbered amongst the participants from the onset, in accordance with Jewish law—and our initial question is pre-empted altogether!

The Mishnah also emphasizes that special caution was to be taken to ensure that the poor of Israel receive enough flour for their *matzot*, and wine as well—"a poor man should not receive less than four cups of wine"—so that they will be able to fulfill their religious obligations. The same practice applied to the sacrifice, as well, and the court's customary procedure ensured that even the destitute would receive a *k'zayit* of meat from the Passover offering.

This insight probably explains why these opening lines of the *Haggadah*, the declaration which invites the poor to come and join in with the Passover bands at the Seder, are conveyed in Aramaic—for this was the language commonly spoken by the masses in the Land of Israel during the era of the Second Temple. The Aramaic language was imported into the land by the earliest returning exiles from Babylon. Although we have explained how this declaration signals to the poor that the time has come for them to participate, it applied equally to all those for whom Aramaic was their mother-tongue—the multitudes of pilgrims who made their way in caravans from Babylon, and converged on Jerusalem to celebrate Passover.

In this light we can appreciate the Torah's requirement that the Passover sacrifice be eaten in a "band," in a large communal meal, as opposed to each man for himself. For by gathering as many people as possible to participate in each "band," the Torah thus brings about harmony and an immense feeling of unity amongst Israel. This feeling amplifies the nation's joy. Such a consideration applies even more to the poverty-stricken; the joy of the Passover celebration is simply not complete unless these individuals are present as part of the community. And if such sensitivity toward the poor should normally be the rule, then it is especially true on this holy night, the night of the Exodus, when we celebrate the transition from slavery to freedom.

Thus Maimonides incorporates these considerations into law: "When one brings festive offerings . . . he should not partake of them alone, joined only by his wife and

מתחיל בגנות

מחזירים את הקערה אל השולחן. עורך הסדר מגלה את המצות 'ומתחיל בגנות' (פסחים קט"ז, א') ופותח ב'עבדים היינו'.

בתשובתו לבן השואל, מספר האב לבנו על אודות ראשית האומה הישראלית, שתחילתה בתרח אבי אברהם, שהיה עובד אלילים. כיצד מתוך טומאת עבודת אלילים קם אברהם אבי האומה והחל לקרוא בשם ה' בעולם. כן יספר האב לבנו כיצד התגלגלו הדברים, וישראל ירדו מצרימה לשנים ארוכות של עבודה קשה, עוני ושעבוד.

עֲבָדִים הָיִינוּ לְפַרְעֹה בְּמִצְרָיִם.

וַיּוֹצִיאֵנוּ יְיָ אֱלֹהֵינוּ מִשָּׁם
בְּיָד חֲזָקָה וּבִזְרֹעַ נְטוּיָה

וְאִלּוּ לֹא
הוֹצִיא הַקָּדוֹשׁ בָּרוּךְ הוּא
אֶת־אֲבוֹתֵינוּ מִמִּצְרַיִם
הֲרֵי אָנוּ וּבָנֵינוּ וּבְנֵי בָנֵינוּ
מְשֻׁעְבָּדִים הָיִינוּ לְפַרְעֹה בְּמִצְרָיִם

וַאֲפִלּוּ
כֻּלָּנוּ חֲכָמִים
כֻּלָּנוּ נְבוֹנִים
כֻּלָּנוּ זְקֵנִים
כֻּלָּנוּ יוֹדְעִים אֶת־הַתּוֹרָה
מִצְוָה עָלֵינוּ
לְסַפֵּר בִּיצִיאַת מִצְרָיִם

וְכָל־הַמַּרְבֶּה לְסַפֵּר בִּיצִיאַת מִצְרַיִם
הֲרֵי זֶה מְשֻׁבָּח

מַעֲשֶׂה
בְּרַבִּי אֱלִיעֶזֶר וְרַבִּי יְהוֹשֻׁעַ
וְרַבִּי אֶלְעָזָר בֶּן עֲזַרְיָה
וְרַבִּי עֲקִיבָא וְרַבִּי טַרְפוֹן
שֶׁהָיוּ מְסֻבִּין בִּבְנֵי בְרָק
וְהָיוּ מְסַפְּרִים בִּיצִיאַת מִצְרַיִם כָּל־אוֹתוֹ הַלַּיְלָה
עַד שֶׁבָּאוּ תַלְמִידֵיהֶם וְאָמְרוּ לָהֶם
רַבּוֹתֵינוּ הִגִּיעַ זְמַן קְרִיאַת שְׁמַע שֶׁל שַׁחֲרִית.

אָמַר רַבִּי אֶלְעָזָר בֶּן עֲזַרְיָה
הֲרֵי אֲנִי כְּבֶן שִׁבְעִים שָׁנָה
וְלֹא זָכִיתִי שֶׁתֵּאָמֵר יְצִיאַת מִצְרַיִם בַּלֵּילוֹת
עַד שֶׁדְּרָשָׁהּ בֶּן זוֹמָא
שֶׁנֶּאֱמַר
לְמַעַן תִּזְכֹּר אֶת־יוֹם צֵאתְךָ מֵאֶרֶץ מִצְרַיִם
כֹּל יְמֵי חַיֶּיךָ
יְמֵי חַיֶּיךָ הַיָּמִים
כֹּל יְמֵי חַיֶּיךָ הַלֵּילוֹת
וַחֲכָמִים אוֹמְרִים
יְמֵי חַיֶּיךָ הָעוֹלָם הַזֶּה
כֹּל יְמֵי חַיֶּיךָ לְהָבִיא לִימוֹת הַמָּשִׁיחַ

בָּרוּךְ הַמָּקוֹם
בָּרוּךְ הוּא
בָּרוּךְ שֶׁנָּתַן תּוֹרָה
לְעַמּוֹ יִשְׂרָאֵל
בָּרוּךְ הוּא

Thus, the style of the questions formulated in our "*Haggadah* of Exile" is different from that of the "*Haggadah* of the Holy Temple." In those days, the son asked questions which were directly related to his desire to understand the commandment he saw before him—the Passover sacrifice. The very nature of that experience deepened the awareness of the Exodus from Egypt. But in our time, the questions in the "*Haggadah* of Exile" are mainly concerned with the explanation for the shankbone and egg, which are merely "Temple reminders," as well as the various singular customs which are practiced this evening, such as leaning. This is all that is left of the "*Haggadah* of Exile."

But it would seem that the true significance of these questions can only be sensed when the Holy Temple stands in its proper place, and the festive participants are able to eat of the festival sacrifices, "with *matzot* and bitter herbs," in Jerusalem. With the destruction of the Temple, the majority of the things eaten at the Seder were demoted from the realm of "obligatory" to that of merely "customary" (with the exception of *matzot*), for without the Temple, even the *mitzvah* of eating *maror* is no longer a Torah obligation. Gone, too, are the *mitzvot* of eating from the *hagigah*, and the roasted Passover sacrifice. What, then, is left for the son to question?

The plate is returned to the table, and the host reveals the *matzot*. The host then "begins with derogatory remarks" (BT Pesahim 116:A) with the words "we were slaves."

By way of answering his son's question, the father begins to recount the earliest history of the Jewish people, which begins with Terah, the father of Abraham. Abraham, the father of our people, sprang forth from the impurity of an idolatrous background—for his own father was an idolator—and began to proclaim God's name in this world. The father explains to his son the progression of events which led to Israel's descent into Egypt for long years of hard labor, affliction and bondage:

BECAUSE WE WERE SLAVES TO PHARAOH IN EGYPT

and the Lord our God brought us out from there "with a mighty hand and an outstretched arm."

And if the Holy One, blessed be He, had not brought our fathers out of Egypt, then we, and our children, and our children's children would still be slaves to Pharaoh in Egypt.

So even if we are
all wise,
all men of knowledge and understanding,
all advanced in years
and all well-versed in the Torah,
we are still nonetheless commanded to relate the story of
the Exodus from Egypt.

And so all those who dwell on the story of the Exodus at great length, they are all the more praiseworthy.

It is related that

Rabbi Eliezer, Rabbi Joshua,
Rabbi Elazar ben Azariah,
Rabbi Akiva and Rabbi Tarfon
once met for the Seder in Bnei Brak and spoke about the Exodus from Egypt all night long, until their students came and said to them: "Masters, the time for reciting the *Shma* of the morning service has arrived!"

Rabbi Elazar ben Azariah said:
"Behold, I am like a man of seventy, yet I was unable to prove why the story of the Exodus from Egypt should be recited at night,
until Ben Zoma explained it.
For it is written:
"That you should remember the day when you came forth out of
the land of Egypt
all the days of your life."
From that, he inferred the following: whereas the expression "the days of your life" would only indicate the days,
"*all* the days of your life"
includes the nights as well.
The sages, however, explain the text in a different way:
"The days of your life" refers to this world only, but "*all* the days of your life" also includes the Messianic era.

Blessed be the All-Present, blessed be He! Blessed be He who gave the Torah to His people Israel, blessed be He!

The Torah speaks about four kinds of sons:

**THE WISE SON,
THE WICKED SON,
THE SIMPLE SON
AND THE SON WHO DOES
NOT KNOW HOW TO ASK.**

כְּנֶגֶד אַרְבָּעָה בָנִים דִּבְּרָה תוֹרָה
אֶחָד חָכָם
וְאֶחָד רָשָׁע
וְאֶחָד תָּם
וְאֶחָד שֶׁאֵינוֹ יוֹדֵעַ לִשְׁאוֹל

What Does the Wise Son Say?

He asks: "What are the testimonies, statutes, and judgments which the Lord our God has commanded you?" *(Deuteronomy 6:20).*

In reply, you should teach him all the ordinances of the Passover, ending with "Do not serve *afikoman* (dessert) after the Passover lamb."

מַה הוּא אוֹמֵר
מָה הָעֵדֹת וְהַחֻקִּים וְהַמִּשְׁפָּטִים אֲשֶׁר צִוָּה יי אֱלֹהֵינוּ אֶתְכֶם
וְאַף אַתָּה אֱמָר־לוֹ כְּהִלְכוֹת הַפֶּסַח
אֵין מַפְטִירִין אַחַר הַפֶּסַח אֲפִיקוֹמָן

The host explains to his son, and to all those present, a sampling of the laws pertaining to the Passover sacrifice, which is eaten on this night in Jerusalem when the Holy Temple is standing. (The illustrations accompanying this *Haggadah* can be utilized for this purpose.)

heaven and you are on the earth . . . therefore, let your words be few" (Ecclesiastes 5:1).

God commands, and it is man's task to fulfill. This is the highest level of wisdom: to understand and to admit that with all our knowledge, with all our sophistication, we do not know at all. "The goal of all knowledge is to know that we know nothing" (Behinat Olam 13:45). All that remains for us is "to learn and teach, to observe and do." This is the Torah's own order: by opening with the wicked son's "question," who attempts to establish his heresy as facts on the ground, and ending with the wise son's question, which establishes that the sacrifices are *hukim*—beyond rhyme and reason. This is the response to the wicked son: we can but fulfill the statutes and laws as we have received them. Indeed, this is his father's immediate answer: "And you shall tell your son: We were slaves to Pharaoh in Egypt . . . and He took us out from there . . . and the Lord commanded us to perform all these *hukim*, for our own benefit, all the days" (Deuteronomy 6:24).

"Do Not Serve Afikoman after the Passover Sacrifice"

Refraining from Sweets at the Meal's Conclusion—Letting the Taste of the *Mitzvah* Remain

This seems to be a strange way to answer the wise son's question. He had asked, "What are the testimonies, statutes, and judgments which the Lord our God has commanded you?" But here, the father seems to be concerned with teaching his son one minute law from amongst many. Indeed, by contrast to the importance of some of the other Passover laws, this particular one he has chosen appears rather peripheral.

For Maimonides, in his introduction to the "Laws of the Passover Sacrifice," enumerates no less than sixteen positive and negative commandments which are to be fulfilled at the time the Passover sacrifice is offered and eaten. Some examples: it must be slaughtered on time, after noon on the fourteenth day; it must be eaten at night, together with matzah and *maror*, it must be eaten roasted and not cooked or boiled; it must be eaten in a "band," and may not be removed from the band; its bones may not be broken; and it is forbidden to leave over from the meat of the sacrifice until morning.

These are only some of the detailed commandments pertaining to the Passover, but out of them all, the *Haggadah* chose this one: that one must not eat *afikoman*, dessert, after eating from the sacrifice. Why was this *halakhah* chosen above all others, to be taught to the wise son?

There are two lessons which the *Haggadah* wishes to impart through this idea. Firstly, the *Haggadah* does not mean to imply that the father should teach his son this law to the exclusion of all the others, but rather, the opposite. This law was chosen as an example precisely because it is applicable to the conclusion of the commandment's performance—that commandment which includes many details of sacrifice, roasting, and eating. The father must teach his son all the laws of the Passover, one by one, until arriving at the very last one, quoted at the conclusion of Tractate Pesahim: "Do not serve *afikoman* after the Passover sacrifice."

And secondly, we are instructed to refrain from partaking of sweets after eating of the Passover sacrifice so that the taste of the *mitzvah* itself should remain in our mouths. Great importance is placed on the small *k'zayit* portion which is eaten at the meal's conclusion—it is to be eaten after one is already satiated from the meal. For it is not eaten out of hunger or desire, but only in order to fulfill a commandment, like a servant who fulfills his master's wishes. As the rabbis said, "I spoke, and they fulfill my wishes" (Rashi on Leviticus 1:9).

It is not the taste of the meat remaining in the mouth which concerns the Torah—it is the taste, the experience, of doing a *mitzvah*, of performing the Creator's will out of love. This is the ideal level of fulfilling the commandments. For the Passover sacrifice in the Holy Temple is not brought because one completely understands the logic behind it, like the wicked son thought; and not out of fear of punishment, or a desire to accrue merit. There is only one objective: to fulfill the commandment—the *hok*—out of a feeling of love and honor for the Creator. This is the highest aspect, "to perform out of love"; the verse "those who love Him go out as mightily as the sun" applies to these individuals (BT Shabbat 88:B). Nothing can overcome the "taste" left in the mouth by fulfilling God's commandments with this type of purity; this is the status of the wise son.

Because He Separates Himself from the People . . . You, Too, Must "Set His Teeth on Edge"

One Who Makes Light of the *Mitzvah* Removes Himself from the Congregation

One negative effect of the wicked son's speech which is felt immediately is that the *ability* to perform the commandment seems to be in doubt. For as long as there are those who remove themselves from the congregation, there is no general consensus amongst Israel to arise as one and renew the Temple service, and bring the Passover sacrifice to Jerusalem. For it would certainly seem that the Holy Temple cannot be rebuilt unless the entire congregation participates in its construction, and the sacrifices cannot be performed unless all of Israel participates—for example, when all of Israel donates the half-shekel to the Temple, the entire nation has participated. But since the wicked son, and those of his ilk, do not lend their hand to the rest of Israel to share in the commandment—and even disagree, and poke fun at it—the commandment cannot be fulfilled.

The issue of congregational participation, as it relates to the subject of the building of the Temple and its service, is discussed in the *Sefer HaHinukh* (Commandment 95). The author writes: "It is a commandment to build the Chosen

What Does the Wicked Son Say?

He asks:
"What do *you* mean by this service?" *(Exodus 12:26).*
By saying "you," and not including himself as well,
he takes himself out of the collective body of the people, and
thus he denies a basic principle of faith.

Therefore you, too, must
"set his teeth on edge" (provoke him),
and tell him: "All of this is because of that which the Lord did for
me when *I* came forth out of Egypt" *(Exodus 13:8),* for if he had
been there, he would not have been redeemed!

רָשָׁע

מַה הוּא אוֹמֵר
מָה הָעֲבוֹדָה הַזֹּאת לָכֶם וְלֹא לוֹ
וּלְפִי שֶׁהוֹצִיא אֶת־עַצְמוֹ מִן הַכְּלָל כָּפַר בָּעִקָּר
וְאַף אַתָּה הַקְהֵה אֶת־שִׁנָּיו וֶאֱמָר־לוֹ
בַּעֲבוּר זֶה עָשָׂה יְיָ לִי בְּצֵאתִי מִמִּצְרָיִם
לִי וְלֹא לוֹ
אִלּוּ הָיָה שָׁם
לֹא הָיָה נִגְאָל

What Does the Wise Son Say?
The Wise and Wicked Sons Are in Conflict Over the Sacrificial Service
In establishing the order of appearance for the four sons, the *Haggadah* places the wise son first. It would seem fitting to begin with this child, for King Solomon—the wisest of all men—stated: "A wise son gladdens his father, but a foolish son is his mother's grief" (Proverbs 10:1). Since a wicked son only causes his parents anguish, we would expect to begin with the one who brings joy. . . .

So, it may surprise us to realize that when the Torah lists these four sons, it does so in the opposite order! The verses begin (Exodus 12:26) with the wicked son's question, placing him first in line—but the wise son's question appears last in the Torah (in Deuteronomy 6:20), and concludes the Torah's listing of the four sons! Why?

It would seem that the wise son's question is more than just a question—it is an answer. It is the answer to the wicked son's "question," which in reality is not a question at all, but a statement of heresy. The Torah begins with his question in the Book of Exodus in order to conclude with a "happy ending"—the wise son, whose words are not only an answer, but a message of consolation and hope as well.

The Jerusalem Talmud (Pesahim 9:4) explains the true meaning of the wicked son's question: "What do you mean by this service? Why must you bother with this business, and put us through this burden year after year?" This son is disgusted with the sacrificial service, and he has the audacity to make fun of the pilgrimage to the Temple in order to offer the Passover sacrifice. He reasons that he is an enlightened individual, who possesses infinitely more understanding than did his own forebears. He knows better. In view of his great wisdom he asks: After all, this service was originally performed in ancient Egypt, at the time of the Exodus . . . but then, it had a specific purpose. It was designed to uproot primitive beliefs which our forefathers may have picked up from the Egyptians—for the latter believed that animals such as sheep and cattle possessed spiritual powers. The ancient Egyptians deified these animals and included them in their idolatrous worship.

Similarly, Maimonides explains (Guide for the Perplexed, Part 3, chs. 32, 46) that this idea of ascribing holiness to animals was widely accepted in those days, and that it is still accepted today in various countries such as India. He goes on to explain that in order to uproot this mistaken belief from the hearts of men, the sacrificial service was established in that particular era as a substitute which was needed at that time. For the Jews at the time of the Exodus, the slaughtering of the sheep, which was holy to their Egyptian hosts, and the placing of its blood on the doorposts, was of paramount significance, for it served to utterly vanquish Egyptian idolatry from the world.

Maimonides makes the additional point that Israel had not yet become accustomed to the abstract belief in One God, and it was difficult for them to dissociate themselves in one fell swoop from the type of service they were familiar with from their surroundings. It would have to be gradual. God therefore decreed that they should be subject to a natural process, whereby they would be able to continue with the style of worship that they had grown accustomed to, but on the condition that they perform it for the sake of Heaven, and not for the sake of idolatry.

But now, hundreds and thousands of years after the Exodus from Egypt, Israel has left these habits far behind. The wicked son reasons that it is high time to cease these practices—"What is this to you?" Why must you insist on keeping up with customs from a bygone era?

The Torah anticipated that one day, sons such as this one would ask these questions. Therefore his question is listed first, before all the others, in order to inform and prepare Israel—even then, at the time of the Exodus—that one day its children would arise and say, "What do you mean by this service?" These children do not ask . . . they do not inquire; they make a statement . . . they establish a fact: the Passover sacrifice is no longer necessary.

In this dispute, it would even appear that the wicked son can corroborate his views by quoting the teachings of Maimonides we have cited, for indeed, the latter's words seem to imply that sacrifices are part of the distant past, and he brings much proof to substantiate his position. Enter the wise son, who will put the wicked son in his place. . . .

What Are the Testimonies, Statutes, and Judgments Which the Lord Our God Has Commanded You?
The Wise Son's Question is the Wicked Son's Answer
The wicked son is self-assured and quite definite in his words, which question the wisdom of fulfilling the Divine commandments, and even wonders aloud if they are eternal—why should they be performed in every generation? In response, the wise son speaks, and his "question" actually cancels out the wicked son's theory, for "the wise son's question is half an answer" (Migdal Oz, Laws of Repentance, ch. 5).

The wise son does not make "statements"; he does not poke fun. The wise son asks: "And it shall come to pass, when your son shall ask you tomorrow, saying. . . ." Even moreso, he requests his father to make his own statement, to teach him the meaning of things and what his duty is. Unlike the wicked son, this son believes that there is a rhyme and reason behind every single commandment the Creator bequeathed to Israel. Yet he also knows that the reasons for many of the Divine commandments are beyond the realm of our comprehension, and that we can never fully understand the Almighty's reasoning. For it is written: "For My thoughts are not your thoughts." But from the very style of his question, we see that the wise son does not attempt to fathom the reason for the commandment. His goal is to simply learn, to understand the details of the commandments: "What are the testimonies, statutes, and judgments which the Lord our God has commanded you?" With this very question itself, the wise son has already answered the wicked son's query—for he emphatically acknowledges that the Holy One's commandments are statutes, *hukim* in Hebrew, meaning, a Divine decree which limited human intellect is incapable of fully comprehending.

Maimonides, too, who attempted to find a satisfactory explanation for the sacrificial system, as he writes in detail in his *Guide for the Perplexed,* arrived at the same conclusion. Thus in *Yad Hazakah* he writes that all of God's commandments in general, and the commandments pertaining to the sacrifices in particular, pertain to the category of *hukim* . . . and cannot be questioned. In his words: "It is fitting for a person to contemplate the ordinances of the holy Torah, and to understand them according to the best of his ability; but as far as those things which he cannot understand, he should take care not to regard them lightly, lest he incur Divine wrath. How much moreso is this true with regard to the commandments which the Holy One decreed to us; one cannot disregard them simply because he does not understand them. Thus the sages state: 'God says, I have decreed laws for you, and you have no permission to question them . . . such as the dietary laws, the red heifer and the scapegoat.' And one should understand that all of the sacrifices fall into this category of *hukim.* The rabbis taught that the entire world only exists on account of the sacrificial service!" (Me'ilah 8:8).

And so the wise son is not too wise; he does not overstep his bounds. He knows that human intellect has its limits; he understands, as the verse states, that "God is in

What Does the Simple Son Say?
He asks: "What is this?" *(Exodus 13:14).*
You should reply: "With a mighty hand,
the Lord brought us out from Egypt,
from the house of bondage" *(Exodus 13:14).*

But as for the Son Who Does Not Know How to Ask,
You must take the initiative, as it is written:
"And you shall tell your son on that day, saying:
'all of this is because of what the Lord did for me when I came
forth out of Egypt'" *(Exodus 13:8).*

תָּם
מַה הוּא אוֹמֵר
מַה־זֹּאת
וְאָמַרְתָּ אֵלָיו
בְּחֹזֶק יָד הוֹצִיאָנוּ יי מִמִּצְרַיִם מִבֵּית עֲבָדִים

fulfilled even if only fifty people or less are present in the Holy Temple (Laws of Passover Sacrifice 1:11). For those fifty who did arrive—they are "the congregation of Israel," and as to those who "willfully refrain from the *mitzvah*, and allow the fourteenth day to pass without bringing the offering—they suffer the penalty of *karet* (to be cut off)," even if they be many. For if they refrained from participating, it is themselves whom they have removed.

Of course, we need to relate to the wicked son, as long as we have an opportunity to engage him, and to draw him close to the Torah and the commandments . . . then we are obligated to do so, lest he be "cast aside" (see II Samuel 14:14). But should he "remove himself" and begin to poke fun, his teeth must be set on edge; he must be distanced. We must help him to correct his ways, but until then, he should not destroy others.

"On Account of This": When the Passover Sacrifice, Matzah and Maror Are Laid Out Before You
In Relating the Story of the Exodus—The Wise Son is Uplifted, the Wicked Son Alienated
The commandment to relate the story of our forefathers' Exodus from Egypt is applicable all year long, not only on Passover. We mention it on many other occasions, and at least twice daily, in the evening and morning service. But this *mitzvah*'s finest hour, and its primary time for fulfillment, is when all the members of the "band" are reclining around the Passover sacrifice, for then they are in the presence of the very vehicle of the *mitzvah*.

Perhaps this in itself is one reason why the Passover sacrifice is partaken of at the meal's conclusion—for as long as it is visible as the center of attention before all those present, it is natural for everyone to continue with the explanation and commentary. As the author of *Shvilei HaLeket* writes, in the time of the Holy Temple the *Haggadah* has the Seder's host declare "when the *Passover sacrifice*, matzah and *maror* are laid out before you. . ."—for the main thrust of the story revolves around the sacrifice.

In this light, we must realize that the wicked son's actions this evening are indeed grave—and they have serious ramifications. For all those present are included in this Passover band and have a portion in the offering; but out of sheer spite, he not only refuses to participate with them but stands contemptuously and mocks them with "What do you mean by this service?" He has "removed himself" from them, by both his word and his deed. In confronting this very phenomenon, the father turns to all those gathered and points to the sacrifice before them: "All of this is because of what the Lord did for *me*"—and not for him. The father stresses that it is in the merit of the very service which is spread before us here this evening, that we were able to leave Egypt. Now it truly becomes clear that had this wicked son been there, he would have declined to participate in the service, and therefore he would not have merited to leave, but would have remained behind.

It is interesting to note the father's expression in responding to this son. He does not say, "for me and not for *you*"—for he does not deem it proper to address the wicked son directly at all. He ignores him. His explanation is actually intended for the benefit of the other sons present; he acts as if the wicked son is not even there. There is no harsher measure of "setting the teeth on edge" than this; the father, children, and all those present are busy with the story and the *Hallel* around the Passover, and they simply ignore the foolish words—and presence—of the wicked son.

When the Passover Sacrifice, Matzah and Maror Are Before You
Children Are Influenced by Teachings—and by Action
The commandment to relate the story of the Exodus to one's children is to be fulfilled in the presence of these three things; they obviously aid in concretizing these concepts and bringing them home. This is the time of "And you shall tell your son," and this is the time for education, for children are not impressed by *words*; they are impressed by *action*. The son is affected by his father's personal example rather than rhetoric; he lets his deeds speak. For "study is not the main thing; action is!" (Avot 1:17). The son observes his father making the pilgrimage to Jerusalem with the entire family; he experiences the hardships of the exhausting trip firsthand; he sees how the sacrifice must be purchased, and checked, and brought to the Temple; how it must be prepared, and offered, and roasted; and the son understands the full significance of serving the Creator with self-sacrifice and dedication. Thus the childen receive their education—not only the "wise" son, but the "simple" one and "he who does not know how to ask," as well. They learn to follow in their father's footsteps; they learn that their desire should be to fulfill the Holy One's commandments as completely as possible. All these tangible deeds are worth ten times more than all the explanations in the world, like the words of the verse indicate (Judges 9:48): "What you have seen, I have done; make haste, and do as I." This is why the *mitzvah* of *Haggadah* is "when the Passover sacrifice, matzah and *maror* are laid out before you."

Even in the wicked son's case, there are times when the proper response— proper from an educational viewpoint—is simply to continue to do. When the latter sees the joyful involvement of all those present, in contrast to his own stark cynicism and detatchment, if he has even the slightest spark of "the fear of God" left within him, he will ultimately awaken, and rejoin the members of his family.

Now, one might think that it is possible to begin relating the story of the Exodus from the first day of the month of Nisan onward, but since the verse states "on that day," it teaches that we are limited to one particular day. "On that day" might suggest that one should relate the story in the daytime, but "all of this" limits it to the time when [*in the time of the Temple:* the Passover sacrifice,] the matzah and *maror* are laid out before you, i.e., Passover eve.

יָכוֹל מֵרֹאשׁ חֹדֶשׁ
תַּלְמוּד לוֹמַר בַּיּוֹם הַהוּא
אִי בַּיּוֹם הַהוּא יָכוֹל מִבְּעוֹד יוֹם
תַּלְמוּד לוֹמַר בַּעֲבוּר זֶה
בַּעֲבוּר זֶה לֹא אָמַרְתִּי
אֶלָּא בְּשָׁעָה שֶׁיֵּשׁ [בזמן המקדש: קָרְבַּן פֶּסַח] מַצָּה וּמָרוֹר מֻנָּחִים לְפָנֶיךָ

מִתְּחִלָּה
עוֹבְדֵי עֲבוֹדָה זָרָה הָיוּ אֲבוֹתֵינוּ

וְעַכְשָׁו
קֵרְבָנוּ הַמָּקוֹם לַעֲבוֹדָתוֹ

IN FORMER DAYS
our fathers
worshiped idols,

BUT NOW
the All-Present has
brought us to His service

House, where we will offer sacrifices to God, and to which the festive pilgrimage shall be made, and to which all of Israel shall gather every year, as it states: 'And you shall build for Me a Sanctuary.'" The author concludes with the words: "And this commandment is in force at a time when the majority of Israel are found in their land. And this commandment is not an obligation on the individual; it is obligatory on the entire congregation."

From the words of the *Sefer HaHinukh* it appears that without the participation of all of Israel, the *mitzvah* of the Temple is not applicable. This would imply that if there is a preponderance of those who resemble the wicked son, who ask "what is this service to you?"—and who complain about this commandment—why then, it would seem that this *mitzvah* cannot be fulfilled at all, Heaven forbid!

In the same way, Rabbi Tzvi Hirsch Hayyot, quoted in *Avodat HaMikdash*, points out that if all of Israel does not contribute the half-shekel to the Temple, it is impossible to fulfill the obligatory daily sacrifice every morning. All this seems to indicate that in a generation wherein the majority of Israel are against the sacrificial service, and many have no intention to donate the half-shekel to the Temple, the entire congregation could be prevented from fulfilling these obligations.

But in reality, this is not the case. If an individual does not desire to participate with the rest of the congregation of Israel in their performance of God's commandments, the body of Israel is unmoved and unchanged—even if those who remain true are in the minority. That one who separates himself from the commandments, it is he who has "removed himself from the congregation and committed heresy," but the damage he causes is only to himself. He cannot affect the entire nation. That which the *Sefer HaHinukh* writes pertaining to the need for all of Israel to participate in order to build the Temple and offer the sacrifices, was not intended to be the final halakhic verdict—and one can find no better proof of this than the historical fact of those who built the Second Temple. For it was only a small minority who returned from Babylonian captivity—altogether, 42,360. The "majority" of Israel refused to return, and the multitudes remained in exile. Despite this, that minority renewed the Temple service. And even within this relatively small congregation there were those who were loathe to participate, yet Ezra and Nehemiah obligated them in a number of Temple-related commandments, such as the separation of *hallah* and the priestly and levitical tithes.

This demonstrates that even if those who are assembled in Jerusalem, and who are interested in the renewal of Temple service, are in the minority—and the majority of Jewry continues to live in the exile—that minority which do occupy themselves with action are considered "the nation of Israel" for all practical purposes. They are fulfilling the commandment, and the others "remove themselves from the congregation."

The author of *Sefer HaHinukh* does not use the expression "at a time when the majority of Israel are found in their land" in a literal sense. His intention is that this commandment can only be fulfilled when many Jews are to be found in Israel; for otherwise, if the land is desolate and abandoned, and few Jews reside there, the *mitzvah* cannot be fulfilled. Physically, it cannot be performed without a large enough congregation.

Those Who Distance Themselves from the Commandments . . . Remove Themselves from the Nation

The *halakhah* does not take into consideration one who is disinterested in the commandments. But not only this—the law establishes that a sacrifice is not accepted from one who deliberately transgresses in public, even if he requests it. Maimonides writes (Laws of Sacrifices 3:4): "We do not accept a sacrifice from a Jew who transgresses the prohibition of idolatry, or who publicly desecrates the Sabbath. If he was accustomed to a certain sin, or this was public knowledge, then he cannot bring an offering for that particular sin." This man who, through his own actions in public, spitefully declared "What is this service to you?"—and denied the commandments of the sacrifices, including the Passover—this same one can no longer bring an offering, even should he so desire.

And so the wicked son is powerless, and ultimately destroys only himself. He not only lacks sufficient power to disturb the commandment or prevent its fulfillment; in the end, he understands that Israel is not interested in his goods. About him it states, "You, too, must set his teeth on edge and tell him: 'It is on account of what God did for *me* when I left Egypt,' me—and not you." Only those who perform the will of the Creator are numbered amongst "the nation of Israel," even if they be the minority. But those who remove themselves from the congregation, they cut themselves off from Israel. Heaven forbid.

The fact is that the *mitzvah* of the Passover sacrifice takes place in the Temple even if the participants are few. Maimonides clarifies that the commandment is

שֶׁנֶּאֱמַר אֶת־אַבְרָהָם
וַיֹּאמֶר יְהוֹשֻׁעַ מֵעֵבֶר הַנָּהָר
אֶל־כָּל־הָעָם וָאוֹלֵךְ אוֹתוֹ בְּכָל־אֶרֶץ כְּנָעַן
כֹּה־אָמַר יְיָ אֱלֹהֵי יִשְׂרָאֵל וָאַרְבֶּה אֶת־זַרְעוֹ
בְּעֵבֶר הַנָּהָר וָאֶתֵּן לוֹ אֶת־יִצְחָק
יָשְׁבוּ אֲבוֹתֵיכֶם מֵעוֹלָם וָאֶתֵּן לְיִצְחָק
תֶּרַח אֲבִי אַבְרָהָם וַאֲבִי נָחוֹר אֶת־יַעֲקֹב וְאֶת־עֵשָׂו
וַיַּעַבְדוּ אֱלֹהִים אֲחֵרִים וָאֶתֵּן לְעֵשָׂו אֶת־הַר שֵׂעִיר
וָאֶקַּח אֶת־אֲבִיכֶם לָרֶשֶׁת אוֹתוֹ

וְיַעֲקֹב וּבָנָיו
יָרְדוּ מִצְרָיִם

בָּרוּךְ שׁוֹמֵר הַבְטָחָתוֹ לְיִשְׂרָאֵל
בָּרוּךְ הוּא

שֶׁהַקָּדוֹשׁ בָּרוּךְ הוּא חִשַּׁב אֶת־הַקֵּץ
לַעֲשׂוֹת כְּמָה שֶׁאָמַר לְאַבְרָהָם אָבִינוּ
בִּבְרִית בֵּין הַבְּתָרִים
שֶׁנֶּאֱמַר
וַיֹּאמֶר לְאַבְרָם יָדֹעַ תֵּדַע כִּי־גֵר יִהְיֶה זַרְעֲךָ
בְּאֶרֶץ לֹא לָהֶם
וַעֲבָדוּם וְעִנּוּ אֹתָם אַרְבַּע מֵאוֹת שָׁנָה
וְגַם אֶת־הַגּוֹי אֲשֶׁר יַעֲבֹדוּ דָּן אָנֹכִי

וְאַחֲרֵי־כֵן יֵצְאוּ בִּרְכֻשׁ גָּדוֹל

(*Overleaf*) **The son poses the question: "Tonight, why do we eat only roasted meat?"** On the Seder night in Jerusalem during the time of the Temple, the *hagigah* sacrifice, the festival offering, is placed on the table—roasted. Two participants can be seen bringing the Passover sacrifice to the table. The son asks one of the famous Four Questions: "Why on all other nights we eat meat either roasted, boiled or cooked, but on this night only roasted?"

As it is said:
"And Joshua said
to all the people:
thus says the Lord God of Israel,
your fathers dwelled on
the other side of the river (the Euphrates) in olden times,
even Terah, the father of Abraham, and the father of Nachor;
and they served other gods.
And I took your father Abraham
from the other side of the river,
and let him go throughout all the land of Canaan,
and multiplied his seed,
and gave him Isaac;
and I gave to Isaac,
Jacob and Esau;
and I gave Mount Seir to Esau
to possess it;

**but Jacob and his children
went down to Egypt"** *(Joshua 24:2–4).*

Blessed be He who fulfills His promise to Israel! Blessed be He!

For the Holy One, blessed be He, determined the end
of the captivity so that He could fulfill what He had said to
Abraham our forefather
in the "Covenant between the Portions":
"And He said to Abram,
Know of a surety that your seed shall be a stranger
in a land which is not theirs,
and shall serve them,
and they shall afflict them four hundred years.
And also that nation, whom they shall serve, I will judge;

and afterwards they shall come out with great wealth"

(Genesis 15:13–14).

"Blessed Be He Who Fulfills His Promise to Israel!"
Abraham Received a Covenant That the Land Will Be for His Children . . . But Only on Condition That Israel Will Build the Temple

"Blessed be He who fulfills His promise to Israel! Blessed be He! For the Holy One, blessed be He, determined the end of the captivity so that He could fulfill what He had said to Abraham our forefather in the 'Covenant between the Portions': '. . .Know of a surety that your seed shall be a stranger . . . and afterwards they shall come out with great wealth'" (Genesis 15:13–14).

The night of Passover is called "a night of vigil" (Exodus 12:42). And just as the "Covenant between the Portions" was conducted at night—at midnight on Passover, to be precise—so too, Israel's redemption from Egypt happened at midnight on Passover night, which was the exact end of the period which God had reckoned. The very night upon which God revealed himself to Abraham was the 15th of Nisan, and it was upon this night that the Holy One decreed for his children to descend into Egypt. At exactly midnight on this very night, 430 years later, the nation of Israel left Egypt. In the succinct language of the *Mechilta* (Exodus 12:40; and Nahmanides): "On this night God said to our forefather, Abraham: 'Abraham! Behold! I now redeem your children!' When the end came, they were not detained."

The Exodus from Egypt to the Land of Israel was the fulfillment of a Divine oath, as the verse states (ibid.), "but the fourth generation shall return to here." Still in all, without the sacrifices the Redemption would not have occurred—for it was the merit of the blood of the Passover sacrifice offered by Israel in Egypt which stood for them, and enabled them to leave (see our comments further on). Likewise, it was in the merit of the future sacrifices that Israel was destined to offer in the Land which stood for them and enabled them to inherit the Land of Israel, continuing to live there for hundreds of years, in spite of their sinful state.

The sages reveal this concept in the Midrash, in explaining the true nature of Abraham's question to God, "How shall I know that I will inherit?" (Genesis 15:8). They make it clear that Abraham did not mean to doubt the word of God, Heaven forbid—rather, the intention of his question was "in what merit will my children be allowed to continue living in the Land?" (see Rashi ibid., also Genesis Rabbah 44:17).

And the Holy One answered Abraham: "In the merit of the sacrifices!"—meaning, in the merit of those sacrifices which Israel is destined to bring to the Tabernacle at Nob, Shiloh and Gibeon, and afterwards, in Jerusalem's Holy Temple. It is this merit which atones for Israel, and allows its people continued presence in the Land, despite their sins and backsliding.

This is the very explanation for the symbolic action which Abraham was commanded to perform as an answer to his own question. God told him: "Take for Me a heifer, three years old"—the Midrash teaches that this is an allusion to the sacrifice of the Day of Atonement; and "a goat three years old"—this is a reference to the offerings of the three festivals; and "a ram three years old"—these are the three types of ram used in the sin offering; "and a turtledove, and a young pigeon"—these are the various sacrifices brought from these species. Through these allusions, the founder of the nation was guaranteed that if his children continue their performance in the Holy Temple, their inheritance will be passed down to the next generations, and their presence in the Land will continue.

Simply put, when Abraham phrased his query of "how will I know that I will inherit," his real concern was "how do I know that my children shall possess this land as an eternal inheritance?" Thus the Holy One's answer: Build Me a Temple! And in the merit of the sacrifices to be brought there, you shall be established in the Land! The first sacrifice ever to be brought collectively by the nation of Israel was the Passover sacrifice, while yet in Egypt. In its merit, Israel was liberated and went from slavery to freedom. The Tabernacle, and the offerings which the Israelites brought in the desert at the time they entered into the Land, played the role of guarantor for Israel's continued presence in the Land, for these offerings have the power to atone for each of their sins, cleansing them from their own iniquity. That is, until the burden becomes too heavy, this leads to destruction, Heaven forbid. After all, every "covenant," every pact or bond, is made between two sides; each has a responsibility.

Here, too, the Holy One assures Abraham: My part of this covenant is to give this land to your descendants, as testified to by the words of conclusion in this section of the Torah, the section of the "Covenant between the Portions" (ibid. 18): "To your seed have I given this land . . . from the river of Egypt unto the great river, the Euphrates"—but this is only on condition that you keep up your end of the agreement: erect a sanctuary in this land, and offer the sacrifices.

וְהִיא שֶׁעָמְדָה לַאֲבוֹתֵינוּ וְלָנוּ
שֶׁלֹּא אֶחָד בִּלְבָד עָמַד עָלֵינוּ לְכַלּוֹתֵנוּ
אֶלָּא שֶׁבְּכָל דּוֹר וָדוֹר עוֹמְדִים עָלֵינוּ לְכַלּוֹתֵנוּ
וְהַקָּדוֹשׁ בָּרוּךְ הוּא מַצִּילֵנוּ מִיָּדָם

צֵא וּלְמַד
מַה בִּקֵּשׁ לָבָן הָאֲרַמִּי
לַעֲשׂוֹת לְיַעֲקֹב אָבִינוּ
שֶׁפַּרְעֹה לֹא גָזַר אֶלָּא עַל הַזְּכָרִים
וְלָבָן בִּקֵּשׁ לַעֲקֹר אֶת הַכֹּל

שֶׁנֶּאֱמַר
אֲרַמִּי אֹבֵד אָבִי
וַיֵּרֶד מִצְרַיְמָה
וַיָּגָר שָׁם
בִּמְתֵי מְעָט
וַיְהִי־שָׁם לְגוֹי
גָּדוֹל עָצוּם
וָרָב

וַיֵּרֶד מִצְרַיְמָה
אָנוּס עַל פִּי הַדִּבּוּר

וַיָּגָר שָׁם
מְלַמֵּד שֶׁלֹּא יָרַד יַעֲקֹב אָבִינוּ
לְהִשְׁתַּקֵּעַ בְּמִצְרַיִם
אֶלָּא לָגוּר שָׁם

שֶׁנֶּאֱמַר וַיֹּאמְרוּ אֶל־פַּרְעֹה לָגוּר בָּאָרֶץ בָּאנוּ
כִּי־אֵין מִרְעֶה לַצֹּאן אֲשֶׁר לַעֲבָדֶיךָ
כִּי־כָבֵד הָרָעָב בְּאֶרֶץ כְּנָעַן
וְעַתָּה יֵשְׁבוּ־נָא עֲבָדֶיךָ בְּאֶרֶץ גֹּשֶׁן

בִּמְתֵי מְעָט
כְּמָה שֶׁנֶּאֱמַר
בְּשִׁבְעִים נֶפֶשׁ יָרְדוּ אֲבֹתֶיךָ מִצְרָיְמָה
וְעַתָּה שָׂמְךָ יְיָ אֱלֹהֶיךָ כְּכוֹכְבֵי הַשָּׁמַיִם לָרֹב

וַיְהִי־שָׁם לְגוֹי
מְלַמֵּד שֶׁהָיוּ יִשְׂרָאֵל מְצֻיָּנִים שָׁם

גָּדוֹל עָצוּם
כְּמָה שֶׁנֶּאֱמַר
וּבְנֵי יִשְׂרָאֵל פָּרוּ וַיִּשְׁרְצוּ
וַיִּרְבּוּ וַיַּעַצְמוּ בִּמְאֹד מְאֹד וַתִּמָּלֵא הָאָרֶץ אֹתָם

וָרָב
כְּמָה שֶׁנֶּאֱמַר רְבָבָה כְּצֶמַח הַשָּׂדֶה נְתַתִּיךְ
וַתִּרְבִּי וַתִּגְדְּלִי וַתָּבֹאִי בַּעֲדִי עֲדָיִים
שָׁדַיִם נָכֹנוּ וּשְׂעָרֵךְ צִמֵּחַ וְאַתְּ עֵרֹם וְעֶרְיָה
וָאֶעֱבֹר עָלַיִךְ וָאֶרְאֵךְ מִתְבּוֹסֶסֶת בְּדָמָיִךְ
וָאֹמַר לָךְ בְּדָמַיִךְ חֲיִי וָאֹמַר לָךְ בְּדָמַיִךְ חֲיִי

---

detail at great length; instead, he abbreviates his speech, and recites only the verse of "My father was a homeless Aramean..."—and this to accommodate all the multitudes of pilgrims who arrive on these two festivals.

But the night of Passover is something else altogether. For at that hour, while reclining comfortably at the Seder table, with the sacrifice and Seder plate placed before him, one is specifically commanded to "tell" all those gathered, to extend and protract the story of the Exodus—to describe and to illustrate to all, just how Abraham's covenant was indeed fulfilled. This is the time for an expansive frame of mind, in order to prolong the explanation of these verses.

For now, the Jew sits together with his family in Jerusalem, the very city which the Almighty informed Abraham He would rest His presence in. Now the father tells his children the whole story, the full story: how our fathers descended to Egypt, how the Egyptians enslaved them and tortured them, and finally, how Israel returned to its land—and to Jerusalem.

Thus, the *Haggadah*, together with the Passover sacrifice, finds full expression through word and action—and this combination of the spoken word together with deed has the strength of many witnesses to demonstrate that indeed, the Covenant has been fulfilled by all its participants.

The host covers the matzot and raises his cup:

And This Same Promise

has stood by our fathers and ourselves.

For not only one man has risen up against us, but in every generation there are those who have risen up against us to destroy us.

But the Holy One, blessed be He, has delivered us out of their hands!

The host puts down his cup and uncovers the matzot.

Go and Learn

what Laban the Aramean sought to do to our father Jacob! For Pharaoh ordered the destruction of the male children only, while Laban intended to uproot everything!

As it is said:

"The Aramean sought to destroy my father; and he went down into Egypt, and sojourned there, few in number, and there he became a nation, great and mighty, and numerous"

(Deuteronomy 26:5).

"And he went down into Egypt,"
impelled by the word of God,

"and sojourned there,"
which indicates that he did not go down to settle, but only to stay.

As it is said: "And they (Joseph's brothers) said to Pharaoh, 'We have come to sojourn in the land, for your servants have no pastures for their flocks, for the famine is great in the land of Canaan; now therefore, we beseech you, let your servants dwell in the land of Goshen'" *(Genesis 47:4).*

"few in number,"
as it is said: "Your fathers went down into Egypt with seventy souls; now the Lord your God has multiplied you like the stars of heaven" *(Deuteronomy 10:22).*

"And there he became a nation,"
which indicates that the Jews were distinguished as a separate people even in Egypt.

"Great and mighty,"
as it is said: "And the Children of Israel were fruitful, and increased abundantly, and multiplied, and waxed exceedingly mighty, and the land was filled with them" *(Exodus 1:7).*

"My Father Was a Homeless Aramean. . ."

The Haggadah—and the Firstfruits in the Holy Temple

We must wonder, how did this section—the teaching of "My father was a homeless Aramean"—wind up being included in the text of the *Haggadah*? For this section of the Torah is recited by the pilgrims who bring their offering of the firstfruits to the Holy Temple, as recorded in Deuteronomy 26:3. What relevance does this bear on the *Haggadah*, and what is their connection?

A close examination of the verses does indeed illuminate the nature of this connection, from a point of view of both language and context. For the expression of "haggadah," which literally means "to tell," is employed by the Torah in connection to both the commandment of relating the story of the Exodus ("And you shall *tell* your son") and in connection with bringing the firstfruits to the Temple: "And you shall come to the priest who shall be in those days, and you shall say to him: 'I tell this day to the Lord your God, that I have come to the country which the Lord swore to our fathers to give us.'"

Whenever the Torah utilizes the concept of "telling," it always refers to the concept of *a story*. The pilgrim, who arrives at the Temple bearing the offering of his firstfruit, relates how God's promise made at the "Covenant between the Portions" had come to pass—for there God vowed that eventually, at the close of four hundred years, Israel will return to the land of its fathers. Now, this individual who humbly stands before the Presence of God in the Temple, declares before Him the chain of events which began with Israel's descent into Egypt and ended with its return home, and he begins his recitation with the words "*I tell*. . ." and this is the very same type of *Haggadah* which the father must relate to his son, as he fulfills the commandment of "And you shall tell your son" on Passover night.

What beautiful simplicity! The omniscient Creator suffers no lack of knowledge; indeed, He knows all that has transpired in His world since the beginning of time, and the thoughts of all men. He certainly knows this story, as well; yet man stands before his Creator in the Holy Temple, and before the *cohen*, the emissary of the One who causes His Presence to dwell in this place, and he recounts the entire chain of events again, beginning with Jacob's trouble with Laban in Aram-naharaim. He continues and relates the story of Israel's descent into Egypt, and concludes with their return home on an outstretched arm, the veritable fulfillment of the verse "and He brought us to this place"—"a reference to the building of the Holy Temple" (Sifre on Deuteronomy 26:9).

So too, on the holiday of Shavuot or Succoth, when the pilgrim brings his offering of firstfruits and stands in the Temple, this is not the time to recount every

"And numerous,"
as it is said:
"I have caused you to multiply like the bud of the field,
and you have increased and waxed great,
and you have come to excellent ornaments;
your breasts are fashioned, and your hair is grown,
yet you are naked and bare" *(Ezekiel 16:7).*

"And when I passed by you, and saw you polluted
in your own blood, I said to you,
In your blood, live! Yes, in your blood, live!" *(Ezekiel 16:6).*

"In Your Blood, Live!"

The Redemption Blossoms—from the Performance of the Passover Sacrifice in Egypt

"And when I passed by you and saw you polluted in your own blood." The commandment of the Passover sacrifice is unique in that it was given *while yet in Egypt*. All of Israel was collectively entrusted with the performance of a *mitzvah*, though they were not in their own land, even though all the other commandments were given in the Sinai desert, within the Land of Israel. The nation received this commandment through the Revelation of the Divine Presence—there, in the depths of the impurity of Egypt. The sages consider this a point for pondering, and wonder what prompted the Creator to reveal Himself to Moses in the midst of idolatrous Egypt, and to issue the command of the Passover sacrifice?

But in reality, were it not for the merit of this very *mitzvah* that stood up and protected Israel, they would never have left Egypt, for the Divine promise given to Abraham, alone, did not possess the strength and force to extricate the nation from Egypt. It was necessary to "add" the force of some merit, some good deeds as well. This thought is explained in the words of the *Mechilta* (Exodus 12:6):

"'And I passed by you, and looked upon you, and behold—your time was the time of love' (Ezekiel 16:8). This means that the time came for the Holy One to keep the vow which He swore to Abraham, to redeem his children. But how? They did not possess Torah knowledge, or *mitzvot* which they could occupy themselves with—and thereby merit redemption; as it states, 'yet you are naked and bare'—'naked,' possessing no good deeds. And so the Holy One, blessed be He, gave them two commandments: the blood of the Passover sacrifice and the blood of circumcision. Let Israel busy themselves with these two commandments, and they will merit redemption—'And when I passed by you and saw you polluted in your own blood, I said to you, In your blood, live! Yes, in your blood, live!'"

This teaches us that the merit of the forefathers alone is not sufficient to aid the children—Israel must possess their own merit; they must deserve to be redeemed. The merit of the commandments which they performed, the circumcision and the Passover sacrifice, justified God's covenant with Abraham and warranted its fulfillment. It was these *mitzvot* which tipped the balance of the scales in favor of Israel's miraculous redemption.

The Passover Sacrifice and Circumcision: Two *Mitzvot* Incumbent Upon Both Congregation and Individual, and Both Declare the Message of God's Kingdom

These two commandments, the blood of the Passover sacrifice and that of the circumcision, share a common factor: each is a sign for the nation of Israel. The "sign" of circumcision is a physical seal, borne by the body, much like the brand on the garment or body of a slave which enables everyone to identify his master. Israel carries a seal which testifies that they have left the bondage of physicality which Egypt represents, and accepted the Heavenly yoke of the King of kings, the Holy One, blessed be He. They have placed themselves in His service exclusively, body and soul alike, and both are eternally sealed.

This concept is reflected in the blessing which every Jew recites after meals: "We give thanks to You, Lord our God . . . that You took us out from the land of Egypt, and redeemed us from the house of bondage; and for Your covenant which You have sealed in our flesh." We have been liberated from the realm of physical servitude, from the service of human beings, and we have exchanged it for spiritual service—to the true King, the Holy One. The commandment of circumcision which we sealed in our flesh while yet in Egypt bears witness that we are in eternal service to the King of kings, the Holy One, blessed be He.

The blood of circumcision, which rectifies each individual Jew, is contrasted to the blood of the Passover sacrifice, which effected a similiar rectification for the

Bringing the Firstfruits in the Temple This picture depicts the festival pilgrims arriving in the Holy Temple with the offering of the firstfruits. Each pilgrim, together with the priest, lifts this special offering—the first produce of his own field—before the presence of God. After this ceremony, the pilgrim sets his offering down at the southwest corner of the altar. Here he would stand opposite the entrance to the Sanctuary and recite the biblical portion of "My father was a homeless Aramean" (Deuteronomy 26:5). In conclusion, each pilgrim bows down before the Lord on a stone set down especially for this purpose, thanking God for all of His kindnesses.

וַיָּרֵעוּ אֹתָנוּ הַמִּצְרִים
כְּמָה שֶׁנֶּאֱמַר
הָבָה נִתְחַכְּמָה לוֹ פֶּן־יִרְבֶּה
וְהָיָה כִּי־תִקְרֶאנָה מִלְחָמָה וְנוֹסַף גַּם־הוּא עַל־שֹׂנְאֵינוּ
וְנִלְחַם־בָּנוּ וְעָלָה מִן־הָאָרֶץ

וַיְעַנּוּנוּ
כְּמָה שֶׁנֶּאֱמַר
וַיָּשִׂימוּ עָלָיו שָׂרֵי מִסִּים לְמַעַן עַנֹּתוֹ בְּסִבְלֹתָם
וַיִּבֶן עָרֵי מִסְכְּנוֹת לְפַרְעֹה
אֶת־פִּתֹם וְאֶת־רַעַמְסֵס

וַיִּתְּנוּ עָלֵינוּ עֲבֹדָה קָשָׁה
כְּמָה שֶׁנֶּאֱמַר
וַיַּעֲבִדוּ מִצְרַיִם אֶת־בְּנֵי יִשְׂרָאֵל בְּפָרֶךְ

וַנִּצְעַק אֶל־יְיָ אֱלֹהֵי אֲבֹתֵינוּ
כְּמָה שֶׁנֶּאֱמַר
וַיְהִי בַיָּמִים הָרַבִּים הָהֵם וַיָּמָת מֶלֶךְ מִצְרַיִם
וַיֵּאָנְחוּ בְנֵי־יִשְׂרָאֵל מִן־הָעֲבֹדָה וַיִּזְעָקוּ
וַתַּעַל שַׁוְעָתָם אֶל־הָאֱלֹהִים מִן־הָעֲבֹדָה

וַיִּשְׁמַע יְיָ אֶת־קֹלֵנוּ
כְּמָה שֶׁנֶּאֱמַר
וַיִּשְׁמַע אֱלֹהִים אֶת־נַאֲקָתָם
וַיִּזְכֹּר אֱלֹהִים אֶת־בְּרִיתוֹ
אֶת־אַבְרָהָם אֶת־יִצְחָק וְאֶת־יַעֲקֹב

וַיַּרְא אֶת־עָנְיֵנוּ
זוֹ פְּרִישׁוּת דֶּרֶךְ אֶרֶץ כְּמָה שֶׁנֶּאֱמַר
וַיַּרְא אֱלֹהִים אֶת־בְּנֵי יִשְׂרָאֵל
וַיֵּדַע אֱלֹהִים

וַנִּצְעַק אֶל־יְיָ אֱלֹהֵי אֲבוֹתֵינוּ
וַיִּשְׁמַע יְיָ אֶת־קֹלֵנוּ
וַיַּרְא אֶת־עָנְיֵנוּ
וְאֶת־עֲמָלֵנוּ
וְאֶת־לַחֲצֵנוּ

---

entire congregation of Israel at once. "Shall we sacrifice the abomination of Egypt before their eyes, and will they not stone us?" (Exodus 8:22). By having such "holy audacity," slaughtering the Passover lamb and vanquishing Egyptian idolatry, Israel informed the entire world that it will not countenance the existence of idolatry, but will wipe out every such manifestation. As the *Yalkut Shimoni* teaches, "Already on the tenth of the month, the Jews tied the lamb to the foot of their beds. When the Egyptians saw this, it made them faint, for they saw that each Jew took the god of Egypt and slaughtered it before their very eyes. Yet they remained silent."

The observance of the Passover sacrifice is conducted in many "bands," and with a multitude of participants. This is how it was done the first time, in ancient Egypt; this is how it was performed in the Holy Temple—all of Israel gathered together as one. Through this yearly action, God's own people declare anew their relentless battle against the forces of idolatry and darkness in this world.

It was this very action of "slaughtering the god of Egypt" and placing its blood upon the doorposts which rescued the Jewish people from Egypt. When God passed over Egypt, He saw the entrance to the Jewish homes, He saw the blood which served to proclaim that no one in this house has any part of Egyptian idolatry; from this point on we are servants to the God of Israel, and no other. It was the merit of this action which had the power to break through the iron gates of Egypt and blaze the trail to freedom.

This is the secret of why the Holy One chose to reveal Himself to Moses in the midst of Egypt, with all its impurity. For had Israel not observed these commandments, they would not have been redeemed.

The "Merit of the Fathers" Still Requires the "Good Deeds of the Sons"—Together, They Bring the Redemption

The rabbis of the Midrash add that several additional merits also stood in Israel's defense: "they did not change their names, neither did they change their language or their style of dress" (Mechilta, ibid.). These "merits" also share a common demoninator—the careful preservation of Jewish identity. But these actions themselves, with all the distinction which they bring to the Jewish people, are only enough to enable an external distinction between Israel and the nations. On the eve of their departure from Egypt, Israel was required to take an extra step, which would distinguish them from the idolators around them beyond any doubt. The act of circumcision, and the slaughter of the Egyptian deity before their very eyes, were the deeds which demonstrated the essential distinction between these two camps, before the eyes of all. This is what tipped the scale, and indicated that the conditions for the fulfillment of the Divine oath at the "Covenant between the Portions" had been met—the conditions which would now enable Israel to exit Egypt, on the path from slavery to freedom.

This is a lesson for all future generations. The time for the conclusion of the Exile is predetermined, but it is not enough for the time simply to come; it must be bolstered by Israel's practical deeds, commandments and merits of significant worth. Israel will not be redeemed unless they themselves play an active role in bringing the redemption about. They must endeavor to free themselves from the chains of exile through the accrued merit of their own good deeds. Then, they will arouse the Divine will to hasten the time of the "end"—and bring on the Final Redemption.

"And the Egyptians ill-treated us, and afflicted us, and laid hard bondage upon us"

(Deuteronomy 26:6).

"Then we cried to the Lord God of our fathers; the Lord heard our voice, and saw our affliction, our sorrow and our oppression"

(Deuteronomy 26:7).

"And the Egyptians ill-treated us,"
as it is said:
"Come, let us deal wisely with them, lest they should multiply; and it will come to pass that when a war comes about, they will also join with our enemies, and fight against us, and then depart from the land" *(Exodus 1:10).*

"And afflicted us,"
as it is said:
"Therefore they set taskmasters over them to afflict them with their burdens. And they built for Pharaoh treasure cities, Pithom and Raamses" *(Exodus 1:11).*

"And laid hard bondage upon us,"
as it is said:
"And the Egyptians compelled the Children of Israel to serve with rigor" *(Exodus 1:13).*

"Then we cried to the Lord God of our fathers,"
as it is said:
"And it came to pass in the process of time, that the King of Egypt died, and the Children of Israel sighed because of the bondage; and they cried, and their cry came up to God because of the bondage" *(Exodus 2:23).*

"And the Lord heard our voice,"
as it is said:
"And God heard their groaning, and God remembered his covenant with Abraham, Isaac, and with Jacob" *(Exodus 2:24).*

"And He saw our affliction"
refers to the forced separation of man and wife, as it is said:
"And God saw the Children of Israel, and knew their condition" *(Exodus 2:25).*

"And the Egyptians compelled the Children of Israel to serve with rigor" (Exodus 1:13).

וְאֶת־עֲמָלֵנוּ
אֵלּוּ הַבָּנִים כְּמָה שֶׁנֶּאֱמַר
כָּל־הַבֵּן הַיִּלּוֹד
הַיְאֹרָה תַּשְׁלִיכֻהוּ
וְכָל־הַבַּת תְּחַיּוּן

וְאֶת־לַחֲצֵנוּ
זֶה הַדְּחַק כְּמָה שֶׁנֶּאֱמַר
וְגַם־רָאִיתִי אֶת־הַלַּחַץ
אֲשֶׁר מִצְרַיִם
לֹחֲצִים אֹתָם

מסיים בשבח

עורך הסדר 'מסיים בשבח' (פסחים קט״ז, א') ומספר בנפלאות היציאה ממצרים והליכת ישראל במדבר, עד הגיעם ליום בניין בית המקדש בירושלים.

וַיּוֹצִיאֵנוּ יְיָ מִמִּצְרַיִם

בְּיָד חֲזָקָה וּבִזְרֹעַ נְטוּיָה וּבְמֹרָא גָּדֹל וּבְאֹתוֹת וּבְמֹפְתִים

וַיּוֹצִיאֵנוּ יְיָ מִמִּצְרַיִם
לֹא עַל־יְדֵי מַלְאָךְ
וְלֹא עַל־יְדֵי שָׂרָף
וְלֹא עַל־יְדֵי שָׁלִיחַ
אֶלָּא הַקָּדוֹשׁ בָּרוּךְ הוּא בִּכְבוֹדוֹ וּבְעַצְמוֹ

שֶׁנֶּאֱמַר
וְעָבַרְתִּי בְאֶרֶץ־מִצְרַיִם בַּלַּיְלָה הַזֶּה
וְהִכֵּיתִי כָל־בְּכוֹר בְּאֶרֶץ מִצְרַיִם
מֵאָדָם וְעַד־בְּהֵמָה
וּבְכָל־אֱלֹהֵי מִצְרַיִם אֶעֱשֶׂה שְׁפָטִים
אֲנִי יְיָ

וְעָבַרְתִּי בְאֶרֶץ־מִצְרַיִם אֲנִי וְלֹא מַלְאָךְ
וְהִכֵּיתִי כָל־בְּכוֹר אֲנִי וְלֹא שָׂרָף
וּבְכָל־אֱלֹהֵי מִצְרַיִם
אֶעֱשֶׂה שְׁפָטִים אֲנִי וְלֹא הַשָּׁלִיחַ

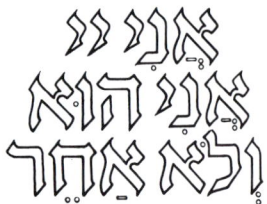

אֲנִי יְיָ
אֲנִי הוּא
וְלֹא אַחֵר

בְּיָד חֲזָקָה — זוֹ הַדֶּבֶר
כְּמָה שֶׁנֶּאֱמַר
הִנֵּה יַד־יְיָ הוֹיָה בְּמִקְנְךָ אֲשֶׁר בַּשָּׂדֶה
בַּסּוּסִים בַּחֲמֹרִים בַּגְּמַלִּים בַּבָּקָר וּבַצֹּאן
דֶּבֶר כָּבֵד מְאֹד

וּבִזְרֹעַ נְטוּיָה — זוֹ הַחֶרֶב
כְּמָה שֶׁנֶּאֱמַר
וְחַרְבּוֹ שְׁלוּפָה בְּיָדוֹ נְטוּיָה עַל־יְרוּשָׁלָיִם

וּבְמֹרָא גָּדֹל — זֶה גִּלּוּי שְׁכִינָה
כְּמָה שֶׁנֶּאֱמַר
אוֹ הֲנִסָּה אֱלֹהִים לָבוֹא לָקַחַת לוֹ גוֹי מִקֶּרֶב גּוֹי
בְּמַסֹּת בְּאֹתֹת וּבְמוֹפְתִים וּבְמִלְחָמָה
וּבְיָד חֲזָקָה וּבִזְרוֹעַ נְטוּיָה וּבְמוֹרָאִים גְּדֹלִים
כְּכֹל אֲשֶׁר־עָשָׂה לָכֶם יְיָ אֱלֹהֵיכֶם
בְּמִצְרַיִם לְעֵינֶיךָ

"And our sorrow"
refers to the destruction of the male children, as it is said: "Every son that is born you shall cast into the river; and every daughter you shall save alive" *(Exodus 1:22)*.

"And our oppression"
refers to the vexation, as it is said: "And I have also seen the oppression with which the Egyptians oppress them" *(Exodus 3:9)*.

"And the Lord brought us forth out of Egypt
with a mighty hand and with an outstretched arm; with great terror and with signs and with wonders" *(Deuteronomy 26:8)*.

"And the Lord brought us forth out of Egypt,"
not through an angel,
not through a seraph and
not through a messenger,
but the Holy One, blessed be He,
alone and in His glory.

As it is said:
"For I will pass through
the land of Egypt this night,
and I will smite all the firstborn in
the land of Egypt,
both man and beast;
and I will execute judgment against all
the gods of Egypt;
I am the Lord" *(Exodus 12:12)*.
"And I will pass through the land of Egypt,"
I, and not an angel.
"And I will smite all the firstborn,"
I, and not a seraph.
"And I will execute judgment against all the gods of Egypt"
I, and not a messenger.

"I am the Lord!"
I, and no other.

"With a mighty hand"
that is the pestilence, as it is said: "Behold, the *hand* of the Lord is upon your cattle in the field, upon the horses, upon the asses, upon the camels, upon the oxen, and upon the sheep; a very grievous pestilence" *(Exodus 9:3)*.

"And with an outstretched arm"
that is the sword, as it is said: "And a drawn *sword* in His hand, stretched out over Jerusalem" *(I Chronicles 21:16)*.

"With great terror"
that is the manifestation of the Divine Presence, as it is said: "Or has God sought to go and take him a nation from the midst of another nation, by proofs, by signs and by wonders; and by war, and by a mighty hand, and by an outstretched arm and by *great terrors*, according to all that the Lord your God did for you in Egypt before your eyes?" *(Deuteronomy 4:34)*.

דָּבָר אַחֵר	וּבְאֹתוֹת זֶה הַמַּטֶּה
בְּיָד חֲזָקָה שְׁתַּיִם	כְּמָה שֶׁנֶּאֱמַר
וּבִזְרֹעַ נְטוּיָה שְׁתַּיִם	וְאֶת־הַמַּטֶּה הַזֶּה תִּקַּח בְּיָדֶךָ
וּבְמֹרָא גָּדֹל שְׁתַּיִם	אֲשֶׁר תַּעֲשֶׂה־בּוֹ אֶת הָאֹתֹת
וּבְאֹתוֹת שְׁתַּיִם	וּבְמֹפְתִים זֶה הַדָּם
וּבְמֹפְתִים שְׁתַּיִם	כְּמָה שֶׁנֶּאֱמַר
	וְנָתַתִּי מוֹפְתִים בַּשָּׁמַיִם וּבָאָרֶץ
	דָּם וָאֵשׁ וְתִימֲרוֹת עָשָׁן

נוהגים להטיף כאן מן הכוס לקערית שלוש פעמים.

אֵלּוּ עֶשֶׂר מַכּוֹת

שֶׁהֵבִיא הַקָּדוֹשׁ בָּרוּךְ הוּא
עַל־הַמִּצְרִים בְּמִצְרַיִם
וְאֵלּוּ הֵן

נוהגים להטיף מן הכוס טיפות יין לקערית על כל מכה ומכה, ואין שותים את היין שבקערית.

בָּרָד	עָרוֹב	דָּם
אַרְבֶּה	דֶּבֶר	צְפַרְדֵּעַ
חֹשֶׁךְ	שְׁחִין	כִּנִּים

מַכַּת בְּכוֹרוֹת

רַבִּי יְהוּדָה הָיָה נוֹתֵן בָּהֶם סִימָנִים
דְּצַ"ךְ עֲדַ"שׁ בְּאַחַ"ב

ממלאים את כוס היין מחדש וממשיכים בקריאת ההגדה.

רַבִּי יוֹסֵי הַגְּלִילִי אוֹמֵר מִנַּיִן אַתָּה אוֹמֵר שֶׁלָּקוּ הַמִּצְרִים בְּמִצְרַיִם עֶשֶׂר מַכּוֹת וְעַל הַיָּם לָקוּ חֲמִשִּׁים מַכּוֹת בְּמִצְרַיִם מָה הוּא אוֹמֵר וַיֹּאמְרוּ הַחַרְטֻמִּם אֶל־פַּרְעֹה אֶצְבַּע אֱלֹהִים הוּא וְעַל הַיָּם מָה הוּא אוֹמֵר וַיַּרְא יִשְׂרָאֵל אֶת־הַיָּד הַגְּדֹלָה אֲשֶׁר עָשָׂה יְיָ בְּמִצְרַיִם וַיִּירְאוּ הָעָם אֶת־יְיָ וַיַּאֲמִינוּ בַּיְיָ וּבְמֹשֶׁה עַבְדּוֹ כַּמָּה לָקוּ בְּאֶצְבַּע עֶשֶׂר מַכּוֹת אֱמֹר מֵעַתָּה בְּמִצְרַיִם לָקוּ עֶשֶׂר מַכּוֹת וְעַל הַיָּם לָקוּ חֲמִשִּׁים מַכּוֹת

"And with signs"
that is the rod (of Moses),
as it is said:
"And you shall take this rod in your hand, with which you shall do *signs*" *(Exodus 4:17).*

"And with wonders"
that is the plague of blood,
as it is said:
"And I will show *wonders* in the heavens, and in the earth, **blood and fire, and pillars of smoke**" *(Joel 2:30).*

It is customary to spill three drops from the cup.

An alternative explanation is this:

"With a mighty hand"
indicates **two** plagues;

"With an outstretched arm,"
another **two**;

"With great terror,"
another **two**;

"And with signs,"
two more;

"And with wonders,"
another **two**.

THESE ARE THE TEN PLAGUES

which the Holy One, blessed be He, brought upon the Egyptians in Egypt, and here they are:

It is customary to spill drops from the cup at the mention of each plague, and also at the three words following. We do not drink the wine which was spilled out.

Blood,   **Pestilence,**   **Locusts,**
Frogs,   **Boils,**   **Darkness,**
Vermin,   **Hail,**   **The Slaying of**
Beasts,   **the Firstborn**

Rabbi Judah arranged them into mnemonic forms:
"Datzach, Adash, Beahab."

The cups of wine are now refilled, and we continue reading the *Haggadah*.

Rabbi Yose the Galilean said: "How do we deduce that the Egyptians were smitten with ten plagues in Egypt, but with fifty on the Red Sea? As follows! Of Egypt, it is said: 'Then the magicians said to Pharaoh, this is the *finger* of God' *(Exodus 8:19).*

But of the Red Sea, it is said: 'And Israel saw the mighty *hand* with which the Lord smote the Egyptians; and the people feared the Lord, and believed in the Lord and in His servant Moses' *(Exodus 14:31).*

Now, if the 'finger' represents the ten plagues of Egypt, the 'hand' at the Red Sea must represent fifty plagues."

◀ (*Overleaf*) **Groups Eating from the Passover Sacrifice in Jerusalem** On the Seder night in Temple times, each group gathers around its pre-arranged Passover sacrifice and conducts the Seder. If two groups, each with its own sacrifice, eat within one house, then a divider must be erected between them, even if it is made from vessels. The groups of celebrants also do not face each other, so as to distinguish to which group each participant belongs.

רִבִּי אֱלִיעֶזֶר אוֹמֵר מִנַּיִן שֶׁכָּל־מַכָּה וּמַכָּה שֶׁהֵבִיא הַקָּדוֹשׁ בָּרוּךְ הוּא עַל הַמִּצְרִים בְּמִצְרַיִם הָיְתָה שֶׁל אַרְבַּע מַכּוֹת שֶׁנֶּאֱמַר יְשַׁלַּח־בָּם חֲרוֹן אַפּוֹ עֶבְרָה וָזַעַם וְצָרָה מִשְׁלַחַת מַלְאֲכֵי רָעִים עֶבְרָה אַחַת וָזַעַם שְׁתַּיִם וְצָרָה שָׁלוֹשׁ מִשְׁלַחַת מַלְאֲכֵי רָעִים אַרְבַּע

אֱמוֹר מֵעַתָּה בְּמִצְרַיִם לָקוּ אַרְבָּעִים מַכּוֹת וְעַל הַיָּם לָקוּ מָאתַיִם מַכּוֹת

רִבִּי עֲקִיבָא אוֹמֵר מִנַּיִן שֶׁכָּל מַכָּה וּמַכָּה שֶׁהֵבִיא הַקָּדוֹשׁ בָּרוּךְ הוּא עַל הַמִּצְרִים בְּמִצְרַיִם הָיְתָה שֶׁל חָמֵשׁ מַכּוֹת שֶׁנֶּאֱמַר יְשַׁלַּח־בָּם חֲרוֹן אַפּוֹ עֶבְרָה וָזַעַם וְצָרָה מִשְׁלַחַת מַלְאֲכֵי רָעִים חֲרוֹן אַפּוֹ אַחַת עֶבְרָה שְׁתַּיִם וָזַעַם שָׁלוֹשׁ וְצָרָה אַרְבַּע מִשְׁלַחַת מַלְאֲכֵי רָעִים חָמֵשׁ

אֱמוֹר מֵעַתָּה בְּמִצְרַיִם לָקוּ חֲמִשִּׁים מַכּוֹת וְעַל הַיָּם לָקוּ חֲמִשִּׁים וּמָאתַיִם מַכּוֹת

---

words, He wrought so many wonders and such fierce judgments against them—then for us, who have received many, many more promises and consolations, how much moreso can we be assured, that He will fulfill His word!"

Rabbenu Saadiah Gaon writes about the future Redemption in a very similar vein (*Emunot V'De'ot*, ch. 8): "When we compare the future Redemption with the Redemption from Egypt, about which we were promised that our oppressors and taskmasters will be judged, and that we would receive great wealth . . . and we have already seen with our own eyes all the miracles which the Holy One did for our forefathers at the Exodus—the splitting of the sea, the manna, the quail, the Revelation at Mount Sinai, the stilling of the sun, etc.—we must realize how much more these promises apply to us, since we have been assured by many prophets of the great goodness which awaits Israel at the time of the Redemption. Certainly, these things will be fulfilled in a far more wondrous manner than that which took place during the first Redemption."

On this basis we can understand the discussion in the *Haggadah* between the sages of Israel, which took place as they gathered together in Rabbi Akiva's home in Bnei Brak. For these sages had witnessed the horrible destruction carried out by Rome with their own eyes. Their own bodies had suffered the affliction and edicts of destruction enacted in the Hadrianic era. We can surely understand the feelings which were aroused within them, as they sat and related the story of the Exodus from Egypt. They reminded each other of the Holy One's promise—the promise couched in the words "I will judge"—and wondrously each of the Egyptian plagues had subdivided into four, and five.

The Almighty will certainly wondrously increase the plagues He will visit upon Rome, "the kingdom of Edom," which subjugates Israel in its post-destruction exile.

Thus it was Rabbi Akiva, who hosted this gathering and in whose academy these discussions took place, who multiplied the tally of the Egyptian plagues more than his other colleagues—for this very gathering took place as a result of the call to rebellion against Rome, and the Sanhedrin's exit from Kerem B'Yavneh, at the start of a long exile. He sought to teach future generations that when the Roman government's Day of Judgment arrives, the Holy One will punish them dearly for the anguish they have caused Israel in its exile.

"Dayenu," It Would Have Been Enough For Us!
How Many Benefits Has God Bestowed Upon Us!

A Song Recited by the Festive Pilgrims Upon the Fifteen Steps

In this classic, well-known song, there are fourteen levels, or "benefits," which are enumerated in the standard *Haggadah* of modern times. However, in the text that was in use in early times—in the days of the *rishonim* (the early rabbinic sages—tenth to fifteenth centuries)—such as the *Haggadot* of the *Shvilei HaLeket*, the *Ritba* and *Hukat ha-Pesach*, a *fifteenth* "benefit" is mentioned as well. Based on this, many commentators explain that originally, the fifteen points included in this song were designed to correspond to the fifteen "Songs of Ascent" in the Book of Psalms. Others maintain that they symbolize the fifteen steps in the Holy Temple leading from the Women's Court to the Nikanor Gates and on through to the Court of Israel (Mishnah Sukkah ch. 5; Tractate Middot).

According to this early text, the additional fifteenth level which is listed at the conclusion reads as follows: "He has brought us forth from Egypt . . . and delivered us into the *Land of Israel*, and built for us the *Holy Temple*, and built for us the *Chosen House*." The meaning behind these words is the fact that when the people of Israel entered into their land, and the Temple had still not been erected "in the place which God will choose" in Jerusalem, the Tabernacle served as the Temple—this was a Holy Temple of sorts, but it was still not the "Chosen House" of God. This is what the sages of the Talmud allude to when they mention that in Shiloh, the Tabernacle was "a house built of stones on the bottom, and skins on top" (BT Zevahim 112:B). It was a temporary arrangement.

This is the order of the ascending levels according to this version:

The thirteenth level: that He brought us into the Land of Israel.

The fourteenth level: He built us the "Holy Temple" in Shiloh, Nob and Gibeon.

The fifteenth level: He built us the "Chosen House" in Jerusalem, through David and Solomon.

In his explanation of the *Haggadah*, the "Rashbatz" (Rabbi Simeon ben Tzemah Duran) writes that this recitation actually forms an extension to the Scriptural verses of "My father was a homeless Aramean" (Deuteronomy 26:15), which are recited as part of the ceremony of bringing the firstfruits to the Temple. Those verses conclude with the words ". . .and He brought us to *this place*, and gave us this land—a land flowing with milk and honey." The rabbis explain (Sifre Deuteronomy 26:9) that the words "and He brought us to *this place*" refer to the Holy Temple in Jerusalem.

We see that, in reality, the biblical section of "My father was a homeless Aramean" is a poetic form of admission, uttered before God by the pilgrims who bring up their firstfruits to the Temple—a declaration of thanks for all the bounty and good which the Creator has bestowed upon His nation, Israel. Now, one might think—of course we must be thankful to God—but is not the listing of these "benefits" perhaps just a bit of an exaggeration? After all, to quote the rabbis, when an individual brings up his firstfruits, all he offers is "one date-seed or a single cluster of grapes"—so why should the ceremony marking this modest offering be accompanied by such a lengthy prayer of thanks?

In truth, the grateful man recites a whole list of undeserved kindnesses which God has dealt him long before he arrived at this point. This awed pilgrim, bringing the modest offering of the firstfruits of his very own produce in humble joy, recalls all the goodness which the Holy One has bestowed upon Israel from the very beginning—the delivery from Egypt, the sustenance in the desert, the giving of the Torah, arrival in Israel . . . up to the building of the Holy Temple. This meager basket of fruit is a minimal offering of thanks, a symbolic gesture by which the bearer attempts to express his deep feelings of thanks for God's many kindnesses, both with him as an individual, and with the entire community as a whole.

The *Dayenu*: An Ancient Song Originally Recited Upon the Temple's Fifteen Steps

In the famed *Meir Ayin Haggadah* by Rabbi Meir Ish Shalom, the author writes: ". . .and my intuition tells me that the stanzas of this song are indeed ancient; they were already known by the talmudic sages of the Land of Israel. And while perhaps this theory cannot be proven by biblical exegesis, nonetheless, an allusion can be found in the Bible. For the verse states (Malachi 3:10): '. . .And I will pour out for you immeasurable blessing.' The Hebrew for immeasurable is *ad b'li dy*, reminiscent of our song's title and refrain, *Dayenu*—it would have been enough for us. Moreover, the sages comment on this verse and state, 'What is meant by the concept of immeasurable blessing? You will give so much thanks to the Lord that your lips will tire of saying *dy*—it is enough!'"

Similarly, the sages of Israel remark on this same verse in Malachi in the conclusion of Tractate Berakhot in the Jerusalem Talmud: "Immeasurable blessing means that the people will exclaim, '*Dayenu*! We have received enough blessings! We have received enough blessings!'"

These sources can be considered an "allusion" since they serve to indicate that the style of the *Dayenu* song is indeed quite ancient, and we find similar expressions of "*dayenu*" used in the rabbinic literature.

In this light, we can now understand that the song's fifteen stanzas which describe the "ascending benefits" are in reality nothing less than an original section of the very song sung by the festival pilgrims who made the journey up to Jerusalem and the Holy Temple, as their feet ascended the fifteen steps which lead up to the Nikanor Gates and into the Courtyard. This realization in itself should not surprise us, for the Jerusalem Talmud (Bikkurim 3:2) bears witness that joyful singing was clearly a part of the procession all along the way to the Temple: "While yet on the road, they would sing, 'I rejoiced when they said to me, Let us go to the House of God.' Once in Jerusalem, they would sing, 'Our feet stood firmly in your gates, O Jerusalem.' On the Temple Mount they sang, 'Hallelujah, praise God in His holy place.' And finally in the Court they sang, 'Let every living soul praise God, Hallelujah!'"

Rabbi Eliezer said: "How can we deduce that every plague which the Holy One, blessed be He, brought upon the Egyptians in Egypt was equivalent to four plagues? It is said: "He cast upon them the fierceness of His anger, wrath, indignation, and trouble, a band of evil angels" *(Psalm 78:49)*. Wrath counts as one; indignation, two; trouble, three; and a band of evil angels, four.

It follows that in Egypt there were forty plagues, and at the Red Sea, two hundred!"

Rabbi Akiva said: "How can we deduce that every plague which the Holy One, blessed be He, brought upon the Egyptians in Egypt was equivalent to five plagues? It is said: "He cast upon them the fierceness of His anger, wrath, and indignation, and trouble, a band of evil angels."

Now, the fierceness of His anger counts as one; wrath, two; indignation, three; trouble, four; and a band of evil angels, five.

It follows that in Egypt there were fifty plagues, and at the Red Sea, two hundred and fifty!"

How Many Benefits Has the Almighty Conferred Upon Us!

"How Can We Deduce That Every Plague Which the Holy One. . ."

What is the Purpose of Calculating the Number of Plagues in Egypt?

"Rabbi Yose the Galilean said: How do we deduce that the Egyptians were smitten with ten plagues in Egypt, but with fifty on the Red Sea?" Three of Israel's greatest sages—Rabbi Yose the Galilean, Rabbi Eliezer, and Rabbi Akiva—deal with the question of the exact number of plagues which were visited upon the Egyptians by the Almighty, both in Egypt and at the shores of the Red Sea. It was these plagues which led to Israel's final exit from Egypt.

Two of these men, Rabbi Eliezer and Rabbi Akiva, were present at the Seder in Bnei Brak. The third, Rabbi Yose the Galilean, is counted amongst Rabbi Akiva's students (Tosafot, BT Avodah Zarah 45:A), so it seems highly probable that he, too, participated in that Seder. It would appear that the lesson of Rabbi Yose before us now was exposited at that very Seder, in Rabbi Akiva's home, for it is quoted by Rabbi Ishmael (*Mechilta* of R. Ishmael, Exodus 24:30), who was a student of both Rabbis Eliezer and Joshua.

As such, it would be useful to understand the gradations between the various opinions as to the number of plagues in Egypt. Rabbi Yose maintains that the grand total of plagues which the Egyptians received was sixty. But Rabbi Eliezer argues that all together, the Egyptians were struck with 240 plagues. Finally, Rabbi Akiva adds even more and counts them as 300, as the *Haggadah* states: "In Egypt there were fifty plagues, and at the Red Sea, two hundred and fifty."

But we wonder: why is it necessary to clarify this information? This point truely seems to be ancient history! For whatever happened, already happened. Since we are unable to prove either side, and each opinion is deduced from biblical exegesis, why bother arguing the point? And, why does Rabbi Akiva "claim" the highest number of plagues?

The Punishment of the Plagues Will Befall Every Kingdom That Enslaved Israel

The answer to our question can again be found in the Torah's account of the "Covenant between the Portions." Abraham was told that the Egyptians will receive their punishment from God: "And also that nation, whom they shall serve, I will judge; and afterwards they shall come out with great wealth" (Genesis 15:14). Rashi points out that the verse's use of the word "and also" seems to be unnecessary, and he answers that this word teaches that the "four kingdoms which have enslaved Israel" will also be punished.

Rashi's words are based on those of the Midrash (Genesis Rabbah 44), which informs us that at the "Covenant between the Portions," Abraham was informed of the identity of each and every nation that would in the future enslave Israel, throughout the successive generations.

This concept explains the use of "and also" in our verse, meaning, not only will the Holy One judge the Egyptians who afflict Israel, and punish them with plagues both in Egypt and on the sea, but every nation which follows in their footsteps, throughout the long and bitter exile, will eventually meet the same judgment and punishment from God, for mistreating His children.

This is the reason why these great scholars found it proper to ponder the assurance which God gave to Abraham, and to compare it with the end result which they were familiar with, for we do find a difference between God's promise, and its actual execution. In the words of the promise, the verse states: "And also that nation, whom they shall serve, I will judge." This verse refers to "judgment" in a generic way, without clarifying its nature or details. But in the final end, this judgment went beyond the limits of what had originally been promised.

Thus the Midrash records: "Rabbi Eliezer said in the name of Rabbi Yose bar Zimra: With these two letters (the Hebrew letters which form the word *dan*, I will "judge") the Holy One promised our father Abraham that He would redeem his children, but if they would only repent—then they would be redeemed through seventy-two letters. For Rabbi Yudan taught: the words of the verse, '. . .to go and take Him a nation from the midst of another nation, by trials, by signs, and by wonders, and by war, and by a mighty hand, and with an outstretched arm, and by great terrors,' consist of 72 letters (in Hebrew)—corresponding to the 72-letter Sacred Name of the Holy One, blessed be He" (Genesis Rabbah 47).

Thus, it transpires that that which God promised through an allusion, was actually fulfilled when it came to the real unfolding of events, for the Exodus was certainly marked by "trials, signs, wonders, war, etc." We should conclude that if the Holy One's assurance to Abraham was fulfilled with regard to the Egyptian captivity, how much moreso can we expect His Divine oath to be fulfilled when the time comes for the judgment of the other nations? For indeed, many prophecies were made concerning the fate which awaits those nations who have oppressed Israel.

The Sages of Israel Deliberate on the Fate Awaiting the Wicked Romans in the Future

The *Midrash HaGadol* (Genesis 15:14) records this statement: "The Holy One assured Abraham that He will judge those nations whom his children will serve in the future, for it is written, 'I will judge.' On account of this guarantee, He will bring many wonders for Abraham's children. For if the Holy One gave an assurance based only on two words regarding the Egyptians—and yet, because of those two

דַּיֵּנוּ	הֶעֱבִירָנוּ בְּתוֹכוֹ בֶּחָרָבָה	אִלּוּ	דַּיֵּנוּ	הוֹצִיאָנוּ מִמִּצְרַיִם	אִלּוּ
דַּיֵּנוּ	שִׁקַּע צָרֵינוּ בְּתוֹכוֹ	וְלֹא	דַּיֵּנוּ	עָשָׂה בָהֶם שְׁפָטִים	וְלֹא
דַּיֵּנוּ	שִׁקַּע צָרֵינוּ בְּתוֹכוֹ	אִלּוּ	דַּיֵּנוּ	עָשָׂה בָהֶם שְׁפָטִים	אִלּוּ
דַּיֵּנוּ	סִפֵּק צָרְכֵּנוּ בַּמִּדְבָּר אַרְבָּעִים שָׁנָה	וְלֹא	דַּיֵּנוּ	עָשָׂה בֵאלֹהֵיהֶם	וְלֹא
דַּיֵּנוּ	סִפֵּק צָרְכֵּנוּ בַּמִּדְבָּר אַרְבָּעִים שָׁנָה	אִלּוּ	דַּיֵּנוּ	עָשָׂה בֵאלֹהֵיהֶם	אִלּוּ
דַּיֵּנוּ	הֶאֱכִילָנוּ אֶת הַמָּן	וְלֹא	דַּיֵּנוּ	הָרַג אֶת בְּכוֹרֵיהֶם	וְלֹא
דַּיֵּנוּ	הֶאֱכִילָנוּ אֶת הַמָּן	אִלּוּ	דַּיֵּנוּ	הָרַג אֶת בְּכוֹרֵיהֶם	אִלּוּ
דַּיֵּנוּ	נָתַן לָנוּ אֶת הַשַּׁבָּת	וְלֹא	דַּיֵּנוּ	נָתַן לָנוּ אֶת מָמוֹנָם	וְלֹא
דַּיֵּנוּ	נָתַן לָנוּ אֶת הַשַּׁבָּת	אִלּוּ	דַּיֵּנוּ	נָתַן לָנוּ אֶת מָמוֹנָם	אִלּוּ
דַּיֵּנוּ	קֵרְבָנוּ לִפְנֵי הַר סִינַי	וְלֹא	דַּיֵּנוּ	קָרַע לָנוּ אֶת הַיָּם	וְלֹא
דַּיֵּנוּ	קֵרְבָנוּ לִפְנֵי הַר סִינַי	אִלּוּ	דַּיֵּנוּ	קָרַע לָנוּ אֶת הַיָּם	אִלּוּ
דַּיֵּנוּ	נָתַן לָנוּ אֶת הַתּוֹרָה	וְלֹא	דַּיֵּנוּ	הֶעֱבִירָנוּ בְּתוֹכוֹ בֶּחָרָבָה	וְלֹא

	נָתַן לָנוּ אֶת הַתּוֹרָה	אִלּוּ
דַּיֵּנוּ	הִכְנִיסָנוּ לְאֶרֶץ יִשְׂרָאֵל	וְלֹא
	הִכְנִיסָנוּ לְאֶרֶץ יִשְׂרָאֵל	אִלּוּ
דַּיֵּנוּ	בָּנָה לָנוּ אֶת הַמִּשְׁכָּן וְהַמִּקְדָּשׁ	וְלֹא
	בָּנָה לָנוּ אֶת הַמִּשְׁכָּן וְהַמִּקְדָּשׁ	אִלּוּ
דַּיֵּנוּ	בָּנָה לָנוּ אֶת בֵּית הַבְּחִירָה	וְלֹא

And He Built for Us His Chosen House, to Atone for All Our Sins

The Temple Is Not a Reward for Good Deeds: It Is a Spiritual Remedy for Sin

Many people seem to be under the erroneous impression that the Holy Temple was given to Israel as a Divine gift, as some sort of "prize" to Israel for good behavior. That is, if the people of Israel follow God's statutes and fulfill His commandments, and behave like "a kingdom of priests and a holy nation," then they deserve to have the Holy Temple. But if the opposite is true, Heaven forbid—then, they do not deserve it. This view sees the Temple as some sort of spiritual apex, a blissful foreshadow and taste of "the world to come"—a reward for Israel's good behavior.

But contrary to this approach, the sages instruct us that the Holy One desires to dwell amongst His creations, in the midst of lowly man—this, despite the fact that they are sinful, and because of it. According to the rabbis, the Temple is neither prize nor reward; it is an intrinsic necessity for the survival of the world. As the Midrash (Tanhuma B'Hukoti 3) states, in the name of Rabbi Ami: "Just as the Holy One, blessed be He, dwells on high, so too, He desired to have a dwelling place down below." This is God's will, to dwell in our world, amongst us. He understands our true nature; that our lives are transient; that we are full of iniquity. But even in our state of impurity, He seeks to dwell amongst us (see BT Yoma 56:B). The Temple's purpose is to atone for Israel and to purify them, and it was for this very reason that Adam, the first man, was created of dust taken from the spot of the altar: since by his very nature, he is destined to sin—"Adam was created from the very spot which atones for him" (JT Nazir 7:8).

Thus the Torah's concept is that the existence of the Holy Temple in Jerusalem, and the daily sacrificial service, are the factors which atone for Israel as it dwells in the Land. The Midrash (Yalkut Shimoni Bo 191) formulates this idea in a most beautiful configuration: "No person ever went to sleep in Jerusalem with sin still in his possession. Why? The daily sacrifice which was offered every morning would atone for sins that were committed at night; the evening offering atoned for sins committed during the day." This idea conveys the true reason for the Holy Temple: to cleanse and banish the accumulated sins of Israel, in order to enable the nation to continue dwelling in the Land. Thus, the inner core idea of the Holy Temple is intended for man's sinful condition, much as a medicinal cure is intended for a state of illness.

The *Haggadah* lists the fifteen benefits which, with God's kindness, Israel merited to receive. The rabbis could have just as easily concluded the litany of *Dayenu* with the phrase, He gave the present, or the prize, to Israel, in that He built them His Chosen House. For what could be higher than receiving a gift from God? But they deemed it necessary to continue and explain just what the "benefit" of this Chosen House is: "to atone for all our sins." The message is clear. The present of the Land of Israel is of the greatest value when it contains the Holy Temple, to atone for Israel in their land. With this system of constant atonement and renewal, the existence of the Holy Temple and its service assure that Israel will enjoy continued presence in their land, in every generation.

If He had brought us out of Egypt, and not executed judgment on them,
it would have been enough!
If He had executed judgment on them, but not upon their gods,
it would have been enough!
If He had executed judgment on their gods, and not slain their firstborn,
it would have been enough!
If He had slain their firstborn, and not given us their wealth,
it would have been enough!
If He had given us their wealth, and not split the sea for us,
it would have been enough!
If He had split the sea for us, and not brought us through on dry land,
it would have been enough!
If He had brought us through on dry land, and not sunk our oppressors in the depths,
it would have been enough!
If He had sunk our oppressors in the depths, and not sustained us in the wilderness for forty years,
it would have been enough!
If He had sustained us in the wilderness for forty years, and not fed us with manna,
it would have been enough!
If He had fed us with manna, and not given us the Sabbath,
it would have been enough!
If He had given us the Sabbath, and not led us to Mount Sinai,
it would have been enough!
If He had led us to Mount Sinai, and not given us the Torah,
it would have been enough!
If He had given us the Torah, and not brought us into the Land of Israel,
it would have been enough!
If He had brought us into the Land of Israel, and not built us the Tabernacle and the Holy Temple,
it would have been enough!
If He had built us the Tabernacle and the Holy Temple, and not built for us His Chosen House,
it would have been enough!

How manifold are the blessings, doubled and redoubled, which the Almighty has bestowed upon us?

He brought us out of Egypt, did judgment on the Egyptians and their gods, slew their firstborn, gave us their wealth, split the Red Sea for us, brought us through its midst on dry land, sank our oppressors in its depths, sustained us in the wilderness for forty years, fed us with manna, gave us the Sabbath, led us to Mount Sinai, gave us the Torah, brought us into the Land of Israel, built for us the Tabernacle and the Holy Temple, and built for us the Chosen House to atone for all our sins.

Based on this information, it would certainly seem logical to conclude that these fifteen stanzas which make up the *Dayenu* were a continuation of these songs of joy, and were recited once the pilgrims reached the fifteen steps leading up from the Women's Court to the Court of Israel. They sang the *Dayenu* verses while ascending these stairs, and while standing in the gates of the Court—for in reality, this song is actually an explanation and elaboration of the verse "And you shall answer and declare before the Lord your God: 'My father was a homeless Aramean,'" and this conjecture can be proven, for the subject matter of these verses matches that of the *Dayenu*'s fifteen stanzas. So too, the section of the "firstfruit verses" is required to be recited out loud, just as the *Haggadah* must be recited.

Like the song of the fruit-bearing pilgrims' procession, the stanzas of the *Dayenu* were chanted by the Passover pilgrims as they ascended to the Temple court—one stanza was sung on each step. Thus, on the first step they sang, "If He had brought us out of Egypt. . ."; on the second step, "If He had executed judgment on them," and so forth. When they reached the last step, at the Gates of Nikanor facing the Court and the Sanctuary, they joyfully sang out, "He built for us the Chosen House, to atone for all our sins."

Dayenu: A Halakhic Solution to the Reading of the "Firstfruit Verses" in the Temple

It would seem that with this new insight, we have now managed to solve a halakhic dilemma as well. For a problem arises when the firstfruits are brought up to the Temple in that the Torah requires each pilgrim to recite the verses of "My father was. . ." before the priest. The Mishnah (Bikkurim 3:4) tells us that this requirement created a problematic situation: "Originally, those who knew how to read would recite these verses themselves, and it was read for those who could not read it themselves. But this practice prevented people from bringing their offerings, and so it was ruled that it would be read aloud for everyone (even for those who could read themselves)." Since the requirement for each pilgrim to read this section aloud had made a great deal of work for the priests—and made things difficult for the pilgrims as well, as each one waited his turn to repeat the section word for word—the rabbis found the solution of reading it for everyone.

But the custom of communal singing along the Temple stairs—and the refrain of *Dayenu*—would satisfy the requirements for this recitation, since the song of both the Passover pilgrims as well as those who bring their firstfruits would reflect the contents of this biblical portion. Since the entire congregation took part in the singing, it would seem that they fulfilled their obligation of reciting the "My father was a homeless Aramean" verses, through the singing of *Dayenu*. Thus, a satisfactory method for the entire assemblage was to recite all the verses—at once.

While it is true that, according to Jewish law, these "firstfruit verses" should preferably be recited in front of the altar, the verses themselves would seem to indicate that they could actually be recited anywhere on the Temple Mount, for it is written: "And you shall take from the firstfruits of your produce . . . *and you shall go to the place which God shall choose* . . . and you shall come to the priest, and you shall say to him, 'I tell this day to the Lord your God, that I have come to the country. . .'" (Deuteronomy 26:2). The subject of the altar is only mentioned after the statement of "I tell this day. . ."—"And the priest shall take the basket out of your hand, and place it before the altar of the Lord your God." This implies that the recital before the priest need not necessarily take place exclusively "before the altar," but could be said anywhere "in the place which God will choose"—in a broader area, the entire expanse of the Temple Mount.

Maimonides' language in the Laws of Firstfruits (3:10) seems to corroborate this concept. He writes: "It is a positive commandment to confess in the Temple, over the firstfruits." He does not write "in the Court"; the concept of "Temple" also includes the Women's Court, where the fifteen steps were located. A similar inference can be drawn from Maimonides' language with regard to another concept: "A place for women was established in the Temple" (Laws of Lulav 8:2). Here he refers to the place in the Women's Court which was prepared for the Festival of the Water Libation. And finally, see the comments of the *Minhat Hinukh* on Commandment 606, where the author opines that it is only a preference for the firstfruit verses to be recited in the court—but they actually could be read outside the court as well, if need be.

In any event, this song is indeed ancient, and dates from the era of the Temple. It was incorporated in this form into the *Haggadah*, for it enumerates the same kindnesses of God which are listed in the "My father was. . ." verses, in a detailed, organized and concise fashion: all the benevolence He has bestowed upon His people from the time they left Egyptian bondage, until they stood before Him in the Temple at Jerusalem.

עַל אַחַת כַּמָּה וְכַמָּה טוֹבָה כְפוּלָה וּמְכֻפֶּלֶת לַמָּקוֹם עָלֵינוּ

שֶׁהוֹצִיאָנוּ מִמִּצְרַיִם	וְהֶעֱבִירָנוּ בְתוֹכוֹ בֶּחָרָבָה
וְעָשָׂה בָהֶם שְׁפָטִים	וְשִׁקַּע צָרֵינוּ בְּתוֹכוֹ
וְעָשָׂה בֵאלֹהֵיהֶם	וְסִפֵּק צָרְכֵּנוּ בַּמִּדְבָּר אַרְבָּעִים שָׁנָה
וְהָרַג אֶת בְּכוֹרֵיהֶם	וְהֶאֱכִילָנוּ אֶת הַמָּן
וְנָתַן לָנוּ אֶת מָמוֹנָם	וְנָתַן לָנוּ אֶת הַשַּׁבָּת
וְקָרַע לָנוּ אֶת הַיָּם	וְקֵרְבָנוּ לִפְנֵי הַר סִינַי
	וְנָתַן לָנוּ אֶת הַתּוֹרָה

וְהִכְנִיסָנוּ לְאֶרֶץ יִשְׂרָאֵל

וּבָנָה לָנוּ אֶת הַמִּשְׁכָּן וְהַמִּקְדָּשׁ

וּבָנָה לָנוּ אֶת בֵּית הַבְּחִירָה לְכַפֵּר עַל כָּל עֲוֹנוֹתֵינוּ.

Cleansing the Courtyard at the Conclusion of the Service When the offering of the Passover sacrifice is concluded, the priests wash down the floor of the courtyard. A specially constructed drainage system facilitated this process.

Rabban Gamliel used to say,
Whoever does not mention these three things

[*in the time of the Holy Temple:*
while eating the Passover sacrifice]

on Passover

has not fulfilled his obligation,

and they are:

PESACH, MATZAH, and MAROR.

[*In the time of the Holy Temple:* **This Passover lamb**
which we are eating—why do we eat it?]

The Passover sacrifice
which our forefathers ate in the time when
the Holy Temple stood—why did they eat it?
Because the Holy One, blessed be He, "passed over"
our fathers' houses in Egypt,
as it is said: "And you shall say, it is the sacrifice of the
Lord's Passover, who passed over the houses of the
Children of Israel in Egypt, when he smote the
Egyptians, and delivered our houses.
And the people bowed the head and worshipped"
(Exodus 12:27).

רַבָּן גַּמְלִיאֵל הָיָה אוֹמֵר
כָּל שֶׁלֹּא אָמַר שְׁלוֹשָׁה דְבָרִים אֵלּוּ

[בזמן המקדש: בְּעֵת אֲכִילַת קָרְבַּן פֶּסַח]

בַּפֶּסַח

לֹא יָצָא יְדֵי חוֹבָתוֹ

וְאֵלּוּ הֵן

פֶּסַח מַצָּה וּמָרוֹר

[בזמן המקדש: קָרְבַּן פֶּסַח זֶה
שֶׁאָנוּ אוֹכְלִים עַל שׁוּם מָה]

פֶּסַח

שֶׁהָיוּ אֲבוֹתֵינוּ אוֹכְלִים בִּזְמַן שֶׁבֵּית הַמִּקְדָּשׁ הָיָה קַיָּם
עַל שׁוּם מָה
עַל שׁוּם שֶׁפָּסַח הַקָּדוֹשׁ בָּרוּךְ הוּא עַל בָּתֵּי אֲבוֹתֵינוּ בְּמִצְרַיִם
שֶׁנֶּאֱמַר וַאֲמַרְתֶּם זֶבַח־פֶּסַח הוּא לַיְיָ
אֲשֶׁר פָּסַח עַל־בָּתֵּי בְנֵי־יִשְׂרָאֵל בְּמִצְרַיִם
בְּנָגְפּוֹ אֶת־מִצְרַיִם וְאֶת־בָּתֵּינוּ הִצִּיל
וַיִּקֹּד הָעָם וַיִּשְׁתַּחֲווּ

This Passover Sacrifice Which Our Forefathers Ate—What Is Its Significance?

The Haggadah's Recollection of the Passover Sacrifice: A Reminder of Both the Passover in Egypt, and the Celebration of the Passover in Jerusalem

"Rabban Gamliel said, Whoever does not mention these three things on Passover has not fulfilled his obligation: the Passover sacrifice (*Pesach*), matzah, and *maror* (the bitter herb)." Rabban Gamliel established that the first thing which must be spoken of on the Seder night is the Passover sacrifice, which was discontinued when the Temple was destroyed. Thus on this night, each father in Israel turns to his son and asks: "The Passover sacrifice—*Pesach*—which *our forefathers ate during the time that the Holy Temple stood*—what was its significance?" And the answer: "It is because the Holy One, Blessed be He, passed over (*pasach*) the houses of our forefathers in Egypt."

And Rabban Gamliel, who lived at the end of the Second Temple era, was an eye-witness to the destruction. According to the Talmud's description (BT Gittin 56:B), when Rabban Yohanan ben Zakkai escaped the siege of Jerusalem and stood before General Vespasian, he requested that the lineage of Rabban Gamliel's presidency be allowed to remain unharmed. For Rabban Yohanan ben Zakkai sought to ensure the continuation of Torah tradition and transmission, and the chain of Davidic kings from which the Messiah would emerge. It was Rabban Gamliel who continued Rabban Yohanan's tradition after the destruction, and the latter authored and established the "Temple Remembrances" to instill the people with faith and hope that the Temple would soon be rebuilt.

From the *Haggadah* itself we learn that mentioning the concept of the Passover sacrifice at the Seder serves two purposes; for when the Temple actually stood, they would say "what is the significance of this Passover sacrifice *which we are eating*?" (Maimonides, Laws of Hametz and Matzah 8:4). Thus they would be reminded of Israel's delivery in Egypt, when God passed over to smite the firstborn. But Rabban Gamliel, in the spirit of the "Temple Remembrances" enacted by Rabban Yohanan ben Zakkai, added another "remembrance" himself: to mention not only the Passover sacrifice on the Seder night, but the Passover sacrifice which our fathers ate in the Temple in Jerusalem as well. Thus: "What is the significance of the Passover sacrifice which our forefathers ate during the time of the Holy Temple?"

This teaches us an important concept: that the *mitzvah* of "and you shall tell your son" applies not only to relating the miracles which occurred in Egypt. Another aspect of the children's education is to inform them that our forefathers ate from the Passover sacrifice in Jerusalem, amidst joy and song. Yes, remember the great miracles of the Exodus from Egypt, as they are recorded in the Torah; only do not forget the great sensation of freedom and redemption which our fathers experienced as they celebrated the Passover festival in Jerusalem. If we will but believe, anticipate and do all we can toward the renewal of this era, we, and our children, shall also merit to celebrate Passover in the courtyards of God, in Jerusalem.

Eating the Passover Sacrifice Without Recitation Is Compared to a Body Without a Soul

Unlike the laws governing the performance of other commandments, such as the wearing of the *tefillin* or the taking of the *lulav*, the Torah commands that when the Passover sacrifice is eaten, one must actually explain its purpose orally—while he performs the act of the commandment. This requirement is not applicable in the case of other *mitzvot*—such as those we have mentioned—for normally, the very action being done (such as shaking the *lulav*, donning *tzitzit*, etc.) is itself a demonstration that the individual is fulfilling the Creator's commandment. This is one of the reasons for the opinion expressed in the Talmud that "the performance of commandments is valid even when done without expressed intent" (BT Pesachim 114:B)—for the very physical action of the commandment itself shows it was this individual's intention to fulfill the command of God.

However, a distinction must be made when it comes to the eating of the Passover sacrifice, for this is the exception to the rule. For when it comes to partaking of this sacrifice, one could erroneously conclude that this is just another meal which is being eaten for enjoyment, like any other night.

This is the actual question which the son poses to his father on this night, as part of the Four Questions: On every other night we are accustomed to eating meat, so why is this night so different—that tonight, the meat may only be served roasted?

This is why the Torah commanded that it is not enough for one to fulfill his Passover obligation merely by eating, but rather, it is incumbent upon the father to explain to his son the purpose of this eating—that the eating of the *k'zayit*, the required amount from the Passover sacrifice, is not eating for taste or pleasure or satiety; it is eaten for its significance: "And you shall declare: 'It is a Passover offering to God!'" In other words, notice was given to all the participants that this meat was not being eaten to satisfy hunger. On the contrary, one is required to already be satiated when he partakes of the Passover sacrifice—for the real reason it is eaten is in order to fulfill God's commandment. This is a spiritual meal, not one designed for the usual physical gratification.

Therefore, one did not fulfill his Divinely ordained, religious requirement unless he actually specified orally for all those present to hear that this Passover sacrifice is "an offering to God!" It is being eaten to fulfill His *mitzvah*, as a remembrance for every generation—to eternalize God's greatness as it was manifest in the slaying of the Egyptian firstborn, when, as the Torah testifies, God killed all their firstborn "and saved our houses."

מגביה המצה ומראה למסובים.

מַצָּה זוֹ

שֶׁאָנוּ אוֹכְלִים עַל שׁוּם מָה
עַל שׁוּם שֶׁלֹּא הִסְפִּיק בְּצֵקָם שֶׁל אֲבוֹתֵינוּ לְהַחֲמִיץ
עַד שֶׁנִּגְלָה עֲלֵיהֶם מֶלֶךְ מַלְכֵי הַמְּלָכִים
הַקָּדוֹשׁ בָּרוּךְ הוּא וּגְאָלָם
שֶׁנֶּאֱמַר וַיֹּאפוּ אֶת־הַבָּצֵק אֲשֶׁר הוֹצִיאוּ מִמִּצְרַיִם
עֻגֹת מַצּוֹת כִּי לֹא חָמֵץ
כִּי־גֹרְשׁוּ מִמִּצְרַיִם וְלֹא יָכְלוּ לְהִתְמַהְמֵהַּ וְגַם־צֵדָה לֹא־עָשׂוּ לָהֶם

מגביה את המרור ומראה למסובים.

מָרוֹר זֶה

שֶׁאָנוּ אוֹכְלִים עַל שׁוּם מָה
עַל שׁוּם שֶׁמֵּרְרוּ הַמִּצְרִים אֶת חַיֵּי אֲבוֹתֵינוּ בְּמִצְרַיִם
שֶׁנֶּאֱמַר וַיְמָרְרוּ אֶת־חַיֵּיהֶם בַּעֲבֹדָה קָשָׁה
בְּחֹמֶר וּבִלְבֵנִים וּבְכָל־עֲבֹדָה בַּשָּׂדֶה
אֵת כָּל־עֲבֹדָתָם אֲשֶׁר־עָבְדוּ בָהֶם בְּפָרֶךְ

בְּכָל־דּוֹר וָדוֹר

חַיָּב אָדָם לִרְאוֹת אֶת־עַצְמוֹ כְּאִלּוּ הוּא יָצָא מִמִּצְרַיִם
שֶׁנֶּאֱמַר
וְהִגַּדְתָּ לְבִנְךָ בַּיּוֹם הַהוּא לֵאמֹר
בַּעֲבוּר זֶה עָשָׂה יְיָ לִי בְּצֵאתִי מִמִּצְרָיִם
לֹא אֶת אֲבוֹתֵינוּ בִּלְבַד גָּאַל הַקָּדוֹשׁ בָּרוּךְ הוּא
אֶלָּא אַף אוֹתָנוּ גָּאַל עִמָּהֶם

שֶׁנֶּאֱמַר
וְאוֹתָנוּ הוֹצִיא מִשָּׁם
לְמַעַן הָבִיא אֹתָנוּ
לָתֶת לָנוּ אֶת־הָאָרֶץ
אֲשֶׁר נִשְׁבַּע לַאֲבוֹתֵינוּ

מכסה את המצות ונוטל את הכוס בידו.

לְפִיכָךְ אֲנַחְנוּ חַיָּבִים
לְהוֹדוֹת לְהַלֵּל לְשַׁבֵּחַ לְפָאֵר לְרוֹמֵם
לְהַדֵּר לְבָרֵךְ לְעַלֵּה וּלְקַלֵּס
לְמִי שֶׁעָשָׂה לַאֲבוֹתֵינוּ וְלָנוּ
אֶת כָּל הַנִּסִּים
הָאֵלֶּה
הוֹצִיאָנוּ מֵעַבְדוּת לְחֵרוּת
מִיָּגוֹן לְשִׂמְחָה מֵאֵבֶל לְיוֹם טוֹב
וּמֵאֲפֵלָה לְאוֹר גָּדוֹל וּמִשִּׁעְבּוּד לִגְאֻלָּה
וְנֹאמַר לְפָנָיו שִׁירָה חֲדָשָׁה
הַלְלוּיָהּ

מניח את הכוס ומגלה את המצות.

הַלְלוּיָהּ

הַלְלוּ עַבְדֵי יְיָ
הַלְלוּ אֶת־שֵׁם יְיָ
יְהִי שֵׁם יְיָ מְבֹרָךְ
מֵעַתָּה וְעַד־עוֹלָם
מִמִּזְרַח־שֶׁמֶשׁ עַד־מְבוֹאוֹ
מְהֻלָּל שֵׁם יְיָ
רָם עַל־כָּל־גּוֹיִם יְיָ
עַל הַשָּׁמַיִם כְּבוֹדוֹ
מִי כַּייָ אֱלֹהֵינוּ
הַמַּגְבִּיהִי לָשָׁבֶת
הַמַּשְׁפִּילִי לִרְאוֹת
בַּשָּׁמַיִם וּבָאָרֶץ
מְקִימִי מֵעָפָר דָּל
מֵאַשְׁפֹּת יָרִים אֶבְיוֹן
לְהוֹשִׁיבִי עִם־נְדִיבִים
עִם נְדִיבֵי עַמּוֹ
מוֹשִׁיבִי עֲקֶרֶת הַבַּיִת
אֵם־הַבָּנִים שְׂמֵחָה

הַלְלוּיָהּ

The host holds up the matzot for all to see.

This matzah

—why do we eat it? Because our fathers' dough did not have time to become leavened before the King of Kings, the Holy One, blessed be He, appeared and redeemed them, as it is written: "And they baked unleavened cakes of the dough which they had brought forth out of Egypt, for it was not leavened; because they were thrust out of Egypt, and could not tarry, neither had they prepared for themselves any victuals" *(Exodus 12:39)*.

The host holds up the bitter herb for all to see.

This bitter herb

—why do we eat it? Because the Egyptians embittered our fathers' lives in Egypt, as it is said: "And they made their lives bitter with hard bondage, in mortar and in brick, and in all manner of labor in the field; all their labor was imposed on them with rigor" *(Exodus 1:14)*.

In Every Generation,

each person is obligated to regard himself as if he personally came out of Egypt, as it is said: "And you shall tell your son on that day, saying, this is because of what the Lord God did for me, when I came forth out of Egypt" *(Exodus 13:8)*. It was not only our fathers who the Holy One, blessed be He, redeemed from Egypt, but ourselves also,

as it is said: "And He brought us out from there that He might bring us in, to give us the Land which He swore to our fathers" *(Deuteronomy 6:23)*.

The host covers the matzot and raises his cup.

So let us thank, praise, laud, glorify, exalt,
honor, bless, extol and adore Him
who did all these miracles
for our fathers and for ourselves.
He brought us out from slavery to freedom,
from anguish to joy, from mourning to holiday,
from darkness to great light,
and from bondage to redemption.
And therefore let us sing to Him a new song.
Hallelujah!

The host puts down his cup and uncovers the matzot.

Praise the Lord.

Praise, O you servants of the Lord,
praise the name of the Lord.
Blessed be the name of the Lord
from this time forth and for evermore.
From the rising of the sun
until the going down of the same
the Lord's name is to be praised.
The Lord is high above all nations,
and His glory above the heavens.
Who can be likened to the Lord our God,
who dwells on high,
who lowers Himself to behold the things
that are in heaven, and in the earth!
He raises the poor out of the dust,
and lifts the needy out of the dunghill;
that He may set him with princes,
even with the princes of His people.
He makes the barren woman to keep house,
and to be a joyful mother of children.

Praise the Lord!

(Psalm 113)

The Praises of "Hallel," in the Holy Temple and in Jerusalem

In the collective consciousness of the Jewish people, Passover night—as the pilgrims partook of the Passover offering and sang the *Hallel* songs of praise—was transformed from an ordinary night into a symbolic climax, a veritable concept which articulates and epitomizes ethereal joy.

This was superbly illustrated by none other than Isaiah the prophet, who celebrated Passover in Jerusalem together with his people, the nation of Israel. When Isaiah sought to describe the great joy which Israel would experience at Sennacherib's downfall, he utilized a parable and stated: "You shall have a song (that you will sing the night of Sennacherib's downfall), as on the night when a holy festival is kept; and gladness of heart…" (30:29). "The night of a holy festival" refers to none other than the night of Passover, as it is written: "And you shall celebrate it as a festival to the Lord" (Exodus 12:14). The rabbis and commentators explain that Isaiah used the night of Passover as his example of rejoicing, for the joy of this night was beyond comparison (Rashi and Radak on Isaiah 30:29).

The sages said (BT Pesahim 75:B) that a "*k'zayit* of the Passover sacrifice, and the singing of *Hallel*, have the power to rise up and break through the roofs of Jerusalem." For the festive *Hallel* was sung as an accompaniment to the eating of the Passover sacrifice, as required by *halakhah*. A *k'zayit*—a biblical measurement, roughly the size of an olive—is the minimum amount which is required to be eaten by each participant. Rashi explains that because of the huge throngs of people that had gathered to offer the sacrifice, the offerings were divided among large groups, each group consisting of at least ten participants, and therefore, each participant naturally received no more than an olive-size portion of the meat. Rashi also mentions that the level of rejoicing was so great, it literally encompassed the masses of festival pilgrims. He writes that "when the multitudes recited the verses of *Hallel* together, the roofs of the houses seemed to burst open" (ibid.).

The First *Hallel* Was Sung at the First Passover Sacrifice—While Yet in Egypt

In reality, the joy experienced on this night is but a continuation of that first great joy—the Exodus from Egypt, when all of Israel sang praises of God together—"on the night when a holy festival is kept," the Festival of Redemption.

In a talmudic discussion (BT Pesahim 117:A), our rabbis discuss the question of the *Hallel*'s source: who sang it the first time, and when? One answer provided by Rabbi Elazar, the son of Rabbi Yose, is that Moses and Israel sang it at the miracle of the sea's splitting. Another opinion maintains that it was originated by King David. But the sages seemed to favor the first opinion, and Rabbi Yose, supporting his son's position, declared in astonishment: "Is it possible that Israel sacrificed their Passover offerings, and took up their palm branches, and did not sing praises?!"

Rabbi Yose does not bring a source to substantiate his reasoning, but it most probably originates in the *Midrash Hallel*. There, too, the question is raised as to the origins of the *Hallel*. This Midrash provides the following answer: "Rabbi Nehemiah stated that David composed it. But what then did Israel do, from the time they left Egypt, until David appeared? Is it possible for them to have eaten from the Passover sacrifice without the *Hallel*? They answered that Moses said *Hallel* when Israel left Egypt. Moses told Israel: "Yesterday, we were slaves to Pharaoh. Now we are slaves to the Holy One, blessed be He." They stood and sung praise to God, for redeeming them from bondage to freedom."

In other words, ever since the time of the Exodus, Israel has sung portions of the *Hallel*, but during King David's life, the latter arranged the order of the psalms and

בֵּית יַעֲקֹב מֵעַם לֹעֵז
הָיְתָה יְהוּדָה לְקָדְשׁוֹ
יִשְׂרָאֵל מַמְשְׁלוֹתָיו
הַיָּם רָאָה וַיָּנֹס
הַיַּרְדֵּן יִסֹּב לְאָחוֹר
הֶהָרִים רָקְדוּ כְאֵילִים
גְּבָעוֹת כִּבְנֵי־צֹאן
מַה־לְּךָ הַיָּם כִּי תָנוּס
הַיַּרְדֵּן תִּסֹּב לְאָחוֹר
הֶהָרִים תִּרְקְדוּ כְאֵילִים
גְּבָעוֹת כִּבְנֵי־צֹאן
מִלִּפְנֵי אָדוֹן חוּלִי אָרֶץ
מִלִּפְנֵי אֱלוֹהַּ יַעֲקֹב
הַהֹפְכִי הַצּוּר אֲגַם־מָיִם
חַלָּמִישׁ לְמַעְיְנוֹ־מָיִם

When Israel Went Out of Egypt,

the house of Jacob from a people of strange language; Judah was His sanctuary, and Israel, His dominion. The sea saw it, and fled: the Jordan was driven back. The mountains skipped like rams, and the little hills like lambs. What ailed you, sea, that you fled? Jordan, why were you driven back? What caused you mountains to skip like rams; and you little hills, like lambs? Tremble, earth, at the presence of the Lord, at the presence of the God of Jacob; who turned the rock into standing water, the flint into a fountain of waters *(Psalm 114).*

question of the son who does not know to ask. By now, everyone is deeply impressed with the sanctity and importance of this night, in which we were released from Egyptian bondage. Now we can celebrate the Passover in Jerusalem as free men, partaking of the sacrifice in joy. This is the moment to acknowledge God, to thank the Creator of heaven and earth for all the kindness He has bestowed upon us—till this very day. This singular blessing was enacted in recognition of these sublime feelings, recited on this night only, once a year: "Blessed is He who has redeemed us!"

In Temple times this blessing expressed complete, perfect joy. Thus, after uttering the words "and brought us to this night on which we eat the Passover sacrifice, matzah and bitter herbs," the participants would conclude with the words "Blessed are You, O Lord, who has redeemed Israel!" (Abrabanel, *Haggadat Zevach Pesach*). But following the destruction of the Holy Temple, the central commandment of this evening is now missing. Without the Passover sacrifice, the sense of joy is diminished, and so the sages of Israel changed the wording, to reflect the new reality. Now, in exile, we declare: "who has brought us to this night on which we eat matzah and *maror*"—only.

And now that our joy is incomplete, we add a prayer and a supplication, to be inserted into the text of the original blessing. We recite: "O Lord our God and God of our fathers, may we live to celebrate in peace other festivals and holy seasons, joyful in the building of Your city and happy in Your service. And there may we eat of the sacrifices and Passover offerings." For today, we are entrenched in Exile, and we are incapable of fulfilling the commandment to offer, and to eat from, the sacrifices. Only when we can once again bring these offerings to Jerusalem as in days of yore will we be able to thank the Creator "for our redemption and for the deliverance of our souls." Our joy will be full only when we can once again fulfill the commandments completely—at the time of the Redemption.

Some Special "Remembrances of the Temple" Contained in the Haggadah

After the destruction of the Holy Temple, a number of laws and customs were enacted and established whose specific purpose was to keep the memory of the Temple alive in the hearts and minds of the Jewish people. A number of these "Temple remembrances" can be found in the *Haggadah* and in the customs for the Seder night, such as the custom to place an egg on the Seder plate as a reminder of the festival (*hagigah*) sacrifice which Israel brought up to the Temple on the 14th day of Nisan, and then ate at the Seder that evening.

However, this egg carries an additional symbolism as well—to remind us of the destruction of the Temple. For the egg is actually a symbol of mourning; it is round, representing the cycle of life—and it has no "mouth," or opening; so too, the grief-stricken mourner finds no words to express his sorrow, but remains silent. Such is the custom which has been adopted by all Jewry; an egg is partaken of in a house of mourning, and eaten by everyone at the meal which precedes the solemn fast of Tishah B'Av (Ninth of Av, the day commemorating the destruction of the Temple, when all of Israel are considered as mourners for the Temple and Jerusalem).

The host covers the *matzot*, raises his cup, and says:

Blessed are You,

O Lord our God, King of the universe, who has redeemed us and our fathers from Egypt and has brought us to this night on which we eat [*in the time of the Holy Temple:* the Passover sacrifice,] matzah and bitter herbs. O Lord our God and God of our fathers, may we live to celebrate in peace other festivals and holy seasons, joyful in the building of Your city and happy in Your service. And there may we eat of the sacrifices and Passover offerings, (*when Passover falls on Saturday night it is said:* of the Passover offerings and the sacrifices) whose blood shall be acceptably sprinkled on the side of Your altar;

then shall we sing to You a new song for our redemption and for the deliverance of our souls.
Blessed are You, O Lord, who has redeemed Israel!

Blessed are You, O Lord our God, King of the universe, who created the fruit of the vine.

The second cup is drunk while in a reclining position.

RAHTSAH — Second Washing of the Hands

The hands are washed a second time and the proper blessing is recited.

Blessed are You, O Lord our God, King of the universe, who has sanctified us with His commandments and commanded us to wash our hands.

MOTSI – MATZAH — The Blessing for Bread and for Matzah

The blessing for bread is said over the matzah, and then the special blessing for the commandment of eating matzah is recited. After these two blessings are said, the matzah is eaten.

The host distributes a k'zayit of matzah shmurah to each person at the Seder, in order to fulfill the commandment of eating matzah. He should prepare enough matzah shmurah in advance, in addition to the matzot on the Seder plate. Each person should receive, as a minimum, about 1/2 of a normal-sized matzah, plus a piece of that which he holds in his hand (it is proper to eat two k'zayitim for the mitzvah of matzah).

The host takes the three matzot in his hands, raises them and recites the blessing:

Blessed are You, O Lord our God, King of the universe, who brings forth bread from the earth.

The host then puts the bottom matzah back in its place, and says the following while still holding the other two:

Blessed are You, O Lord our God, King of the universe, who has sanctified us with His commandments, and commanded us to eat matzah.

The host dips the matzot in salt, breaks off a portion of both the upper and middle matzah for himself, and breaks the rest into portions which he distributes to everyone present. All eat their k'zayit of matzah while reclining on the left side.

מכסה את המצות ונוטל את הכוס בידו.

בָּרוּךְ אַתָּה יְיָ אֱלֹהֵינוּ מֶלֶךְ הָעוֹלָם אֲשֶׁר גְּאָלָנוּ וְגָאַל אֶת אֲבוֹתֵינוּ מִמִּצְרַיִם וְהִגִּיעָנוּ הַלַּיְלָה הַזֶּה לֶאֱכָל בּוֹ [בזמן המקדש: פֶּסַח] מַצָּה וּמָרוֹר כֵּן יְיָ אֱלֹהֵינוּ וֵאלֹהֵי אֲבוֹתֵינוּ יַגִּיעֵנוּ לְמוֹעֲדִים וְלִרְגָלִים אֲחֵרִים הַבָּאִים לִקְרָאתֵנוּ לְשָׁלוֹם שְׂמֵחִים בְּבִנְיַן עִירֶךָ וְשָׂשִׂים בַּעֲבוֹדָתֶךָ וְנֹאכַל שָׁם מִן הַזְּבָחִים וּמִן הַפְּסָחִים אֲשֶׁר יַגִּיעַ דָּמָם עַל קִיר מִזְבַּחֲךָ לְרָצוֹן וְנוֹדֶה לְךָ שִׁיר חָדָשׁ עַל גְּאֻלָּתֵנוּ וְעַל פְּדוּת נַפְשֵׁנוּ בָּרוּךְ אַתָּה יְיָ גָּאַל יִשְׂרָאֵל:

הִנְנִי מוּכָן וּמְזֻמָּן לְקַיֵּם מִצְוַת כּוֹס שֵׁנִי שֶׁל אַרְבָּעָה כוֹסוֹת, כְּנֶגֶד לָשׁוֹן שֵׁנִי שֶׁל אַרְבָּעָה לְשׁוֹנוֹת גְּאֻלָּה, שֶׁנֶּאֱמַר: וְהִצַּלְתִּי אֶתְכֶם מֵעֲבֹדָתָם.

בָּרוּךְ אַתָּה יְיָ אֱלֹהֵינוּ מֶלֶךְ הָעוֹלָם בּוֹרֵא פְּרִי הַגָּפֶן.

שׁוֹתִים בַּהֲסִבָּה.

רָחְצָה נוֹטְלִים יָדַיִם לִסְעוּדָה בִּבְרָכָה.

בָּרוּךְ אַתָּה יְיָ אֱלֹהֵינוּ מֶלֶךְ הָעוֹלָם אֲשֶׁר קִדְּשָׁנוּ בְּמִצְוֹתָיו וְצִוָּנוּ עַל נְטִילַת יָדָיִם

מוֹצִיא מַצָּה

עוֹרֵךְ הַסֵּדֶר מְחַלֵּק לְכָל אֶחָד מִן הַמְסֻבִּים 'כְּזַיִת', לְמַצַּת מִצְוָה. לְשֵׁם כָּךְ יָכִין לְפָנָיו מַצּוֹת 'שְׁמוּרָה', בְּנוֹסָף עַל הַמַּצּוֹת שֶׁבְּקַעֲרַת הַסֵּדֶר, וִיחַלֵּק לְכָל אֶחָד חֲצִי מַצָּה מְכֻוָּנָה לִפְחוֹת, בְּצֵרוּף חֵלֶק מִן הַמַּצּוֹת שֶׁבְּיָדוֹ. (וְרָאוּי לֶאֱכֹל שְׁנֵי 'כְּזַיתִים' בַּאֲכִילַת מַצַּת מִצְוָה).

הָעוֹרֵךְ נוֹטֵל אֶת שְׁלוֹשׁ הַמַּצּוֹת בְּיָדָיו וּמְבָרֵךְ:

בָּרוּךְ אַתָּה יְיָ אֱלֹהֵינוּ מֶלֶךְ הָעוֹלָם הַמּוֹצִיא לֶחֶם מִן הָאָרֶץ

מַנִּיחַ אֶת הַמַּצָּה הַתַּחְתּוֹנָה מִיָּדוֹ וּמְבָרֵךְ:

בָּרוּךְ אַתָּה יְיָ אֱלֹהֵינוּ מֶלֶךְ הָעוֹלָם אֲשֶׁר קִדְּשָׁנוּ בְּמִצְוֹתָיו וְצִוָּנוּ עַל אֲכִילַת מַצָּה

הָעוֹרֵךְ בּוֹצֵעַ אֶת שְׁתֵּי הַמַּצּוֹת שֶׁבְּיָדָיו, אֶת הַמַּצָּה הָעֶלְיוֹנָה וְאֶת הַמַּצָּה הַחֲצוּיָה, יִטְבֹּל בְּמֶלַח, יְחַלֵּק לַמְסֻבִּים וְיֹאכְלוּ בַּהֲסִבַּת שְׂמֹאל.

---

completed the songs with additional chapters. Obviously, since the Torah commands that the Passover sacrifice should be celebrated with song and praise to God, this commandment was fulfilled by Israel before David's time as well, by the singing of those parts which had accompanied Israel at the time of the Exodus.

With regard to the sages' expression "Could Israel have then sacrificed the Passover, and taken up the *lulav*, without *Hallel*?"—they do not refer to the *lulavim* which are used to fulfill the holiday obligations on the Festival of Succoth, but this is rather meant generically, as an expression of authentic festival joy which was characteristic of Israel's golden age. For in ancient days Israel's joy was classically expressed through the waving of branches, as illustrated by King David and Israel's rejoicing before the Ark of God "with all manner of cypress wood" (II Samuel 6). Similarly, the *Yalkut Shimoni* (Leviticus 651) brings this parable: "The matter can be likened to two individuals who appear before a magistrate to be judged. We do not know who will emerge the victor . . . but when one leaves the judge's chamber with a palm branch in his hand, we know that he is the victor."

Israel's joy at the Exodus was a joy of victory, of victors who had successfully slaughtered the pagan gods of Egypt without fear; they take up the "*lulav* of victory." The joy which they experienced on the night they were liberated from Egyptian bondage is the source of their joy in later generations, in the Temple at Jerusalem.

Songs of *Hallel* in the Temple and Jerusalem

While the recitation of *Hallel* is a commandment which is applicable to all the festivals, and in fact, the sages list 18 days during the year wherein the *Hallel* is said, still, in the course of the entire year, there is only one *night* in which it is recited—and that is "the night of the holy holiday," Passover night.

On the day of the Passover sacrifice, the 14th of Nisan, the *Hallel* is sung more than on any other day of the year. For as the Mishnah taught us, the members of each band who offer the Passover sacrifice read the *Hallel* several times, while the Levites, too, accompany them from atop the platform, adding the sounds of their harps, lyres and cymbols to the joyous harmony.

The Levites stand atop the platform and sing the entire *Hallel*. Those Israelites present in the court are also commanded to accompany their sacrificial service with song; these join in with the Levites' song. Thus the sound of the festive *Hallel* was practically constant in the courtyards of the Holy Temple, and around Jerusalem, throughout the entire 14th of Nisan. To the Jewish people, this day became the symbol of the ideal joy; in the words of the prophet, "the night of the holy festival."

And He Has Brought Us to This Night, on Which We Eat the Passover Sacrifice, Matzah and *Maror*

Without a doubt, the *Haggadah* reaches its emotional and spiritual climax with the words of this blessing: "Who has redeemed us and redeemed our fathers from Egypt, and brought us to this night on which we eat the Passover sacrifice, matzah and bitter herbs." This was the version of the blessing which was uttered in Jerusalem when the Temple stood, as the Passover sacrifice was mentioned as well. This was recited after all those present at the Seder had related the story of the Exodus and spoken about the Passover, matzah and *maror*, after they had already answered the questions posed by the first three sons, and "helped along" the

מָרוֹר
MAROR — Eating the bitter herbs

The host distributes a *k'zayit* portion of the lettuce (about 27 grams) to all the participants. Everyone dips the *maror* into the haroseth and recites the blessing for eating *maror*. It is then eaten without reclining.

The blessing to be recited:
Blessed are You, O Lord our God, King of the universe, who has sanctified us with His commandments, and commanded us to eat bitter herbs.

עוֹרֵךְ הַסֵדֶר יַחְלֹק לְכֹל אֶחָד מִן הַמְסֻבִּים 'כְּזַיִת' (כְּעֶשְׂרִים וְשִׁבְעָה גְּרַם) מִן הַמָּרוֹר (מִן הַחַסָה), הַמְסֻבִּים יִטְבְּלוּ אוֹתָהּ 'טִיבּוּל שֵׁנִי' בַּחֲרוֹסֶת, יְבָרְכוּ 'עַל אֲכִילַת מָרוֹר' וְיֹאכְלוּ בְּלִי הֲסִיבָה.

בָּרוּךְ אַתָּה יְיָ אֱלֹהֵינוּ מֶלֶךְ הָעוֹלָם אֲשֶׁר קִדְּשָׁנוּ בְּמִצְוֹתָיו וְצִוָּנוּ עַל אֲכִילַת מָרוֹר.

[In the time of the Holy Temple, after the matzah and *maror* were eaten, the following blessing was recited: "Blessed are You, O Lord our God, King of the universe, who has sanctified us with His commandments, and commanded us to eat from the sacrifice." They would then partake of the *hagigah* offering. Likewise, in the time of the Holy Temple, after eating from the *hagigah* offering, all the participants would then partake of the Passover sacrifice as well. First this blessing is recited: "Blessed are You, O Lord our God, King of the universe, who has sanctified us with His commandments, and commanded us to eat of the Passover sacrifice."]

[בִּזְמַן הַמִּקְדָּשׁ, אַחַר אֲכִילַת מַצָּה וּמָרוֹר מְבָרְכִים:

בָּרוּךְ אַתָּה יְיָ אֱלֹהֵינוּ מֶלֶךְ הָעוֹלָם אֲשֶׁר קִדְּשָׁנוּ בְּמִצְוֹתָיו וְצִוָּנוּ עַל אֲכִילַת הַזֶּבַח.

וְאוֹכְלִים מִבְּשַׂר קָרְבַּן הַחֲגִיגָה].

[בִּזְמַן הַמִּקְדָּשׁ אַחַר אֲכִילַת קָרְבַּן חֲגִיגָה מְבָרְכִים:

בָּרוּךְ אַתָּה יְיָ אֱלֹהֵינוּ מֶלֶךְ הָעוֹלָם אֲשֶׁר קִדְּשָׁנוּ בְּמִצְוֹתָיו וְצִוָּנוּ עַל אֲכִילַת הַפֶּסַח.

וְאוֹכְלִים מִבְּשַׂר הַפֶּסַח].

כּוֹרֵךְ
KOREKH — Matzah Combined with Bitter Herbs

The host takes a *k'zayit* from the bottom matzah, and a *k'zayit* of *maror* (lettuce leaves), dips it in haroseth and combines them together. All the other Seder participants do likewise, and all eat while reclining on the left side. Before eating, they should say:

This is a remembrance of the Temple; this is what Hillel did in the time when the Holy Temple stood. He took the Passover sacrifice, matzah and bitter herb and ate them together, in order to fulfill what is written: "With unleavened bread and bitter herbs they shall eat it" *(Numbers 9:11).*

Those of Sephardic descent have a custom to say: "A remembrance of the Temple; may it be renewed in our days!"

עוֹרֵךְ הַסֵדֶר יִקַּח 'כְּזַיִת' מִן הַמַּצָּה הַשְּׁלִישִׁית, הַתַּחְתּוֹנָה, וּ'כְזַיִת' מָרוֹר (חַסָה) יִטְבּוֹל בַּחֲרוֹסֶת וְיִכְרְכֵם בְּיַחַד. כָּךְ יַעֲשׂוּ שְׁאָר הַמְסֻבִּים וְיֹאכְלוּ בַּהֲסִיבָה. לִפְנֵי אֲכִילָתָם יֹאמְרוּ הַמְסֻבִּים: 'זֵכֶר לַמִּקְדָּשׁ כְּהִלֵּל'. וּמִנְהַג בְּנֵי סְפָרַד לוֹמַר:

"זֵכֶר לַמִּקְדָּשׁ, בִּמְהֵרָה יְחֻדַּשׁ".

זֵכֶר לְמִקְדָּשׁ כְּהִלֵּל
כֵּן עָשָׂה הִלֵּל בִּזְמַן שֶׁבֵּית הַמִּקְדָּשׁ הָיָה קַיָּם
הָיָה כּוֹרֵךְ פֶּסַח מַצָּה וּמָרוֹר וְאוֹכֵל בְּיַחַד
לְקַיֵּם מַה שֶּׁנֶּאֱמַר עַל מַצּוֹת וּמְרוֹרִים יֹאכְלֻהוּ

שֻׁלְחָן עוֹרֵךְ
SHULHAN OREKH — The Meal is Served

סוֹעֲדִים אֶת סְעוּדַת הֶחָג

[בִּזְמַן הַמִּקְדָּשׁ, לְאַחַר סְעוּדַת הֶחָג, אוֹכְלִים פַּעַם נוֹסֶפֶת 'כְּזַיִת' בְּשַׂר מִקָּרְבַּן הַפֶּסַח בְּסוֹף הַסְעוּדָה, כְּדֵי שֶׁיִּשָׁאֵר טַעַם אֲכִילַת מִצְוַת הַפֶּסַח בְּפִי הַמְסֻבִּים].

[In the time of the Holy Temple, once the festive meal was concluded, an additional *k'zayit* of meat from the Passover sacrifice was eaten, in order for "the taste of the *mitzvah*" of the Passover sacrifice to remain in the mouth.]

צָפוּן
TSAFUN — The Afikoman

When the festive meal is concluded, the host takes a *k'zayit* from the matzah which he has hidden and distributes a piece of it to all present (he supplements this with additional *matzah shmurah* so that all receive the proper *k'zayit* amount—about 1/2 of a normal-sized matzah). It is proper to eat two *k'zayitim*. They are eaten in remembrance of the Passover sacrifice and the *hagigah* offering eaten in the time of the Holy Temple. Before eating the *afikoman*, all should say:

"This is a remembrance for the Passover sacrifice, which is to be eaten when we are satiated."

With the exception of the third and fourth cups of wine (and according to the custom of some, a "fifth" cup as well—see our explanation to follow), nothing may be eaten after partaking of the *afikoman*. However, one who stays awake after the Seder in order to study the laws of the Passover sacrifice, or to relate the story of the Exodus, is permitted to drink coffee or tea in order to remain alert.

לְאַחַר גְּמַר הַסְעוּדָה יִקַּח עוֹרֵךְ הַסֵדֶר 'כְּזַיִת' מִפְּרוּסַת הָאֲפִיקוֹמָן שֶׁהִצְנִיעַ, וִיחַלֵּק לְכָל אֶחָד מִן הַמְסֻבִּים, מִמֶּנָה וּמִמַּצָּה שְׁמוּרָה אַחֶרֶת, 'כְּזַיִת' בְּיַחַד (חֲצִי מַצָּה לִפְחוֹת). וְרָאוּי לֶאֱכוֹל שְׁנֵי 'כְּזֵיתִים'. וְיֹאכְלֵם כְּזֵכֶר לְקָרְבַּן פֶּסַח וּכְזֵכֶר לְקָרְבַּן חֲגִיגָה הַנֶּאֱכָלִים בְּלַיְלָה זֶה בִּזְמַן הַבַּיִת.

לִפְנֵי אֲכִילַת הָאֲפִיקוֹמָן יֹאמְרוּ הַמְסֻבִּים:

זֵכֶר לְקָרְבַּן פֶּסַח הַנֶּאֱכָל עַל הַשּׂוֹבַע.

אֵין לֶאֱכוֹל אַחַר אֲכִילַת אֲפִיקוֹמָן כִּי אִם לִשְׁתּוֹת כּוֹס שְׁלִישִׁי וְכוֹס רְבִיעִי (וְיֵשׁ נוֹהֲגִים 'כּוֹס חֲמִישִׁי', רְאֵה לְהַלָּן). וְאִם מַמְשִׁיךְ בְּסִפּוּר יְצִיאַת מִצְרַיִם וְלִמּוּד הִלְכוֹת קָרְבַּן פֶּסַח, וְרוֹצֶה לִשְׁמוֹר עַל עֵרָנוּתוֹ בַּלַּיְלָה, רַשַּׁאי לִשְׁתּוֹת קָפֶה אוֹ תֵּה.

In reflecting upon this inclusion in the Seder plate, it is interesting to note that according to the fixed calendar, each year the holiday of Passover falls out on the same day of the week on which several months later, the fast of Tishah B'Av will occur as well.

The well-known custom Hillel the Elder enacted while the Holy Temple yet stood, to make a "sandwich" of *matzot* and bitter herbs and to eat them together (in the days of the Temple, he ate them together with the roasted meat of the sacrifice, and to fulfill the words of the biblical verse, "You shall eat the Passover sacrifice with *matzot* and bitter herbs"), was also included in the *Haggadah*. It was Hillel's opinion that the meat of the Passover sacrifice must be eaten while it is wrapped together with the matzah and bitter herb (BT Pesahim 115:A), and it was incorporated into the text of the *Haggadah* as another "Temple Remembrance."

Because of halakhic doubt, all of Israel has adopted Hillel's custom, and in addition to the matzah and *maror* which are first eaten separately this evening, we also wrap them and eat them together afterwards, in keeping with Hillel's opinion. Maimonides maintains (Laws of Hametz and Matzah, ch. 8) that Hillel the Elder's sandwich consisted of only matzah and bitter herbs, and he ate them without the Passover sacrifice; that he ate separately. Nowadays, the *afikoman* is our "remembrance of the Temple," and is eaten at the conclusion of our Seder meal as a substitute for the Passover sacrifice. For like the Passover itself, the sages adopted the custom of eating the *afikoman* last, so that we will remain with the taste of the matzah, just as they remained with the taste of the Passover offering in the days of the Holy Temple. So too, it was also ruled that the *afikoman* be eaten before midnight, and this is also a "Temple remembrance"—for such was the law with regard to the Passover sacrifice.

The establishment and enactment of these "remembrances" serves to deepen awareness of the laws and customs which were in effect in the era of the Holy Temple, and they also aid in strengthening the faith that "the Temple will be rebuilt speedily." Therefore, in order to ensure that these ordinances are remembered and recognized by all of Israel—thus preparing them for the rebuilding of the Temple—many such reminders were incorporated into the structure of the Seder and its *mitzvot*, so that the Temple will remain at the forefront of our consciousness.

בָּרֵךְ

<small>מוזגין כוס שלישי לברכת המזון.</small>

הִנְנִי מוּכָן וּמְזֻמָּן לְקַיֵּם מִצְוַת עֲשֵׂה שֶׁל בִּרְכַּת הַמָּזוֹן
כְּמוֹ שֶׁכָּתוּב בַּתּוֹרָה וְאָכַלְתָּ וְשָׂבָעְתָּ וּבֵרַכְתָּ אֶת־יְיָ אֱלֹהֶיךָ
עַל הָאָרֶץ הַטֹּבָה אֲשֶׁר נָתַן־לָךְ

<small>אם יש שלשה בני מצוה, מזמנים</small>

הַמְזַמֵּן	רַבּוֹתַי נְבָרֵךְ
הַמְסֻבִּים	יְהִי שֵׁם יְיָ מְבֹרָךְ מֵעַתָּה וְעַד־עוֹלָם
הַמְזַמֵּן	בִּרְשׁוּת מָרָנָן וְרַבָּנָן וְרַבּוֹתַי נְבָרֵךְ (בעשרה מוסיפים אֱלֹהֵינוּ) שֶׁאָכַלְנוּ מִשֶּׁלּוֹ
הַמְסֻבִּים	בָּרוּךְ (בעשרה מוסיפים אֱלֹהֵינוּ) שֶׁאָכַלְנוּ מִשֶּׁלּוֹ וּבְטוּבוֹ חָיִינוּ
	בָּרוּךְ הוּא וּבָרוּךְ שְׁמוֹ

<small>אם אין שלשה מתחילין כאן</small>

בָּרוּךְ

אַתָּה יְיָ אֱלֹהֵינוּ מֶלֶךְ הָעוֹלָם הַזָּן אֶת־הָעוֹלָם כֻּלּוֹ בְּטוּבוֹ בְּחֵן בְּחֶסֶד וּבְרַחֲמִים הוּא נוֹתֵן לֶחֶם לְכָל־בָּשָׂר כִּי לְעוֹלָם חַסְדּוֹ וּבְטוּבוֹ הַגָּדוֹל תָּמִיד לֹא חָסַר לָנוּ וְאַל יֶחְסַר לָנוּ מָזוֹן לְעוֹלָם וָעֶד בַּעֲבוּר שְׁמוֹ הַגָּדוֹל כִּי הוּא אֵל זָן וּמְפַרְנֵס לַכֹּל וּמֵטִיב לַכֹּל וּמֵכִין מָזוֹן לְכָל־בְּרִיּוֹתָיו אֲשֶׁר בָּרָא בָּרוּךְ אַתָּה יְיָ הַזָּן אֶת הַכֹּל

נוֹדֶה

לְךָ יְיָ אֱלֹהֵינוּ עַל שֶׁהִנְחַלְתָּ לַאֲבוֹתֵינוּ אֶרֶץ חֶמְדָּה טוֹבָה וּרְחָבָה וְעַל שֶׁהוֹצֵאתָנוּ יְיָ אֱלֹהֵינוּ מֵאֶרֶץ מִצְרַיִם וּפְדִיתָנוּ מִבֵּית עֲבָדִים וְעַל בְּרִיתְךָ שֶׁחָתַמְתָּ בִּבְשָׂרֵנוּ וְעַל תּוֹרָתְךָ שֶׁלִּמַּדְתָּנוּ וְעַל חֻקֶּיךָ שֶׁהוֹדַעְתָּנוּ וְעַל חַיִּים חֵן וָחֶסֶד שֶׁחוֹנַנְתָּנוּ וְעַל אֲכִילַת מָזוֹן שֶׁאַתָּה זָן וּמְפַרְנֵס אוֹתָנוּ תָּמִיד בְּכָל יוֹם וּבְכָל עֵת וּבְכָל שָׁעָה

וְעַל הַכֹּל יְיָ אֱלֹהֵינוּ אֲנַחְנוּ מוֹדִים לָךְ וּמְבָרְכִים אוֹתָךְ יִתְבָּרַךְ שִׁמְךָ בְּפִי כָּל חַי תָּמִיד לְעוֹלָם וָעֶד כַּכָּתוּב וְאָכַלְתָּ וְשָׂבָעְתָּ וּבֵרַכְתָּ אֶת יְיָ אֱלֹהֶיךָ עַל הָאָרֶץ הַטֹּבָה אֲשֶׁר נָתַן לָךְ בָּרוּךְ אַתָּה יְיָ עַל הָאָרֶץ וְעַל הַמָּזוֹן

רַחֶם־נָא

יְיָ אֱלֹהֵינוּ עַל יִשְׂרָאֵל עַמֶּךָ וְעַל יְרוּשָׁלַיִם עִירֶךָ וְעַל צִיּוֹן מִשְׁכַּן כְּבוֹדֶךָ וְעַל מַלְכוּת בֵּית דָּוִד מְשִׁיחֶךָ וְעַל הַבַּיִת הַגָּדוֹל וְהַקָּדוֹשׁ שֶׁנִּקְרָא שִׁמְךָ עָלָיו אֱלֹהֵינוּ אָבִינוּ רְעֵנוּ זוּנֵנוּ פַּרְנְסֵנוּ וְכַלְכְּלֵנוּ וְהַרְוִיחֵנוּ וְהַרְוַח לָנוּ יְיָ אֱלֹהֵינוּ מְהֵרָה מִכָּל צָרוֹתֵינוּ וְנָא אַל תַּצְרִיכֵנוּ יְיָ אֱלֹהֵינוּ לֹא לִידֵי מַתְּנַת בָּשָׂר וָדָם וְלֹא לִידֵי הַלְוָאָתָם כִּי אִם לְיָדְךָ הַמְּלֵאָה הַפְּתוּחָה הַקְּדוֹשָׁה וְהָרְחָבָה שֶׁלֹּא נֵבוֹשׁ וְלֹא נִכָּלֵם לְעוֹלָם וָעֶד

בשבת

רְצֵה וְהַחֲלִיצֵנוּ יְיָ אֱלֹהֵינוּ בְּמִצְוֹתֶיךָ וּבְמִצְוַת יוֹם הַשְּׁבִיעִי הַשַּׁבָּת הַגָּדוֹל וְהַקָּדוֹשׁ הַזֶּה כִּי יוֹם זֶה גָּדוֹל וְקָדוֹשׁ הוּא לְפָנֶיךָ לִשְׁבָּת־בּוֹ וְלָנוּחַ בּוֹ בְּאַהֲבָה כְּמִצְוַת רְצוֹנֶךָ וּבִרְצוֹנְךָ הָנִיחַ לָנוּ יְיָ אֱלֹהֵינוּ שֶׁלֹּא תְהֵא צָרָה וְיָגוֹן וַאֲנָחָה בְּיוֹם מְנוּחָתֵנוּ וְהַרְאֵנוּ יְיָ אֱלֹהֵינוּ בְּנֶחָמַת צִיּוֹן עִירֶךָ וּבְבִנְיַן יְרוּשָׁלַיִם עִיר קָדְשֶׁךָ כִּי אַתָּה הוּא בַּעַל הַיְשׁוּעוֹת וּבַעַל הַנֶּחָמוֹת

BAREKH — Grace after Meals

The third cup of wine is poured before the Grace.
A Song of Ascents. When the Lord returned the exiles of Zion, we were like dreamers. Then our mouths will be filled with laughter, and our tongues with song; then they will say among the nations, the Lord has done great things for them. The Lord has done great things for us; we are glad. Return our exiles again, O Lord, as the streams in the south. They that sow in tears shall reap in joy. He that goes forth and weeps bearing precious seed, shall doubtless come again with rejoicing, bringing his sheaves with him.

ZIMUN — When three or more people have eaten together.
One of them begins: Gentlemen, Let us say Grace!
The others answer: Blessed be the Name of the Lord for ever and ever!
He continues: Masters, teachers, gentlemen, by your leave, let us bless Him (*when ten men are present, say,* our God) whose food we have eaten.
The others answer: Blessed be He (*when ten men are present, say,* our God) whose food we have eaten and through whose goodness we live! Blessed be He and blessed be His Name!

If less than three men are present, begin here:

Blessed are You, O Lord our God, King of the universe, who feeds the whole world in His goodness, with grace, mercy and compassion. "He gives food to every creature, for His mercy endures forever" *(Psalm 136:25)*. And in His great goodness, food has never failed us, and may it never fail us for ever and ever, for His great Name's sake, for He feeds and sustains all, is good to all, and provides food for every creature which He has created. Blessed are You, O Lord, who feeds us all!

We thank You, O Lord our God, for the pleasant, good, and ample land which You gave to our fathers as an inheritance, and for having brought us, O Lord our God, out of the land of Egypt and redeemed us from the house of bondage. For the Covenant which You have sealed in our flesh, for the Law which You have taught us and for Your statutes which You have made known to us; for the life, grace, and mercy with which You have favored us, and for the food with which You feed and sustain us continually, every day, at every time and at every hour.
And for all this, O Lord our God, we thank and bless You, blessed be Your Name in the mouth of all that lives, continually for evermore! As it is written: "When you have eaten and are satisfied, then you shall bless the Lord your God, for the good land which He has given you" *(Deuteronomy 8:10)*. Blessed are You, O Lord, for the land and for the sustenance!

Have mercy, O Lord our God, upon Your people Israel, upon Jerusalem Your city, upon Zion the seat of Your glory, on the kingdom of the house of David Your anointed *and on the great and holy House which is called by Your Name.* O God our father, shepherd and sustainer, keeper and deliverer, may we be delivered speedily, O Lord our God, from all our troubles. And may we never stand in need, O Lord our God, of gifts of men, nor of their loans, but only of Your full, open, holy, and generous hand, that we may not be ashamed nor confounded for ever and ever.

אֱלֹהֵינוּ וֵאלֹהֵי אֲבוֹתֵינוּ

יַעֲלֶה וְיָבֹא וְיַגִּיעַ וְיֵרָאֶה וְיֵרָצֶה וְיִשָּׁמַע וְיִפָּקֵד וְיִזָּכֵר זִכְרוֹנֵנוּ וּפִקְדוֹנֵנוּ וְזִכְרוֹן אֲבוֹתֵינוּ וְזִכְרוֹן מָשִׁיחַ בֶּן דָּוִד עַבְדֶּךָ וְזִכְרוֹן יְרוּשָׁלַיִם עִיר קָדְשֶׁךָ וְזִכְרוֹן כָּל עַמְּךָ בֵּית יִשְׂרָאֵל לְפָנֶיךָ לִפְלֵיטָה לְטוֹבָה לְחֵן וּלְחֶסֶד וּלְרַחֲמִים לְחַיִּים וּלְשָׁלוֹם בְּיוֹם חַג הַמַּצּוֹת הַזֶּה זָכְרֵנוּ יְיָ אֱלֹהֵינוּ בּוֹ לְטוֹבָה וּפָקְדֵנוּ בוֹ לִבְרָכָה וְהוֹשִׁיעֵנוּ בוֹ לְחַיִּים וּבִדְבַר יְשׁוּעָה וְרַחֲמִים חוּס וְחָנֵּנוּ וְרַחֵם עָלֵינוּ וְהוֹשִׁיעֵנוּ כִּי אֵלֶיךָ עֵינֵינוּ כִּי אֵל חַנּוּן וְרַחוּם אָתָּה

וּבְנֵה יְרוּשָׁלַיִם עִיר הַקֹּדֶשׁ בִּמְהֵרָה בְיָמֵינוּ
בָּרוּךְ אַתָּה יְיָ בּוֹנֵה בְרַחֲמָיו יְרוּשָׁלַיִם אָמֵן

בָּרוּךְ אַתָּה יְיָ אֱלֹהֵינוּ מֶלֶךְ הָעוֹלָם הָאֵל אָבִינוּ מַלְכֵּנוּ אַדִּירֵנוּ בּוֹרְאֵנוּ גּוֹאֲלֵנוּ יוֹצְרֵנוּ קְדוֹשֵׁנוּ קְדוֹשׁ יַעֲקֹב רוֹעֵנוּ רוֹעֵה יִשְׂרָאֵל הַמֶּלֶךְ הַטּוֹב וְהַמֵּטִיב לַכֹּל שֶׁבְּכָל יוֹם וָיוֹם הוּא הֵיטִיב הוּא מֵיטִיב הוּא יֵיטִיב לָנוּ הוּא גְמָלָנוּ הוּא גוֹמְלֵנוּ הוּא יִגְמְלֵנוּ לָעַד לְחֵן וּלְחֶסֶד וּלְרַחֲמִים וּלְרֶוַח הַצָּלָה וְהַצְלָחָה בְּרָכָה וִישׁוּעָה נֶחָמָה פַּרְנָסָה וְכַלְכָּלָה וְרַחֲמִים וְחַיִּים וְשָׁלוֹם וְכָל טוֹב וּמִכָּל טוּב לְעוֹלָם אַל יְחַסְּרֵנוּ

הָרַחֲמָן הוּא יִמְלֹךְ עָלֵינוּ לְעוֹלָם וָעֶד
הָרַחֲמָן הוּא יִתְבָּרַךְ בַּשָּׁמַיִם וּבָאָרֶץ
הָרַחֲמָן הוּא יִשְׁתַּבַּח לְדוֹר דּוֹרִים וְיִתְפָּאַר בָּנוּ לָנֶצַח נְצָחִים וְיִתְהַדַּר בָּנוּ לָעַד וּלְעוֹלְמֵי עוֹלָמִים
הָרַחֲמָן הוּא יְפַרְנְסֵנוּ בְּכָבוֹד
הָרַחֲמָן הוּא יִשְׁבֹּר עֻלֵּנוּ מֵעַל צַוָּארֵנוּ וְהוּא יוֹלִיכֵנוּ קוֹמְמִיּוּת לְאַרְצֵנוּ
הָרַחֲמָן הוּא יִשְׁלַח לָנוּ בְּרָכָה מְרֻבָּה בַּבַּיִת הַזֶּה וְעַל שֻׁלְחָן זֶה שֶׁאָכַלְנוּ עָלָיו
הָרַחֲמָן הוּא יִשְׁלַח לָנוּ אֶת אֵלִיָּהוּ הַנָּבִיא זָכוּר לַטּוֹב וִיבַשֵּׂר לָנוּ בְּשׂוֹרוֹת טוֹבוֹת יְשׁוּעוֹת וְנֶחָמוֹת

On the Sabbath say:

Be pleased, O Lord our God, to make us happy through keeping Your commandments, and through the commandment of the seventh day, this great and holy Sabbath. For this is a great and holy day before You, to rest and be at ease, in love, according to Your will. And may it be Your will, O Lord our God, that there be no trouble, sorrow, or affliction on our day of rest, and may we see, O Lord our God, the consolation of Zion Your city and the building of Jerusalem Your holy city, for You are Lord of redemption and the Lord of consolations.

O God and God of our fathers!

May there rise, and come and arrive, and be seen and accepted and heard, and be visited and remembered, our remembrance and the remembrance of our fathers, the remembrance of the Messiah, son of David Your servant, the remembrance of Jerusalem Your holy city and the remembrance of all Your people, the house of Israel: for deliverance, for good and for grace, for kindness, for mercy, for life and for peace before You on this day, the Feast of Matzot. In this season remember us, O Lord our God, for good, and visit us for a blessing and save us for life: and with the word of salvation and mercy, pity us and show us grace, be merciful to us and redeem us, for our eyes look always toward You, O God, who are merciful and gracious!

O Build Jerusalem, the holy city, soon, in our days. Blessed are You, O Lord, who in His mercy builds Jerusalem, Amen!

Blessed are You, O Lord our God, King of the universe! O God, our father, our King, our ruler, creator, redeemer, maker, our Holy One, the Holy One of Jacob; our shepherd, the shepherd of Israel; the good King who does good to all, and each and every day did, does, and will do good to us! He did, does, and will deal kindly with us always, for grace, favor, mercy, and deliverance; freedom, protection, prosperity, blessing, salvation, comfort, support, sustenance, mercy, life, peace, and all good; and may every good never be lacking us!

May the All-Merciful reign over us for ever and ever!

May the All-Merciful be blessed in heaven and on earth!

May the All-Merciful be praised throughout all generations!

May the All-Merciful May He be glorified amongst us for all ages, and honored among us now and for all eternity!

May the All-Merciful sustain us in honor!

May the All-Merciful break the yoke from off our necks and lead us upright into our Land!

May the All-Merciful multiply blessings on this house, and on this table at which we have eaten!

May the All-Merciful send us Elijah the Prophet (may he be remembered for good) to bring us good tidings of comfort and salvation!

בן הסמוך על שלחן הוריו אומר

הָרַחֲמָן הוּא יְבָרֵךְ אֶת־אָבִי מוֹרִי בַּעַל הַבַּיִת הַזֶּה וְאֶת אִמִּי מוֹרָתִי בַּעֲלַת הַבַּיִת הַזֶּה אוֹתָם וְאֶת בֵּיתָם וְאֶת זַרְעָם וְאֶת כָּל אֲשֶׁר לָהֶם

בעל הבית אומר

הָרַחֲמָן הוּא יְבָרֵךְ אוֹתִי וְאֶת אִשְׁתִּי וְאֶת זַרְעִי וְאֶת כָּל אֲשֶׁר לִי

בעלת הבית אומרת

הָרַחֲמָן הוּא יְבָרֵךְ אוֹתִי וְאֶת בַּעְלִי וְאֶת זַרְעִי וְאֶת כָּל אֲשֶׁר לִי

אורח אומר

הָרַחֲמָן הוּא יְבָרֵךְ אֶת־בַּעַל הַבַּיִת הַזֶּה וְאֶת בַּעֲלַת הַבַּיִת הַזֶּה וְאֶת כָּל הַמְסֻבִּין כָּאן אוֹתָם וְאֶת בֵּיתָם וְאֶת זַרְעָם וְאֶת כָּל אֲשֶׁר לָהֶם

אוֹתָנוּ וְאֶת כָּל אֲשֶׁר לָנוּ כְּמוֹ שֶׁנִּתְבָּרְכוּ אֲבוֹתֵינוּ אַבְרָהָם יִצְחָק וְיַעֲקֹב בַּכֹּל מִכֹּל כֹּל כֵּן יְבָרֵךְ אוֹתָנוּ כֻּלָּנוּ יַחַד בִּבְרָכָה שְׁלֵמָה וְנֹאמַר אָמֵן

בַּמָּרוֹם יְלַמְּדוּ עֲלֵיהֶם וְעָלֵינוּ זְכוּת שֶׁתְּהֵא לְמִשְׁמֶרֶת שָׁלוֹם וְנִשָּׂא בְרָכָה מֵאֵת יְיָ וּצְדָקָה מֵאֱלֹהֵי יִשְׁעֵנוּ וְנִמְצָא חֵן וְשֵׂכֶל טוֹב בְּעֵינֵי אֱלֹהִים וְאָדָם

בשבת

הָרַחֲמָן הוּא יַנְחִילֵנוּ יוֹם שֶׁכֻּלּוֹ שַׁבָּת וּמְנוּחָה לְחַיֵּי הָעוֹלָמִים

הָרַחֲמָן הוּא יַנְחִילֵנוּ יוֹם שֶׁכֻּלּוֹ טוֹב

הָרַחֲמָן הוּא יְזַכֵּנוּ לִימוֹת הַמָּשִׁיחַ וּלְחַיֵּי הָעוֹלָם הַבָּא מִגְדּוֹל יְשׁוּעוֹת מַלְכּוֹ וְעֹשֶׂה־חֶסֶד לִמְשִׁיחוֹ לְדָוִד וּלְזַרְעוֹ עַד עוֹלָם עֹשֶׂה שָׁלוֹם בִּמְרוֹמָיו הוּא יַעֲשֶׂה שָׁלוֹם עָלֵינוּ וְעַל כָּל יִשְׂרָאֵל וְאִמְרוּ אָמֵן

יְראוּ אֶת־יְיָ קְדֹשָׁיו כִּי־אֵין מַחְסוֹר לִירֵאָיו כְּפִירִים רָשׁוּ וְרָעֵבוּ וְדֹרְשֵׁי יְיָ לֹא־יַחְסְרוּ כָל־טוֹב הוֹדוּ לַייָ כִּי־טוֹב כִּי לְעוֹלָם חַסְדּוֹ פּוֹתֵחַ אֶת־יָדֶךָ וּמַשְׂבִּיעַ לְכָל־חַי רָצוֹן בָּרוּךְ הַגֶּבֶר אֲשֶׁר יִבְטַח בַּייָ וְהָיָה יְיָ מִבְטַחוֹ נַעַר הָיִיתִי גַּם זָקַנְתִּי וְלֹא־רָאִיתִי צַדִּיק נֶעֱזָב וְזַרְעוֹ מְבַקֶּשׁ־לָחֶם

יְיָ עֹז לְעַמּוֹ יִתֵּן יְיָ יְבָרֵךְ אֶת־עַמּוֹ

A son sitting at his parents' table says:

May the All-Merciful bless my father and teacher, the master of this house, and my mother and teacher, the mistress of this house, them, their children, and all that is theirs!

A guest says:

May the All-Merciful bless the master of this house, the mistress of this house, them, their children, and all that is theirs.

The head of the household says:

May the All-Merciful bless me, my wife, my children, and all that is mine!

Us, and all that belongs to us! As our fathers Abraham, Isaac and Jacob were blessed with all and every good, so may He bless us all together with a perfect blessing. And let us say, Amen!

May their merits and may ours, made known on high, be a store of peace treasured up for us! And may we receive a blessing from the Lord and righteousness from the God of our salvation. And may we find grace and favor in the eyes of God and men!

On the Sabbath say:

May the All-Merciful bring us to a day that is entirely Sabbath, and the rest of everlasting life!

May the All-Merciful bring us to a day that is entirely good!

May the All-Merciful make us worthy of the days of the Messiah and the life of the world to come!

"He is a tower of salvation to His king, and shows mercy to His anointed, to David and his seed for evermore" *(II Samuel 22:51)*. He who makes peace in His high places, may He make peace upon us and upon all Israel. And let us say, Amen!

"O fear the Lord, you His saints, for those that fear Him do not want. The young lions lack, and suffer hunger, but they that seek the Lord shall not be wanting any good thing" *(Psalm 34:9–10)*. "O give thanks to the Lord, for He is good: for His mercy endures forever" *(Psalm 118:1)*. "You open Your hand, and satisfy the desire of every living thing" *(Psalm 145:16)*. "Blessed is the man that trusts in the Lord, and whose hope the Lord is" *(Jeremiah 17:7)*. "I have been young, now I am old; yet I have not seen the righteous forsaken, nor his seed begging bread" *(Psalm 37:25)*.

"The Lord will give strength to His people: the Lord will bless His people with

PEACE"

(Psalm 29:11).

The Priests Ascend the Ramp The priests take from every sacrifice the portions that will be offered up on the altar. These portions are placed in a vessel and brought up the ramp to the top of the altar, where they are placed on the fire.

הנני מוכן ומזומן לקיים מצוות כוס שלישי של ארבעה כוסות, כנגד לשון שלישי של ארבעה לשונות גאולה, שנאמר: וְגָאַלְתִּי אֶתְכֶם בִּזְרוֹעַ נְטוּיָה וּבִשְׁפָטִים גְּדֹלִים.

בָּרוּךְ אַתָּה יְיָ אֱלֹהֵינוּ מֶלֶךְ הָעוֹלָם בּוֹרֵא פְּרִי הַגָּפֶן

ושותים בהסיבה.

מוזגין כוס גדול לכבודו של אליהו הנביא מבשר הגאולה. את כוסו של אליהו יניח בקערת הסדר.

פותחין את הדלת לכבודו של אליהו ואומרים: **הרחמן הוא ישלח לנו את אליהו הנביא זכור לטוב ויבשר לנו בשורות טובות ישועות ונחמות.**

שְׁפֹךְ

חֲמָתְךָ אֶל-הַגּוֹיִם אֲשֶׁר לֹא-יְדָעוּךָ וְעַל-מַמְלָכוֹת אֲשֶׁר בְּשִׁמְךָ לֹא קָרָאוּ כִּי אָכַל אֶת-יַעֲקֹב וְאֶת-נָוֵהוּ הֵשַׁמּוּ שְׁפֹךְ-עֲלֵיהֶם זַעְמֶךָ וַחֲרוֹן אַפְּךָ יַשִּׂיגֵם תִּרְדֹּף בְּאַף וְתַשְׁמִידֵם מִתַּחַת שְׁמֵי יְיָ

הלל

מוזגין כוס רביעי לכל המסובין ומוזגין מעט מכוסו של אליהו לכל אחד מן המסובים.

לֹא לָנוּ יְיָ לֹא לָנוּ כִּי-לְשִׁמְךָ תֵּן כָּבוֹד עַל-חַסְדְּךָ עַל-אֲמִתֶּךָ לָמָּה יֹאמְרוּ הַגּוֹיִם אַיֵּה-נָא אֱלֹהֵיהֶם וֵאלֹהֵינוּ בַשָּׁמָיִם כֹּל אֲשֶׁר-חָפֵץ עָשָׂה עֲצַבֵּיהֶם כֶּסֶף וְזָהָב מַעֲשֵׂה יְדֵי אָדָם פֶּה-לָהֶם וְלֹא יְדַבֵּרוּ עֵינַיִם לָהֶם וְלֹא יִרְאוּ אָזְנַיִם לָהֶם וְלֹא יִשְׁמָעוּ אַף לָהֶם וְלֹא יְרִיחוּן יְדֵיהֶם וְלֹא יְמִישׁוּן רַגְלֵיהֶם וְלֹא יְהַלֵּכוּ לֹא-יֶהְגּוּ בִּגְרוֹנָם כְּמוֹהֶם יִהְיוּ עֹשֵׂיהֶם כֹּל אֲשֶׁר-בֹּטֵחַ בָּהֶם יִשְׂרָאֵל בְּטַח בַּיְיָ עֶזְרָם וּמָגִנָּם הוּא בֵּית אַהֲרֹן בִּטְחוּ בַיְיָ עֶזְרָם וּמָגִנָּם הוּא יִרְאֵי יְיָ בִּטְחוּ בַיְיָ עֶזְרָם וּמָגִנָּם הוּא

יְיָ זְכָרָנוּ יְבָרֵךְ יְבָרֵךְ אֶת-בֵּית יִשְׂרָאֵל יְבָרֵךְ אֶת-בֵּית אַהֲרֹן יְבָרֵךְ יִרְאֵי יְיָ הַקְּטַנִּים עִם-הַגְּדֹלִים יֹסֵף יְיָ עֲלֵיכֶם עֲלֵיכֶם וְעַל-בְּנֵיכֶם בְּרוּכִים אַתֶּם לַיְיָ עֹשֵׂה שָׁמַיִם וָאָרֶץ הַשָּׁמַיִם שָׁמַיִם לַיְיָ וְהָאָרֶץ נָתַן לִבְנֵי-אָדָם לֹא הַמֵּתִים יְהַלְלוּ-יָהּ וְלֹא כָּל-יֹרְדֵי דוּמָה וַאֲנַחְנוּ נְבָרֵךְ יָהּ מֵעַתָּה וְעַד-עוֹלָם

הַלְלוּיָהּ

אָהַבְתִּי כִּי-יִשְׁמַע יְיָ אֶת-קוֹלִי תַּחֲנוּנָי כִּי-הִטָּה אָזְנוֹ לִי וּבְיָמַי אֶקְרָא אֲפָפוּנִי חֶבְלֵי-מָוֶת וּמְצָרֵי שְׁאוֹל מְצָאוּנִי צָרָה וְיָגוֹן אֶמְצָא וּבְשֵׁם-יְיָ אֶקְרָא אָנָּה יְיָ מַלְּטָה נַפְשִׁי חַנּוּן יְיָ וְצַדִּיק וֵאלֹהֵינוּ מְרַחֵם שֹׁמֵר פְּתָאיִם יְיָ דַּלּוֹתִי וְלִי יְהוֹשִׁיעַ שׁוּבִי נַפְשִׁי לִמְנוּחָיְכִי כִּי-יְיָ גָּמַל עָלָיְכִי כִּי חִלַּצְתָּ נַפְשִׁי מִמָּוֶת אֶת-עֵינִי מִן-דִּמְעָה אֶת-רַגְלִי מִדֶּחִי אֶתְהַלֵּךְ לִפְנֵי יְיָ בְּאַרְצוֹת הַחַיִּים הֶאֱמַנְתִּי כִּי אֲדַבֵּר אֲנִי עָנִיתִי מְאֹד אֲנִי אָמַרְתִּי בְחָפְזִי כָּל-הָאָדָם כֹּזֵב

---

destruction, and according to Rashi, there is a reason for singing: we thank the Holy One that He vented His anger on wood and stones—on the Holy Temple—and not on His people. The verse reads: "A psalm of Asaph. O God, nations have come into Your inheritance; they have defiled Your holy Sanctuary, they have laid Jerusalem in heaps." It is evident that the plain meaning of this verse refers to the destruction of the Holy Temple, which is inexorably bound up with the Festival of Passover, the actual beginning of the destruction, as we have stated. The main target of these verses is obviously the Roman Empire, which destroyed Jerusalem, burned the Holy Temple and exiled Israel.

The Custom to Open the Door Originates with the Priests in the Holy Temple
In the *Haggadah Shleimah*, Rabbi M. M. Kasher cites an opinion which maintains that the custom to open the door when these verses are recited is also rooted in the era of the Temple, *for a well-established custom that was practiced by the priests in the Holy Temple was to open the Temple gates at midnight on the night of Passover*. Once again, Josephus testifies to the accuracy of this claim: "On the Festival of Passover, the Priests were accustomed to open the gates of the Temple immediately after midnight." Josephus continues to relate that on one occasion, the Samaritans took advantage of this custom and used the opportunity to defile the Temple with human bones. From that time onward, security in the Temple was increased.

Thus, we have seen that the custom to open the doors at midnight and to recite these verses of anger and revenge, is based on a combination of two concepts, both of which are rooted in the Temple, and connected with Passover. On the one hand, these verses express rage over the destruction which Rome caused—the same Rome which is "Edom," those who have ruled over Israel ever since its dispersion amongst the nations. And at the same time, the opening of the doors expresses our hope that we will once again merit to practice that ancient custom—opening wide the Temple gates on the Festival of Redemption, as in days gone by.

Pour Out Your Wrath Upon the Nations Who Do Not Know You

Many commentators on the *Haggadah* have already wondered as to the source for the custom of reciting verses during the Seder which speak of vengeance against Israel's enemies. The generally accepted view is that this custom came about in response to the attacks perpetrated against various Jewish communities during the long course of their exile—attacks which invariably took place during the holiday of Passover, the blood libels of Europe, the Inquisition of Spain, and many others.

But it would seem that the actual origin for the recital of these verses is yet rooted in the Temple's destruction by the Roman Empire. For the siege which the Romans laid on Jerusalem, eventually leading to the destruction of the Holy Temple, was begun during the festival of Passover. The historian Josephus testifies to this fact in his book, *The Jewish Wars* (Book 6,9; 3,4): "Many people were gathered to Jerusalem to celebrate the Festival of Matzot, and suddenly the war closed in on them; it was as if it had been decreed to close the nation in, as in a prison. And when the war broke out in the environs of Jerusalem, the city was filled with many people." The Festival of Passover at the time of the rebellion was the last Passover in Jerusalem, and it was in these days that Titus' siege against the city was begun. According to Josephus' description, more than one million pilgrims arrived in Jerusalem that year to offer the Passover sacrifice.

A close examination of the verses selected here in the *Haggadah* to express the wrath against Israel's enemies reveals that the underlying reason for this wrath, and the desire for revenge, is the destruction of the Temple. This is the meaning of the verse, "Pour out Your wrath upon the nations that do not know You . . . for they have devoured Jacob and laid waste his dwelling place" (Psalm 79:6–7). "Dwelling place" is a reference to none other than the Holy Temple, as it is called in the Song of the Sea: "You have guided them in strength to Your holy dwelling place" (Exodus 15:13). The Aramaic translation of the verse in the Book of Psalms actually translates the word "dwelling place" as "Holy Temple."

From the outset of this chapter of Psalms, its subject is clearly a song about the

The host says:
Blessed are You, O Lord our God, King of the universe, who created the fruit of the vine.

All drink while reclining on the left side. It is customary at this point to fill a large glass with wine for Elijah the Prophet, messenger of Redemption. "Elijah's Cup" is placed by the Seder plate.

The door is now opened in honor of Elijah the Prophet, and the following is said:
"May the All-Merciful send us Elijah the Prophet (may he be remembered for good) to bring us good tidings of comfort and salvation!"

"Pour out

Your wrath upon the heathens that have not known You, and upon the kingdoms that have not called upon Your name. For they have devoured Jacob and laid waste his dwelling place" *(Psalm 79:6–7)*.
"Pour out Your indignation upon them, and let Your wrathful anger take hold of them" *(Psalm 69:24)*. "Pursue them and destroy them in anger from under the heavens of the Lord" *(Lamentations 3:66)*.

THE HALLEL

The fourth cup is now poured for all the participants. A bit from "Elijah's Cup" is poured out to each participant.

Not to us, O Lord, not to us, but to Your Name give glory, for Your mercy, and for Your truth's sake.
Why should the heathens say, where is their God?
Our God is in the heavens: He has done whatever He pleased.
Their idols are silver and gold, the work of men's hands.
They have mouths, but they do not speak; they have eyes, but they do not see; they have ears, but they do not hear; they have noses, but they do not smell; they have hands, but they do not handle; they have feet, but they do not walk; neither do they speak through their throat.
Those who make them are just like them;
so is every one that trusts them.
O Israel, trust in the Lord: He is their help and their shield.
O house of Aaron, trust in the Lord: He is their help and their shield.
You that fear the Lord, trust in the Lord:
He is their help and their shield.
The Lord has been mindful of us: He will bless us;
He will bless the house of Israel; He will bless the house of Aaron.
He will bless them that fear the Lord, both small and great.
The Lord shall increase you more and more, you and your children.
You are blessed of the Lord who made heaven and earth.
The heaven, even the heavens, are the Lord's; but He has given the earth to the children of men. The dead do not praise the Lord, neither do they who go down to silence.
But we will bless the Lord from now and forever.
Praise the Lord *(Psalm 115)*.

I love the Lord, because He has heard my voice and my supplications. Because He has inclined His ear to me, therefore I will call upon Him as long as I live. The sorrows of death compassed me, and the pains of hell got hold upon me: I found trouble and sorrow.

Then I called upon the Name of the Lord: I beseech You, O Lord, deliver my soul. Gracious is the Lord, and righteous; our God is merciful. The Lord preserves the simple: I was brought low, and He helped me. Return to your rest, O my soul; for the Lord has dealt bountifully with you. For you have delivered my soul from death, my eyes from tears, and my feet from falling. I will walk before the Lord in the land of the living. I believed, therefore I have spoken: I was greatly afflicted; I said in my haste, all men are liars.

הוֹדוּ לַיָי כִּי טוֹב כִּי לְעוֹלָם חַסְדּוֹ

כָּל־תַּגְמוּלוֹהִי עָלָי	מָה־אָשִׁיב לַיָי
וּבְשֵׁם יְיָ אֶקְרָא	כּוֹס־יְשׁוּעוֹת אֶשָּׂא
נֶגְדָה־נָּא לְכָל־עַמּוֹ	נְדָרַי לַיָי אֲשַׁלֵּם
הַמָּוְתָה לַחֲסִידָיו	יָקָר בְּעֵינֵי יְיָ
אֲנִי עַבְדְּךָ בֶּן־אֲמָתֶךָ	אָנָּה יְיָ כִּי־אֲנִי עַבְדֶּךָ
	פִּתַּחְתָּ לְמוֹסֵרָי
וּבְשֵׁם יְיָ אֶקְרָא	לְךָ־אֶזְבַּח זֶבַח תּוֹדָה
נֶגְדָה־נָּא לְכָל־עַמּוֹ	נְדָרַי לַיָי אֲשַׁלֵּם
בְּתוֹכֵכִי יְרוּשָׁלָיִם	בְּחַצְרוֹת בֵּית יְיָ
	הַלְלוּיָהּ

הַלְלוּ אֶת־יְיָ כָּל־גּוֹיִם שַׁבְּחוּהוּ כָּל־הָאֻמִּים
כִּי גָבַר עָלֵינוּ חַסְדּוֹ וֶאֱמֶת־יְיָ לְעוֹלָם

הַלְלוּיָהּ

יֹאמַר־נָא יִשְׂרָאֵל	
כִּי לְעוֹלָם חַסְדּוֹ	
יֹאמְרוּ־נָא בֵית־אַהֲרֹן	
כִּי לְעוֹלָם חַסְדּוֹ	
יֹאמְרוּ־נָא יִרְאֵי יְיָ	
כִּי לְעוֹלָם חַסְדּוֹ	

עָנָנִי בַמֶּרְחָב יָהּ	מִן־הַמֵּצַר קָרָאתִי יָּהּ
מַה־יַּעֲשֶׂה לִי אָדָם	יְיָ לִי לֹא אִירָא
וַאֲנִי אֶרְאֶה בְשֹׂנְאָי	יְיָ לִי בְּעֹזְרָי
מִבְּטֹחַ בָּאָדָם	טוֹב לַחֲסוֹת בַּיָי
מִבְּטֹחַ בִּנְדִיבִים	טוֹב לַחֲסוֹת בַּיָי
בְּשֵׁם יְיָ כִּי אֲמִילַם	כָּל־גּוֹיִם סְבָבוּנִי
בְּשֵׁם יְיָ כִּי אֲמִילַם	סַבּוּנִי גַם־סְבָבוּנִי
סַבּוּנִי כִדְבוֹרִים דֹּעֲכוּ כְּאֵשׁ קוֹצִים בְּשֵׁם יְיָ כִּי אֲמִילַם	
וַיְיָ עֲזָרָנִי	דָּחֹה דְחִיתַנִי לִנְפֹּל
וַיְהִי־לִי לִישׁוּעָה	עָזִּי וְזִמְרָת יָהּ
קוֹל רִנָּה וִישׁוּעָה בְּאָהֳלֵי צַדִּיקִים יְמִין יְיָ עֹשָׂה חָיִל	
יְמִין יְיָ רוֹמֵמָה	יְמִין יְיָ עֹשָׂה חָיִל
וַאֲסַפֵּר מַעֲשֵׂי יָהּ	לֹא־אָמוּת כִּי־אֶחְיֶה
וְלַמָּוֶת לֹא נְתָנָנִי	יַסֹּר יִסְּרַנִּי יָּהּ
אָבֹא־בָם אוֹדֶה יָהּ	פִּתְחוּ־לִי שַׁעֲרֵי־צֶדֶק
צַדִּיקִים יָבֹאוּ בוֹ	זֶה־הַשַּׁעַר לַיָי

וַתְּהִי־לִי לִישׁוּעָה	אוֹדְךָ כִּי עֲנִיתָנִי
וַתְּהִי־לִי לִישׁוּעָה	אוֹדְךָ כִּי עֲנִיתָנִי
הָיְתָה לְרֹאשׁ פִּנָּה	אֶבֶן מָאֲסוּ הַבּוֹנִים
הָיְתָה לְרֹאשׁ פִּנָּה	אֶבֶן מָאֲסוּ הַבּוֹנִים
הִיא נִפְלָאת בְּעֵינֵינוּ	מֵאֵת יְיָ הָיְתָה זֹּאת
הִיא נִפְלָאת בְּעֵינֵינוּ	מֵאֵת יְיָ הָיְתָה זֹּאת
נָגִילָה וְנִשְׂמְחָה בוֹ	זֶה־הַיּוֹם עָשָׂה יְיָ
נָגִילָה וְנִשְׂמְחָה בוֹ	זֶה־הַיּוֹם עָשָׂה יְיָ

אָנָּא יְיָ הוֹשִׁיעָה נָּא
אָנָּא יְיָ הוֹשִׁיעָה נָּא
אָנָּא יְיָ הַצְלִיחָה נָּא
אָנָּא יְיָ הַצְלִיחָה נָּא

What shall I render to the Lord for all His benefits toward me? I will take the cup of salvation, and call upon the Name of the Lord. I will pay my vows to the Lord now in the presence of all His people.
Precious in the sight of the Lord is the death of His saints.
O Lord, I am truly Your servant; I am Your servant, and the son of Your handmaid: You have loosened my bonds.
I will offer You the sacrifice of thanksgiving, and will call upon the Name of the Lord. I will pay my vows to the Lord now,
in the presence of all His people, in the courts of the Lord's house, in your midst, O Jerusalem.
Praise the Lord *(Psalm 116)*.

Praise the Lord, all you nations: praise Him, all you people. For His merciful kindness is great toward us, and the truth of the Lord endures forever.

Praise the Lord *(Psalm 117)*.

**Give thanks to the Lord;
for He is good:
because
His mercy
endures forever.**

Let Israel now say,
that His mercy endures forever.
Let the house of Aaron now say,
that His mercy endures forever.
Let them now that fear the Lord say,
that His mercy endures forever.

I called upon the Lord in distress: The Lord answered me, and set me in a large place. The Lord is on my side; I will not fear: What can man do to me? The Lord takes my part with those who help me; therefore I shall see my desire upon those who hate me. It is better to trust in the Lord than to put confidence in man. It is better to trust in the Lord than to put confidence in princes. All nations compassed me about: but in the name of the Lord I will destroy them. They compassed me about, yes, they compassed me about: but in the name of the Lord I will destroy them. They compassed me about like bees; they are quenched as the fire of thorns: for in the name of the Lord I will destroy them. You have thrust sore at me, that I might fall: but the Lord helped me. The Lord is my strength and song; He has become my salvation. The voice of rejoicing and salvation is in the tabernacles of the righteous: the right hand of the Lord does valiantly. I shall not die, but live, and declare the works of the Lord. The Lord has sorely chastened me; but He has not given me over to death. Open up to me the gates of righteousness: I will go into them, and I will praise the Lord; this is the gate of the Lord, into which the righteous will enter.

I will praise You: for You have heard me, and have become my salvation. I will praise You: for You have heard me, and have become my salvation. The stone which the builders refused has become the head of the corner. The stone which the builders refused has become the head of the corner. This is the Lord's doing; it is marvelous in our eyes. This is the Lord's doing; it is marvelous in our eyes. This is the day which the Lord has made; we will rejoice and be glad of it. This is the day which the Lord has made; we will rejoice and be glad of it.

**Save now, I beseech You, O Lord!
Save now, I beseech You, O Lord!
O Lord, I beseech You, send now prosperity!
O Lord, I beseech You, send now prosperity!**

The Altar Depicted here is the surface of the altar and the arrangements of wood for the sacrifices. There were three separate arrangements on the altar. The sacrifices were offered upon the largest pile, located on the eastern side of the altar (at the front of the picture). At the southwestern corner stood the arrangement which provided the fire and coals for the incense offering that took place on the golden incense altar within the Sanctuary itself. The third pile was appointed to keep the fire burning perpetually. In the center of the altar, we see the accumulation of coals and ashes which were gathered there from the different arrangements in order to remove them to a pre-designated location outside the confines of the Temple.

◄ *(Overleaf)* **To the Holy Temple** The festival pilgrims stream toward the Temple. Approaching the holy mountain on foot or mounted, musicians accompanying the caravans led the people in joyous song. Numerous entrances, bridges and plazas brought the great throngs, which converged on Jerusalem to celebrate the sacred festivals, into the Temple complex.

בָּרוּךְ הַבָּא בְּשֵׁם יְיָ	בֵּרַכְנוּכֶם מִבֵּית יְיָ
בָּרוּךְ הַבָּא בְּשֵׁם יְיָ	בֵּרַכְנוּכֶם מִבֵּית יְיָ
אֵל יְיָ וַיָּאֶר לָנוּ	אִסְרוּ־חַג בַּעֲבֹתִים
עַד קַרְנוֹת הַמִּזְבֵּחַ	
אֵל יְיָ וַיָּאֶר לָנוּ	אִסְרוּ־חַג בַּעֲבֹתִים
עַד קַרְנוֹת הַמִּזְבֵּחַ	
אֵלִי אַתָּה וְאוֹדֶךָּ	אֱלֹהַי אֲרוֹמְמֶךָּ
אֵלִי אַתָּה וְאוֹדֶךָּ	אֱלֹהַי אֲרוֹמְמֶךָּ
הוֹדוּ לַיְיָ כִּי־טוֹב	כִּי לְעוֹלָם חַסְדּוֹ
הוֹדוּ לַיְיָ כִּי־טוֹב	כִּי לְעוֹלָם חַסְדּוֹ

יְהַלְלוּךָ יְיָ אֱלֹהֵינוּ כָּל מַעֲשֶׂיךָ
וַחֲסִידֶיךָ צַדִּיקִים עוֹשֵׂי רְצוֹנֶךָ
וְכָל עַמְּךָ בֵּית יִשְׂרָאֵל
בְּרִנָּה יוֹדוּ וִיבָרְכוּ וִישַׁבְּחוּ
וִיפָאֲרוּ וִירוֹמְמוּ וְיַעֲרִיצוּ
וְיַקְדִּישׁוּ וְיַמְלִיכוּ אֶת שִׁמְךָ מַלְכֵּנוּ
כִּי לְךָ טוֹב לְהוֹדוֹת וּלְשִׁמְךָ נָאֶה לְזַמֵּר
כִּי מֵעוֹלָם וְעַד עוֹלָם אַתָּה אֵל

הוֹדוּ לַיְיָ כִּי־טוֹב	כִּי לְעוֹלָם חַסְדּוֹ
הוֹדוּ לֵאלֹהֵי הָאֱלֹהִים	כִּי לְעוֹלָם חַסְדּוֹ
הוֹדוּ לַאֲדֹנֵי הָאֲדֹנִים	כִּי לְעוֹלָם חַסְדּוֹ
לְעוֹשֵׂה נִפְלָאוֹת גְּדֹלוֹת לְבַדּוֹ	כִּי לְעוֹלָם חַסְדּוֹ
לְעוֹשֵׂה הַשָּׁמַיִם בִּתְבוּנָה	כִּי לְעוֹלָם חַסְדּוֹ
לְרוֹקַע הָאָרֶץ עַל־הַמָּיִם	כִּי לְעוֹלָם חַסְדּוֹ
לְעוֹשֵׂה אוֹרִים גְּדֹלִים	כִּי לְעוֹלָם חַסְדּוֹ
אֶת־הַשֶּׁמֶשׁ לְמֶמְשֶׁלֶת בַּיּוֹם	כִּי לְעוֹלָם חַסְדּוֹ
אֶת־הַיָּרֵחַ וְכוֹכָבִים לְמֶמְשְׁלוֹת בַּלָּיְלָה	כִּי לְעוֹלָם חַסְדּוֹ
לְמַכֵּה מִצְרַיִם בִּבְכוֹרֵיהֶם	כִּי לְעוֹלָם חַסְדּוֹ
וַיּוֹצֵא יִשְׂרָאֵל מִתּוֹכָם	כִּי לְעוֹלָם חַסְדּוֹ
בְּיָד חֲזָקָה וּבִזְרוֹעַ נְטוּיָה	כִּי לְעוֹלָם חַסְדּוֹ
לְגוֹזֵר יַם־סוּף לִגְזָרִים	כִּי לְעוֹלָם חַסְדּוֹ
וְהֶעֱבִיר יִשְׂרָאֵל בְּתוֹכוֹ	כִּי לְעוֹלָם חַסְדּוֹ
וְנִעֵר פַּרְעֹה וְחֵילוֹ בְיַם־סוּף	כִּי לְעוֹלָם חַסְדּוֹ
לְמוֹלִיךְ עַמּוֹ בַּמִּדְבָּר	כִּי לְעוֹלָם חַסְדּוֹ
לְמַכֵּה מְלָכִים גְּדֹלִים	כִּי לְעוֹלָם חַסְדּוֹ
וַיַּהֲרֹג מְלָכִים אַדִּירִים	כִּי לְעוֹלָם חַסְדּוֹ
לְסִיחוֹן מֶלֶךְ הָאֱמֹרִי	כִּי לְעוֹלָם חַסְדּוֹ
וּלְעוֹג מֶלֶךְ הַבָּשָׁן	כִּי לְעוֹלָם חַסְדּוֹ
וְנָתַן אַרְצָם לְנַחֲלָה	כִּי לְעוֹלָם חַסְדּוֹ
נַחֲלָה לְיִשְׂרָאֵל עַבְדּוֹ	כִּי לְעוֹלָם חַסְדּוֹ
שֶׁבְּשִׁפְלֵנוּ זָכַר לָנוּ	כִּי לְעוֹלָם חַסְדּוֹ
וַיִּפְרְקֵנוּ מִצָּרֵינוּ	כִּי לְעוֹלָם חַסְדּוֹ
נֹתֵן לֶחֶם לְכָל־בָּשָׂר	כִּי לְעוֹלָם חַסְדּוֹ
הוֹדוּ לְאֵל הַשָּׁמָיִם	כִּי לְעוֹלָם חַסְדּוֹ

המהדרין לקיים מצוות כוס חמישי מסיימים כאן בברכה:

ברוך אתה ה' מלך מהולל בתשבחות

ואומרים:

הנני מוכן ומזומן לקיים מצוות כוס רביעי של ארבעה כוסות, שהוא כנגד לשון רביעי של ארבעה לשונות גאולה, שנאמר: ולקחתי אתכם לי לעם והייתי לכם לאלקים.

ברוך אתה יי אלהינו מלך העולם בורא פרי הגפן

שותין בהסיבה ומוזגין כוס חמישי.

המקיימים מצוות ארבע כוסות ממשיכים ואומרים:

הודו לה' כי טוב.

Rabbi Tarfon, Who Served as a Priest in the Holy Temple, Established the Custom of the Fifth Cup—To Hasten the Rebuilding of the Temple

Rabbi Tarfon, whose opinion that drinking the fifth cup is obligatory, is also counted amongst the sages of Israel who were gathered together in Bnei Brak. It would seem that as one who himself served as a priest in the Holy Temple, he felt that adding this fifth cup was the correct thing to do—for it corresponds with the expression of "And I will bring you," which alludes to the Holy Temple.

These are the "four expressions of redemption": "And I will bring you out"; "And I will deliver you"; "And I will redeem you"; and "And I will take you," and each refers to a specific stage in the redemptive process of Israel's Exodus from Egypt. As opposed to these four stages, the fifth expression of "And I will bring you" refers to the building of the Holy Temple in Jerusalem.

Similarly, we find in the biblical section of "My father was a homeless Aramean" that several expressions are used: "And God *took us out* of Egypt . . . and He has brought us to this place" (Deuteronomy 26:8–9). The rabbis of the *Sifre* explain: "What is meant by the words, 'And He has brought us to this place?' *This is a reference to the construction of the Holy Temple!*" And the *Sifre* adds: "As a reward for coming to *this place* (the Holy Temple) He has given us this land!"

The meaning of this midrashic statement is clear. The true portent and meaning of "And I will bring you" is a concept—not just entering into the land, but entering into Jerusalem and building the Holy Temple. For it is this action which gives meaning and purpose to Israel's presence in its land. Without the Temple, the act of entering into the land loses its significance. The main idea of the verse "And I will bring you into the land" has Jerusalem and the Holy Temple as its goal and the measure of its fulfillment.

In this light, we can understand the difference between the language of the Mishnah, which mentions only the four cups, and the *baraita* which the Talmud cites that includes Rabbi Tarfon and the fifth cup as well. The Mishnah mentions neither the concept of the "fifth cup" nor that of the "Great Hallel," for the Mishnah discusses the version of the *Haggadah* which was in use while the Temple stood—*Haggadat HaMikdash*, the "Temple *Haggadah*."

This fact explains why the Mishnah only recognizes four cups: when Israel dwelled in Jerusalem during the era of the Temple, the main purpose of drinking the cups was to recall the four expressions of redemption, and thus review the stages of the Exodus from Egypt. However, once the Temple was destroyed and its lacking was sorely felt by the participants at the Seder, Rabbi Tarfon offered an innovation: to drink a fifth cup, symbolizing "And I will bring you" during the *Haggadah*—and thus, to give expression to our prayers and hopes that our lives shall bear witness to the fulfillment of the verse wherein the Holy One promises, "And He has brought us to this place." The fifth cup was drunk and all thoughts turned toward Jerusalem and the Temple: may He bring us to Jerusalem as He brought us forth from Egypt, and may we merit the rebuilding of the Holy Temple.

The "Great Hallel": Remembering the Bitterness of Exile, and Yearning to Return to the Hallowed Courtyards of God

It is in this light that we can understand the Talmud's discussion (BT Pesahim 118:A) regarding which verses should be included in the Great *Hallel* and recited over the "fifth cup." The anonymous opinion mentioned in the *baraita* maintains that one should recite the 23rd Psalm—which begins with the words, "The Lord is my shepherd; I shall not be lacking. . ." and continues with the words, "Though I walk in the valley of death (*and exile*), I shall not fear, for You are with me . . . You anoint my head with oil; my cup runs over. Surely goodness and mercy shall follow me all the days of my life: and I will dwell in *the house of the Lord* forever."

This chapter thus contains an allusion that although one has already drunk his full with the four cups, he should nonetheless drink an additional cup, to demonstrate the degree of his faith through action—his faith and belief that the Holy One will yet liberate us from the shadow of death caused by our exile, and that the day will come when the Temple will be rebuilt, and we shall witness the fulfillment of the verse "And I shall dwell in the house of the Lord forever" in our own lives.

Rabbi Yohanan's opinion, in that same talmudic reference, holds that the verses of the Great *Hallel* must begin with the words of Psalm 134: "A song of ascents. Behold, bless the Lord, all you servants of the Lord, who stand by night in the house of the Lord. . . ." The following psalm contains the words "Praise Him, O servants of the Lord, you who stand in the house of the Lord, in the courts of the house of our God. . ." (Psalm 135). These verses are an explicit indication that the intention of the recitation of the Great *Hallel* as the fifth cup is drunk is intended to express the anticipation of "the servants of the Lord who stand in the house of the Lord" and in His courtyards, even throughout the "night" of destruction and exile. Thus the Great *Hallel* acts as a vehicle by which one can express his hope that even "in our degradation He has remembered us" and that though we be in exile, God will still "remove our yoke." For the great kindness which He did for Israel in Egypt is forever; whenever we are in distress, God comes to our aid and delivers us to "this place"—to the Holy Temple. Thus, the additional fifth cup was especially enacted for the "*Haggadah* of Exile," so that we may see the fulfillment of "And I will bring you" in our own lives.

Blessed is he that comes in the name of the Lord: we have blessed you out of the house of the Lord. Blessed is he that comes in the name of the Lord: we have blessed you out of the house of the Lord.

God is the Lord, which has showed us light: bind the sacrifice with cords, even to the horns of the altar. God is the Lord, which has showed us light: bind the sacrifice with cords, even to the horns of the altar.

You are my God, and I will praise You; You are my God, I will exalt You. You are my God, and I will praise You; You are my God, I will exalt You.

O give thanks to the Lord, for He is good: for His mercy endures forever! O give thanks to the Lord, for He is good: for His mercy endures forever!

(Psalm 118)

All Your works, O Lord our God, shall praise You,
and Your pious ones, the just who do Your will
and all Your people of the house of Israel,
with song shall ever thank, bless, praise,
extol, exalt, honor, hallow,
and acknowledge Your Name, O our King!
For to You it is good to give thanks,
and it is becoming to sing praises to Your name;
for You are God from everlasting to everlasting.
Blessed are You, O Lord, a King extolled with praises.

At this point, those who are scrupulous to observe the "fifth cup"
conclude with the blessing:
Blessed are You, O Lord our God, a King extolled with praises.

They then recite:
I am now ready and prepared to fulfill the commandment of the fourth cup, which corresponds with the fourth of the "four expressions of redemption," as the Torah states: "And I will take you to Me for a people, and I shall be for you a God" *(Exodus 6:7)*.
Blessed are You, O Lord our God, King of the universe, who created the fruit of the vine.
All drink the fourth cup while reclining on the left side. The fifth cup is then poured out.

Those who do not observe the custom of the "fifth cup" continue here:
Give thanks to the Lord; for He is good:
> *for His mercy endures forever.*

O give thanks to the God of gods:
> *for His mercy endures forever.*

O give thanks to the Lord of lords:
> *for His mercy endures forever.*

To Him who alone does great wonders:
> *for His mercy endures forever.*

To Him that by wisdom made the heavens:
> *for His mercy endures forever.*

To Him that stretched out the earth above the waters:
> *for His mercy endures forever.*

To Him that made great lights:
> *for His mercy endures forever.*

The sun to rule by day:
> *for His mercy endures forever.*

The moon and stars to rule by night:
> *for His mercy endures forever.*

To Him that smote Egypt in their firstborn:
> *for His mercy endures forever.*

And brought out Israel from among them:
> *for His mercy endures forever.*

With a strong hand, and with an outstretched arm:
> *for His mercy endures forever.*

To Him who divided the Red Sea into parts:
> *for His mercy endures forever.*

And made Israel to pass through the midst of it:
> *for His mercy endures forever.*

But overthrew Pharaoh and his host in the Red Sea:
> *for His mercy endures forever.*

To Him who led His people through the wilderness:
> *for His mercy endures forever.*

To Him who smote great kings:
> *for His mercy endures forever.*

And slew famous kings:
> *for His mercy endures forever.*

Sihon king of the Amorites:
> *for His mercy endures forever.*

And Og the king of Bashan:
> *for His mercy endures forever.*

And gave their land for a heritage:
> *for His mercy endures forever.*

A heritage for Israel His servant:
> *for His mercy endures forever.*

Who remembered us in our low state:
> *for His mercy endures forever.*

And has redeemed us from our enemies:
> *for His mercy endures forever.*

Who gives food to all flesh:
> *for His mercy endures forever.*

O give thanks to the God of heaven:
> *for His mercy endures forever.*

(Psalm 136)

The Fifth Cup—For the Holy Temple

Sources for the Fifth Cup: The Talmud, Geonic and Responsa Literature

The rabbis established the custom of drinking four cups at the Seder, and this is the practice which has been accepted by Israel. The earlier and later authorities have written that these four cups represent the "four expressions of redemption" which were specified to Moses at the time of the Exodus from Egypt: "And I will bring you out," "And I will deliver you," "And I will redeem you," "And I will take you." These four terms are used by the Holy One to express His actions in delivering the Children of Israel from Egyptian bondage.

At the same time, it is praiseworthy to add an extra fifth cup as well, and to recite the "Great *Hallel*" over this cup, and to drink it upon concluding the *Haggadah*—for this cup symbolizes the fifth expression, "And I will bring you" (Exodus 6:8). Maimonides actually incorporates this practice into law, and after he explains the obligation of drinking the four cups, he adds: "And it is proper to pour out a fifth cup as well, and to recite the Great *Hallel* over it, but this cup is not obligatory, like the other four" (Laws of Hametz and Matzah 8:10).

The original source for drinking a fifth cup at the Seder can be found in Tractate Pesahim of the Talmud. There it states: "The rabbis taught: One should finish the *Hallel* over the fifth cup, and recite the Great *Hallel*—this according to Rabbi Tarfon" (118:A).

In addition to Maimonides, many scholars of the geonic period, as well as those from the earlier schools, also accepted Rabbi Tarfon's words as legally binding, and conducted themselves accordingly in their respective communities. On the other hand, other authorities such as the Rashbam and other Tosafists did not accept this version of the Talmud. While this is not the place to enter into a lengthy explanation or debate on the various versions of the Talmud and the redeeming value of each (since Rabbi M. M. Kasher has already done this in a special essay found in his work, *Haggadah Shleimah*), still, it is imperative that we investigate one particular detail of this subject as it applies to the "Temple *Haggadah*"—and it is this point which Rabbi Kasher does not elaborate upon, namely, *the reasons for the fifth cup*.

59

נִשְׁמַת כָּל חַי תְּבָרֵךְ אֶת שִׁמְךָ יְיָ אֱלֹהֵינוּ

וְרוּחַ כָּל בָּשָׂר תְּפָאֵר וּתְרוֹמֵם זִכְרְךָ מַלְכֵּנוּ תָּמִיד
מִן הָעוֹלָם וְעַד הָעוֹלָם אַתָּה אֵל וּמִבַּלְעָדֶיךָ אֵין לָנוּ מֶלֶךְ
גּוֹאֵל וּמוֹשִׁיעַ פּוֹדֶה וּמַצִּיל וּמְפַרְנֵס וּמְרַחֵם
בְּכָל עֵת צָרָה וְצוּקָה אֵין לָנוּ מֶלֶךְ אֶלָּא אַתָּה
אֱלֹהֵי הָרִאשׁוֹנִים וְהָאַחֲרוֹנִים אֱלוֹהַּ כָּל בְּרִיּוֹת
אֲדוֹן כָּל תּוֹלָדוֹת הַמְהֻלָּל בְּרֹב הַתִּשְׁבָּחוֹת
הַמְנַהֵג עוֹלָמוֹ בְּחֶסֶד וּבְרִיּוֹתָיו בְּרַחֲמִים
וַייָ לֹא יָנוּם וְלֹא יִישָׁן
הַמְעוֹרֵר יְשֵׁנִים וְהַמֵּקִיץ נִרְדָּמִים וְהַמֵּשִׂיחַ אִלְּמִים
וְהַמַּתִּיר אֲסוּרִים וְהַסּוֹמֵךְ נוֹפְלִים וְהַזּוֹקֵף כְּפוּפִים
לְךָ לְבַדְּךָ אֲנַחְנוּ מוֹדִים

אִלּוּ פִינוּ מָלֵא שִׁירָה כַּיָּם וּלְשׁוֹנֵנוּ רִנָּה כַּהֲמוֹן גַּלָּיו
וְשִׂפְתוֹתֵינוּ שֶׁבַח כְּמֶרְחֲבֵי רָקִיעַ וְעֵינֵינוּ מְאִירוֹת כַּשֶּׁמֶשׁ וְכַיָּרֵחַ
וְיָדֵינוּ פְרוּשׂוֹת כְּנִשְׁרֵי שָׁמָיִם וְרַגְלֵינוּ קַלּוֹת כָּאַיָּלוֹת
אֵין אֲנַחְנוּ מַסְפִּיקִים לְהוֹדוֹת לְךָ יְיָ אֱלֹהֵינוּ וֵאלֹהֵי אֲבוֹתֵינוּ
וּלְבָרֵךְ אֶת שְׁמֶךָ עַל אַחַת מֵאָלֶף אֶלֶף אַלְפֵי אֲלָפִים
וְרִבֵּי רְבָבוֹת פְּעָמִים הַטּוֹבוֹת שֶׁעָשִׂיתָ עִם אֲבוֹתֵינוּ וְעִמָּנוּ

מִמִּצְרַיִם גְּאַלְתָּנוּ יְיָ אֱלֹהֵינוּ וּמִבֵּית עֲבָדִים פְּדִיתָנוּ
בְּרָעָב זַנְתָּנוּ וּבְשָׂבָע כִּלְכַּלְתָּנוּ
מֵחֶרֶב הִצַּלְתָּנוּ וּמִדֶּבֶר מִלַּטְתָּנוּ וּמֵחֳלָיִם רָעִים וְנֶאֱמָנִים דִּלִּיתָנוּ
עַד הֵנָּה עֲזָרוּנוּ רַחֲמֶיךָ וְלֹא עֲזָבוּנוּ חֲסָדֶיךָ
וְאַל תִּטְּשֵׁנוּ יְיָ אֱלֹהֵינוּ לָנֶצַח

עַל כֵּן אֵבָרִים שֶׁפִּלַּגְתָּ בָּנוּ וְרוּחַ וּנְשָׁמָה שֶׁנָּפַחְתָּ בְּאַפֵּנוּ
וְלָשׁוֹן אֲשֶׁר שַׂמְתָּ בְּפִינוּ
הֵן הֵם יוֹדוּ וִיבָרְכוּ וִישַׁבְּחוּ וִיפָאֲרוּ וִירוֹמְמוּ
וְיַעֲרִיצוּ וְיַקְדִּישׁוּ וְיַמְלִיכוּ אֶת שִׁמְךָ מַלְכֵּנוּ
כִּי כָל פֶּה לְךָ יוֹדֶה וְכָל לָשׁוֹן לְךָ תִשָּׁבַע
וְכָל בֶּרֶךְ לְךָ תִכְרַע וְכָל קוֹמָה לְפָנֶיךָ תִשְׁתַּחֲוֶה
וְכָל לְבָבוֹת יִירָאוּךָ וְכָל קֶרֶב וּכְלָיוֹת יְזַמְּרוּ לִשְׁמֶךָ
כַּדָּבָר שֶׁכָּתוּב כָּל עַצְמוֹתַי תֹּאמַרְנָה יְיָ מִי כָמוֹךָ
מַצִּיל עָנִי מֵחָזָק מִמֶּנּוּ וְעָנִי וְאֶבְיוֹן מִגֹּזְלוֹ
מִי יִדְמֶה לָּךְ וּמִי יִשְׁוֶה לָּךְ וּמִי יַעֲרָךְ לָךְ
הָאֵל הַגָּדוֹל הַגִּבּוֹר וְהַנּוֹרָא אֵל עֶלְיוֹן קוֹנֵה שָׁמַיִם וָאָרֶץ
נְהַלֶּלְךָ וּנְשַׁבֵּחֲךָ וּנְפָאֶרְךָ וּנְבָרֵךְ אֶת שֵׁם קָדְשֶׁךָ
כָּאָמוּר לְדָוִד בָּרֲכִי נַפְשִׁי אֶת יְיָ וְכָל קְרָבַי אֶת שֵׁם קָדְשׁוֹ
הָאֵל בְּתַעֲצֻמוֹת עֻזֶּךָ הַגָּדוֹל בִּכְבוֹד שְׁמֶךָ
הַגִּבּוֹר לָנֶצַח וְהַנּוֹרָא בְּנוֹרְאוֹתֶיךָ
הַמֶּלֶךְ הַיּוֹשֵׁב עַל כִּסֵּא רָם וְנִשָּׂא שׁוֹכֵן עַד מָרוֹם וְקָדוֹשׁ שְׁמוֹ
וְכָתוּב רַנְּנוּ צַדִּיקִים בַּייָ לַיְשָׁרִים נָאוָה תְהִלָּה
בְּפִי יְשָׁרִים תִּתְהַלָּל וּבְדִבְרֵי צַדִּיקִים תִּתְבָּרַךְ
וּבִלְשׁוֹן חֲסִידִים תִּתְרוֹמָם וּבְקֶרֶב קְדוֹשִׁים תִּתְקַדָּשׁ
וּבְמַקְהֲלוֹת רִבְבוֹת עַמְּךָ בֵּית יִשְׂרָאֵל
בְּרִנָּה יִתְפָּאֵר שִׁמְךָ מַלְכֵּנוּ בְּכָל דּוֹר וָדוֹר
שֶׁכֵּן חוֹבַת כָּל הַיְצוּרִים לְפָנֶיךָ יְיָ אֱלֹהֵינוּ וֵאלֹהֵי אֲבוֹתֵינוּ
לְהוֹדוֹת לְהַלֵּל לְשַׁבֵּחַ לְפָאֵר לְרוֹמֵם לְהַדֵּר לְבָרֵךְ לְעַלֵּה וּלְקַלֵּס
עַל כָּל דִּבְרֵי שִׁירוֹת וְתִשְׁבָּחוֹת דָּוִד בֶּן יִשַׁי עַבְדְּךָ מְשִׁיחֶךָ

יִשְׁתַּבַּח שִׁמְךָ לָעַד מַלְכֵּנוּ
הָאֵל הַמֶּלֶךְ הַגָּדוֹל וְהַקָּדוֹשׁ בַּשָּׁמַיִם וּבָאָרֶץ
כִּי לְךָ נָאֶה יְיָ אֱלֹהֵינוּ וֵאלֹהֵי אֲבוֹתֵינוּ שִׁיר וּשְׁבָחָה הַלֵּל וְזִמְרָה
עֹז וּמֶמְשָׁלָה נֶצַח גְּדֻלָּה וּגְבוּרָה תְּהִלָּה וְתִפְאֶרֶת
קְדֻשָּׁה וּמַלְכוּת בְּרָכוֹת וְהוֹדָאוֹת מֵעַתָּה וְעַד עוֹלָם

המהדרים לקיים מצוות כוס חמישי אומרים כאן:

הנני מוכן ומזומן לקיים מצוות כוס חמישי כנגד לשון חמישי של לשונות הגאולה, שנאמר: וְהֵבֵאתִי אֶתְכֶם אֶל הָאָרֶץ אֲשֶׁר נָשָׂאתִי אֶת יָדִי לָתֵת אֹתָהּ לְאַבְרָהָם לְיִצְחָק וּלְיַעֲקֹב וְנָתַתִּי אֹתָהּ לָכֶם מוֹרָשָׁה אֲנִי ה'.

ושותה כוס חמישי בלי ברכה.
לאחר שתיית הכוס מברך ברכה אחרונה.

המקיימים מצוות ארבע כוסות ממשיכים ואומרים: ברוך אתה ה'...

בָּרוּךְ אַתָּה יְיָ אֱלֹהֵינוּ מֶלֶךְ גָּדוֹל בַּתִּשְׁבָּחוֹת אֵל הַהוֹדָאוֹת
אֲדוֹן הַנִּפְלָאוֹת הַבּוֹחֵר בְּשִׁירֵי זִמְרָה מֶלֶךְ אֵל חֵי הָעוֹלָמִים

The breath of all life shall praise Your name, O Lord our God,

and the spirit of all flesh shall glorify and exalt Your remembrance continually, O King! From everlasting to everlasting You are God, and besides You we have no king, redeemer, savior, deliverer, sustainer and comforter at all times of trouble and distress; we have no king but You. You are God of the first and God of the last, God of all creatures, Lord of all generations, adored with many praises, who rules His world with tenderness and His creatures with mercy. "The Lord neither slumbers nor sleeps."

He wakens the sleeping and rouses the slumbering, gives speech to the dumb, releases the bound, supports the fallen and raises up those who are bowed. To Him alone do we give thanks! Though our mouths were filled with songs like the sea and our tongues as the crash of its waves, our lips filled with praises like the boundless sky, our eyes shining like the sun and moon, our hands outspread like the eagle's wings and our feet swift as hinds; we would still not know how to thank You, O Lord our God and God of our fathers, or to bless Your name, for even one of the countless kindnesses You have bestowed on our fathers and on us.

You did deliver us from Egypt, O Lord our God, and released us from the house of bondage; in hunger You did feed us, and in famine nourish us. You delivered us from the sword, You saved us from the pestilence, and from sore and grievous sicknesses You did preserve us. Until now Your mercies have sustained us, and Your kindness has not forsaken us, and You, O Lord our God, may You never forsake us!

And therefore, the limbs which You have formed in us, the breath which You have breathed in us, and the tongue which You have put into our mouths, they shall thank, praise, glorify, extol, honor, hallow, and proclaim Your name, our King! For to You, every mouth shall give thanks, and to You, every tongue shall swear; every knee shall bend to You and before You every stature shall bow down. Every heart shall fear You, and all the inward parts and reins shall sing praises to Your name. As it is written: "All my bones shall say, Lord, who is like You, who delivers the poor from him that is too strong for him, and the poor and needy from him who spoils him?" *(Psalm 35:10).*

Who is like You? Who is equal to You? Who can be compared to You? Great, mighty and tremendous God, God most high, to whom heaven and earth belong! We will praise, adore, glorify, and bless Your holy name, as it is said: "A psalm of David. Bless the Lord, O my soul, and all that is within me, bless His holy name!" *(Psalm 103:1).*

God, mighty in His power, great in the honor of His Name, valiant forever, terrible in His fearful deeds!

The King, seated on His high and lofty throne!

He dwells in the heavens and His name is holy, as it is written: "Rejoice in the Lord, you righteous, for praise becomes the upright" *(Psalm 33:1).* In the mouth of the upright shall You be praised, with the words of the righteous You shall be blessed, by the tongue of the pious You shall be extolled, and in the midst of the holy You shall be hallowed.

And in the assemblies of the multitudes of Your people, of the house of Israel, shall Your name, O our King, be glorified in song in every generation. For such is the duty of every creature before You, O Lord our God and God of our fathers, to thank, praise, extol, glorify, exalt, honor, bless, and adore You beyond all the words of the songs and praises of David, son of Jesse, Your servant and anointed!

Praised be Your Name for ever, O our King! God and King, great and holy in heaven and on earth. For to You are becoming, O Lord our God and God of our fathers, song and praise, hymn and psalm, strength and dominion, victory, power and greatness, praise and glory, holiness and sovereignty, blessing and thanksgiving to Your great and holy name; for You are God from everlasting to everlasting.

Those who are scrupulous to observe the custom of the "fifth cup" recite here:
**I am now ready and prepared to fulfill the commandment of the fifth cup,
which corresponds with the fifth of the "expressions of redemption," as the Torah states:
"And I will bring you into the land, which I swore to give to Abraham, to Isaac, and to Jacob,
and I will give it to you as a heritage; I am the Lord** *(Exodus 6:8).*
The fifth cup is then drunk without reciting a blessing.
After drinking the cup, the appropriate grace for wine is recited.

Those who do not observe the custom of the "fifth cup" continue here: Blessed are you. . . .

Blessed are You, O Lord, Almighty King, great beyond all praises, God of thanksgiving,
Lord of wonders, extolled in songs of praise, Ruler, Almighty and Eternal God!

בָּרוּךְ אַתָּה יְיָ אֱלֹהֵינוּ מֶלֶךְ הָעוֹלָם
עַל הַגֶּפֶן וְעַל פְּרִי הַגֶּפֶן וְעַל תְּנוּבַת הַשָּׂדֶה
וְעַל אֶרֶץ חֶמְדָּה טוֹבָה וּרְחָבָה
שֶׁרָצִיתָ וְהִנְחַלְתָּ לַאֲבוֹתֵינוּ
לֶאֱכֹל מִפִּרְיָהּ
וְלִשְׂבּוֹעַ מִטּוּבָהּ
רַחֶם נָא יְיָ אֱלֹהֵינוּ עַל יִשְׂרָאֵל עַמֶּךָ וְעַל יְרוּשָׁלַיִם עִירֶךָ
וְעַל צִיּוֹן מִשְׁכַּן כְּבוֹדֶךָ וְעַל מִזְבְּחֶךָ וְעַל הֵיכָלֶךָ
וּבְנֵה יְרוּשָׁלַיִם עִיר הַקֹּדֶשׁ בִּמְהֵרָה בְיָמֵינוּ וְהַעֲלֵנוּ לְתוֹכָהּ
וְשַׂמְּחֵנוּ בְּבִנְיָנָהּ וְנֹאכַל מִפִּרְיָהּ וְנִשְׂבַּע מִטּוּבָהּ
וּנְבָרֶכְךָ עָלֶיהָ בִּקְדֻשָּׁה וּבְטָהֳרָה
וּרְצֵה וְהַחֲלִיצֵנוּ בְּיוֹם הַשַּׁבָּת הַזֶּה
וְשַׂמְּחֵנוּ בְּיוֹם חַג הַמַּצּוֹת הַזֶּה כִּי אַתָּה יְיָ טוֹב וּמֵטִיב לַכֹּל
וְנוֹדֶה לְךָ עַל הָאָרֶץ וְעַל פְּרִי הַגֶּפֶן
בָּרוּךְ אַתָּה יְיָ עַל הָאָרֶץ וְעַל פְּרִי הַגֶּפֶן

הִנְנִי מוּכָן וּמְזֻמָּן לְקַיֵּם מִצְוַת כּוֹס רְבִיעִי שֶׁל אַרְבָּעָה כּוֹסוֹת, כְּנֶגֶד
לָשׁוֹן רְבִיעִי שֶׁל אַרְבָּעָה לְשׁוֹנוֹת גְּאוּלָה, שֶׁנֶּאֱמַר: וְלָקַחְתִּי אֶתְכֶם לִי
לְעָם וְהָיִיתִי לָכֶם לֵאלֹקִים.

בָּרוּךְ אַתָּה יְיָ אֱלֹהֵינוּ מֶלֶךְ הָעוֹלָם בּוֹרֵא פְּרִי הַגָּפֶן

שׁוֹתִים בַּהֲסִיבָה.

נִרְצָה

חֲסַל סִדּוּר פֶּסַח כְּהִלְכָתוֹ
כְּכָל מִשְׁפָּטוֹ וְחֻקָּתוֹ
כַּאֲשֶׁר זָכִינוּ לְסַדֵּר אוֹתוֹ
כֵּן נִזְכֶּה לַעֲשׂוֹתוֹ
זָךְ שׁוֹכֵן מְעוֹנָה
קוֹמֵם קְהַל עֲדַת מִי מָנָה
קָרֵב נַהֵל נִטְעֵי כַנָּה
פְּדוּיִים לְצִיּוֹן בְּרִנָּה

I am now ready and prepared to fulfill the commandment of the fourth cup, which corresponds with the fourth of the "four expressions of redemption," as the Torah states: "And I will take you to Me for a people, and I shall be for you a God" *(Exodus 6:7).*
The host says:
Blessed are You, O Lord our God, King of the universe, who created the fruit of the vine.

All drink the fourth cup while reclining.

Blessed are You, O Lord our God, King of the universe, for the vine and for the fruit of the vine, and for the produce of the field and for the pleasant, good and ample land which You have loved and which You have given to our fathers as an inheritance, to eat of its fruits and to be satisfied with its goodness.
Have mercy, O Lord our God, upon Your people Israel, upon Jerusalem Your city, upon Zion the seat of Your glory, upon Your altar and upon Your Temple, and build Jerusalem, the holy city soon, in our days. Bring us up into its midst, that we may rejoice in its building and eat of its fruits, be satisfied with its goodness and bless You in holiness and purity;
(and be pleased to make us happy on this Sabbath day)
and may we rejoice on this day, the Feast of Matzot, for You, O Lord, are good and does good to all, and we thank You for the land and for the fruit of the vine. Blessed are You, O Lord, for the land and for the fruit of the vine.

NIRTSAH — Conclusion

May the Seder which we have now concluded
be acceptable in the eyes of God.

**The ordering of the Passover has been
completed according to its precepts,
with all its customs and ordinances.
Just as it has been granted us to order it now,
so may we be found worthy
to fulfill it in the future.
Pure One, dwelling on High,
raise up to Yourself a congregation
without number! Bring us back soon,
the plants of Your vineyard,
redeemed into Zion with joyful song.**

The Seder Is Concluded
Reciting the Passover Seder Orally Will Hasten the Time of Action
The concluding hymn dates from a later period, and was written especially for those who recite the "*Haggadah* of Exile." For them, the destruction and ensuing exile seem to drag on endlessly, and hope of rebuilding seems remote indeed. It is for these weary exiled celebrants that this hymn is intended; it actually constitutes the final answer to the wise son.

After the *afikoman* has been eaten, and this son observes that the Passover sacrifice was neither brought to the table nor eaten—and in its place, more matzah was eaten as a substitute, as a remembrance—a new question is raised almost automatically: How long must we suffice ourselves with symbolic gestures? How long shall this situation continue, when we must satisfy ourselves with lip service?

It is this last point which the father now answers: "We have completed the order of Passover, according to its laws." In speech, we have reenacted the proper order of events for Passover night. Today we have done this in word, not in deed, like something which is not applicable to us. But for this very reason the father continues and expresses his hope that "Just as we have merited to order it, so may we merit to fulfill it"—in deed; through action. And in Jerusalem.

The rabbis taught, "Great is the power of study, for it leads to action" (BT Kiddushin 40:B). The end result of speech, and desire, is always action. Indeed, only when one recognizes the true nature of these things, and he is filled with the desire to renew the Passover "according to all its precepts and ordinances," only then is he licensed to seal the *Haggadah* with the proclamation: "Next Year in Jerusalem!"

לְשָׁנָה הַבָּאָה בִּירוּשָׁלַיִם הַבְּנוּיָה

NEXT YEAR IN THE REBUILT JERUSALEM!

Temple Vessels — On the Setting of a Remnant from the Second Temple
The following photographs depict several groupings of various sacred vessels restored by the Temple Institute.
The vessels are displayed on a stone decorated with a floral motif which is an actual remnant from the Second Temple complex.

The Temple Remnant with Instruments of the Festival Sacrifice The large brass vessel is used to prepare the meal offering, and the brass cups are for measuring the proper amounts of flour, oil and wine for each offering. The golden flask is designed to pour the wine libation on the altar. It is poured into the silver cup which is located at the corner of the altar. In the background, the "three-pronged fork" is for turning over the sacrifice upon the altar.

The Temple Remnant with the Instruments of the *Omer* (Barley) Sacrifice Pictured here: the basket (called *kupah*) of barley picked for the *mitzvah* of the *Omer*, the sifter for sifting the barley; and the *abuv*, a perforated brass vessel in which the grains of barley are roasted over a fire, in keeping with the commandment.

The Temple Remnant with Instruments of the Passover Sacrifice The large brass tray (called *magas*) is used to carry parts of the sacrifice to the altar. A silver shovel is used to stir the fire on the altar. Vessels known as *mizrakim* of varying sizes are used to gather the blood of the sacrifice for sprinkling on the altar. One of these, the largest, is made of silver and its weight is "70 shekels (talents) of silver, by the Sanctuary weight" (Numbers 7:13).

The Temple Remnant with Stone Vessels The vessels shown here are designed for the preparation of the ashes of the red heifer, the Torah's process for ritual purification (Numbers 19). They are made especially of stone, since this is the only material which is impervious to the penetration of ritual impurity. The stone cups here date to the First Temple period. The stone mortar in the foreground is also ancient. The marble flask is for drawing water from the Shiloh Spring. Also included is a stone dish used in preparing the solution of the ashes, and the stone *kallal* vessel for storing the ashes in purity.

וּבְכֵן וַיְהִי בַּחֲצִי הַלַּיְלָה
It Happened At Midnight

Often You did perform miracles at night.
At the beginning of the watches of this night.
The righteous convert (Abraham) prevailed when he divided his company at night.

And it happened at midnight.

The blasphemer raised his hand against Your dwelling place; You shamed his dead by night.
Bel and his image were overthrown in the darkness of night.
To the much-beloved (Daniel) the secret vision was revealed at night.

And it happened at midnight.

You did threaten the king of Gerar (Abimelech) with death in a dream at night.
The Aramean (Laban) was struck with terror in the dead of night.
Israel strove with God and prevailed at night.

And it happened at midnight.

He who caroused from the holy vessels (Belshazzar) was slain that same night.
He was delivered from the lion's den, revealed Your fearful dreams of the night.
The Agagite who cherished hatred (Haman) wrote missives at night.

And it happened at midnight.

You smote the firstborn of the Egyptians at midnight.
They did not find their host when they arose at night.
Sennacherib's host was defeated through the stars at night.

And it happened at midnight.

You did rouse Your power against him when sleep fled at night.
You will tread the winepress for him who asked, "Watchman, what of the night?"
The watchman of Israel shall cry out: "The morning will come after the night."

And it happened at midnight.

Let the day come near that is neither day nor night.
Most High, make it known that the day and the night is Yours!
Appoint watchmen to Your city by day and by night,
Make light as day the darkness of the night!

And it happened at midnight.

וּבְכֵן וַאֲמַרְתֶּם זֶבַח פֶּסַח
And You Shall Say, "It is the Sacrifice of the Passover"

You have displayed Your mighty power at Passover.
You set up the Passover above all the feasts.
To the Ezrahite (Abraham) You revealed Your midnight miracles at Passover.

And you shall say, "It is the sacrifice of the Passover."

Lord! You smote each firstborn's head on Passover.
All-Powerful! But Your firstborn, You spared on Passover.
Not letting a destroyer pass my doors on Passover.

And you shall say, "It is the sacrifice of the Passover."

You knocked at his door in the heat of the day on Passover.
He fed the angels with *matzot* on Passover.
And he ran to the herd in memory of the ox, on Passover.

And you shall say, "It is the sacrifice of the Passover."

The enclosed city (Jericho) was taken at the time of Passover.
Midian was destroyed by a barley cake, the offering on the Passover.
The princes of Pul and Lud were consumed in a great fire on Passover.

And you shall say, "It is the sacrifice of the Passover."

The furious men of Sodom were consumed with fire on Passover.
Lot was brought out, and he baked *matzot* at the end of Passover.
You swept the land of Moph and Noph, and went through it on Passover.

And you shall say, "It is the sacrifice of the Passover."

He stayed one more day in Nob till the approach of Passover.
A hand wrote the fate of Zul on Passover.
The "watch was set, the table spread" on Passover.

And you shall say, "It is the sacrifice of the Passover."

Hadassah assembled the people for a three-day fast on Passover.
You hung the head of an evil house (Haman) on a fifty-cubit gallows on Passover.
"Both of these" You will bring in a moment on Utz (Edom) on Passover.
Your hand will be strong and Your right arm lifted up, as when You sanctified the Passover.

And you shall say, "It is the sacrifice of the Passover."

כִּי לוֹ נָאֶה כִּי לוֹ יָאֶה

To Him It Is Becoming, Him It Shall Become

אַדִּיר בִּמְלוּכָה ⸱ בָּחוּר כַּהֲלָכָה ⸱ גְּדוּדָיו יֹאמְרוּ לוֹ
Mighty in His kingdom, chosen as of right,
The hosts of angels say to Him,
לְךָ וּלְךָ, לְךָ כִּי לְךָ, לְךָ אַף לְךָ, לְךָ יְיָ הַמַּמְלָכָה
To You, To You, To You, To You,
To You, O Lord, is sovereignty!
כִּי לוֹ נָאֶה כִּי לוֹ יָאֶה
To Him it is becoming, Him it shall become!

דָּגוּל בִּמְלוּכָה ⸱ הָדוּר כַּהֲלָכָה ⸱ וָתִיקָיו יֹאמְרוּ לוֹ
Foremost in His kingdom, glorious as of right,
His ministers say to Him,
לְךָ וּלְךָ, לְךָ כִּי לְךָ, לְךָ אַף לְךָ, לְךָ יְיָ הַמַּמְלָכָה
To You, To You, To You, To You,
To You, O Lord, is sovereignty!
כִּי לוֹ נָאֶה כִּי לוֹ יָאֶה
To Him it is becoming, Him it shall become!

זַכַּאי בִּמְלוּכָה ⸱ חָסִין כַּהֲלָכָה ⸱ טַפְסְרָיו יֹאמְרוּ לוֹ
Pure is His kingdom, powerful as of right,
His angels say to Him,
לְךָ וּלְךָ, לְךָ כִּי לְךָ, לְךָ אַף לְךָ, לְךָ יְיָ הַמַּמְלָכָה
To You, To You, To You, To You,
To You, O Lord, is sovereignty!
כִּי לוֹ נָאֶה כִּי לוֹ יָאֶה
To Him it is becoming, Him it shall become!

יָחִיד בִּמְלוּכָה ⸱ כַּבִּיר כַּהֲלָכָה ⸱ לִמּוּדָיו יֹאמְרוּ לוֹ
Single in His kingdom, omnipotent as of right,
His servitors say to Him,
לְךָ וּלְךָ, לְךָ כִּי לְךָ, לְךָ אַף לְךָ, לְךָ יְיָ הַמַּמְלָכָה
To You, To You, To You, To You,
To You, O Lord, is sovereignty!
כִּי לוֹ נָאֶה כִּי לוֹ יָאֶה
To Him it is becoming, Him it shall become!

מֶלֶךְ בִּמְלוּכָה ⸱ נוֹרָא כַּהֲלָכָה ⸱ סְבִיבָיו יֹאמְרוּ לוֹ
Ruler in His kingdom, awesome as of right,
Those about Him say to Him,
לְךָ וּלְךָ, לְךָ כִּי לְךָ, לְךָ אַף לְךָ, לְךָ יְיָ הַמַּמְלָכָה
To You, To You, To You, To You,
To You, O Lord, is sovereignty!
כִּי לוֹ נָאֶה כִּי לוֹ יָאֶה
To Him it is becoming, Him it shall become!

עָנָו בִּמְלוּכָה ⸱ פּוֹדֶה כַּהֲלָכָה ⸱ צַדִּיקָיו יֹאמְרוּ לוֹ
Most meek in His kingdom, redeemer as of right,
The righteous say to Him,
לְךָ וּלְךָ, לְךָ כִּי לְךָ, לְךָ אַף לְךָ, לְךָ יְיָ הַמַּמְלָכָה
To You, To You, To You, To You,
To You, O Lord, is sovereignty!
כִּי לוֹ נָאֶה כִּי לוֹ יָאֶה
To Him it is becoming, Him it shall become!

קָדוֹשׁ בִּמְלוּכָה ⸱ רַחוּם כַּהֲלָכָה ⸱ שִׁנְאַנָּיו יֹאמְרוּ לוֹ
Most Holy in His kingdom, merciful as of right,
The multitudes say to Him,
לְךָ וּלְךָ, לְךָ כִּי לְךָ, לְךָ אַף לְךָ, לְךָ יְיָ הַמַּמְלָכָה
To You, To You, To You, To You,
To You, O Lord, is sovereignty!
כִּי לוֹ נָאֶה כִּי לוֹ יָאֶה
To Him it is becoming, Him it shall become!

תַּקִּיף בִּמְלוּכָה ⸱ תּוֹמֵךְ כַּהֲלָכָה ⸱ תְּמִימָיו יֹאמְרוּ לוֹ
Almighty in His kingdom, upholding as of right,
His perfect ones, they say to Him,
לְךָ וּלְךָ, לְךָ כִּי לְךָ, לְךָ אַף לְךָ, לְךָ יְיָ הַמַּמְלָכָה
To You, To You, To You, To You,
To You, O Lord, is sovereignty!
כִּי לוֹ נָאֶה כִּי לוֹ יָאֶה
To Him it is becoming, Him it shall become!

אַדִּיר הוּא

Mighty Is He!
He will build His house soon:
Speedily, speedily,
Soon, in our days.
Build it, Lord, build it, build Your House soon!

יִבְנֶה בֵיתוֹ בְּקָרוֹב
בִּמְהֵרָה בִּמְהֵרָה בְּיָמֵינוּ בְּקָרוֹב
אֵל בְּנֵה אֵל בְּנֵה
בְּנֵה בֵיתְךָ בְּקָרוֹב

בָּחוּר גָּדוֹל דָּגוּל הָדוּר וָתִיק זַכַּאי
הוּא הוּא הוּא הוּא הוּא הוּא הוּא
חָסִיד טָהוֹר יָחִיד כַּבִּיר לָמוּד
הוּא הוּא הוּא הוּא הוּא
מֶלֶךְ נוֹרָא סַגִּיב עִזּוּז
הוּא הוּא הוּא הוּא
פּוֹדֶה צַדִּיק קָדוֹשׁ
הוּא הוּא הוּא
רַחוּם שַׁדַּי
הוּא הוּא
תַּקִּיף
הוּא

Choice, great, and high is He!
He will build His house soon:
Speedily, speedily,
Soon, in our days.
Build it, Lord, build it, build Your House soon!

Honored, worthy, pure is He!
He will build His house soon:
Speedily, speedily,
Soon, in our days.
Build it, Lord, build it, build Your House soon!

Righteous, pure, and One is He!
He will build His house soon:
Speedily, speedily,
Soon, in our days.
Build it, Lord, build it, build Your House soon!

Mighty, wise, and sovereign is He!
He will build His house soon:
Speedily, speedily,
Soon, in our days.
Build it, Lord, build it, build Your House soon!

Tremendous, high and strong is He!
He will build His house soon:
Speedily, speedily,
Soon, in our days.
Build it, Lord, build it, build Your House soon!

Redeemer, just, and holy is He!
He will build His house soon:
Speedily, speedily,
Soon, in our days.
Build it, Lord, build it, build Your House soon!

Compassionate, almighty is He!
He will build His house soon:
Speedily, speedily,
Soon, in our days.
Build it, Lord, build it, build Your House soon!

יִבְנֶה בֵיתוֹ בְּקָרוֹב
בִּמְהֵרָה בִּמְהֵרָה בְּיָמֵינוּ בְּקָרוֹב
אֵל בְּנֵה אֵל בְּנֵה
בְּנֵה בֵיתְךָ בְּקָרוֹב

ספירת העומר
THE COUNTING OF THE OMER

The custom of those Jews living in the Diaspora who conduct the Seder on the second night of Passover, is to recite the blessing over the "counting of the *omer*" after the hymn *Adir Hu* ("Mighty Is He!"), since the theme of this song is the rebuilding of the Holy Temple.

Blessed are You, O Lord our God, King of the universe, who has sanctified us with His commandments, and commanded us to count the *omer*.

Today is the first day of the *omer*.

May it be Your will, O Lord, our God and God of our fathers, that the Holy Temple be rebuilt speedily in our days, and grant us our portion in Your Torah.

מנהג ישראל היושבים מחוץ לארץ ישראל, ועורכים 'סדר שני' כמנהג בני חוץ לארץ, לומר את ברכת ספירת העומר בסיום הפיוט 'אדיר הוא יבנה ביתו בקרוב', שכולו בקשה על בנין בית המקדש.

בָּרוּךְ אַתָּה יי אֱלֹהֵינוּ מֶלֶךְ הָעוֹלָם אֲשֶׁר קִדְּשָׁנוּ בְּמִצְוֹתָיו וְצִוָּנוּ עַל סְפִירַת הָעֹמֶר

הַיּוֹם יוֹם אֶחָד לָעֹמֶר

יהי רצון מלפניך יי אלהינו ואלהי אבותינו, שיבנה בית המקדש במהרה בימינו ותן חלקנו בתורתך.

Abuv This perforated copper vessel was used to roast the kernels of barley. A tray holding the burning coals was placed underneath.

Harvesting the *Omer* (Barley) The barley for the *omer* offering was harvested with a scythe at the conclusion of the first day of the festival of Passover, among a multitude of people.

◀ (*Overleaf*) **The Sifting of the *Omer* in the Temple Courtyard** After the barley is cut, the priests bring it to the courtyard in baskets and containers. They then grind down the grains and roast them in the *abuv* over the fire. This roasting is a biblical commandment. After the grains are ground in a millstone, they are sifted through 13 separate sifters. The offering is then waved before the presence of God in the eastern section of the courtyard. A portion is burned on the altar, and the remainder is eaten by the priests.

אֶחָד מִי יוֹדֵעַ אֶחָד אֲנִי יוֹדֵעַ
Who Knows One? I Know One!
One is our God in heaven and on earth.

שְׁנַיִם מִי יוֹדֵעַ שְׁנַיִם אֲנִי יוֹדֵעַ
שְׁנֵי לוּחוֹת הַבְּרִית

Who knows *two*? I know two!
Two are the tablets of the Law,
One is our God in heaven and on earth.

שְׁלוֹשָׁה מִי יוֹדֵעַ שְׁלוֹשָׁה אֲנִי יוֹדֵעַ
שְׁלוֹשָׁה אָבוֹת
שְׁנֵי לוּחוֹת הַבְּרִית

Who knows *three*?
I know three!
Three are the patriarchs,
Two are the tablets of the Law,
One is our God in heaven and on earth.

אַרְבַּע מִי יוֹדֵעַ אַרְבַּע אֲנִי יוֹדֵעַ
אַרְבַּע אִמָּהוֹת
שְׁלוֹשָׁה אָבוֹת
שְׁנֵי לוּחוֹת הַבְּרִית

Who knows *four*? I know four!
Four are the matriarchs,
Three are the patriarchs,
Two are the tablets of the Law,
One is our God in heaven and on earth.

חֲמִשָּׁה מִי יוֹדֵעַ חֲמִשָּׁה אֲנִי יוֹדֵעַ
חֲמִשָּׁה חֻמְשֵׁי תוֹרָה
אַרְבַּע אִמָּהוֹת
שְׁלוֹשָׁה אָבוֹת
שְׁנֵי לוּחוֹת הַבְּרִית

Who knows *five*? I know five!
Five are the books of the Torah,
Four are the matriarchs,
Three are the patriarchs,
Two are the tablets of the Law,
One is our God in heaven and on earth.

שִׁשָּׁה מִי יוֹדֵעַ שִׁשָּׁה אֲנִי יוֹדֵעַ
שִׁשָּׁה סִדְרֵי מִשְׁנָה
חֲמִשָּׁה חֻמְשֵׁי תוֹרָה
אַרְבַּע אִמָּהוֹת
שְׁלוֹשָׁה אָבוֹת
שְׁנֵי לוּחוֹת הַבְּרִית

Who knows *six*? I know six!
Six are the orders of the Mishnah,
Five are the books of the Torah,
Four are the matriarchs,
Three are the patriarchs,
Two are the tablets of the Law,
One is our God in heaven and on earth.

שִׁבְעָה מִי יוֹדֵעַ שִׁבְעָה אֲנִי יוֹדֵעַ
שִׁבְעָה יְמֵי שַׁבַּתָּא
שִׁשָּׁה סִדְרֵי מִשְׁנָה
חֲמִשָּׁה חֻמְשֵׁי תוֹרָה
אַרְבַּע אִמָּהוֹת
שְׁלוֹשָׁה אָבוֹת
שְׁנֵי לוּחוֹת הַבְּרִית

Who knows *seven*?
I know seven!
Seven are the days of the week,
Six are the orders of the Mishnah,
Five are the books of the Torah,
Four are the matriarchs,
Three are the patriarchs,
Two are the tablets of the Law,
One is our God in heaven and on earth.

אַחַד עָשָׂר מִי יוֹדֵעַ אַחַד עָשָׂר אֲנִי יוֹדֵעַ
אַחַד עָשָׂר כּוֹכְבַיָּא
עֲשָׂרָה דִבְּרַיָּא
תִּשְׁעָה יַרְחֵי לֵידָה
שְׁמוֹנָה יְמֵי מִילָה
שִׁבְעָה יְמֵי שַׁבְּתָא
שִׁשָּׁה סִדְרֵי מִשְׁנָה
חֲמִשָּׁה חֻמְשֵׁי תוֹרָה
אַרְבַּע אִמָּהוֹת
שְׁלוֹשָׁה אָבוֹת
שְׁנֵי לוּחוֹת הַבְּרִית

Who knows *eleven*?
I know eleven!
Eleven are the stars in Joseph's dream,
Ten are the commandments,
Nine are the months of bearing,
Eight are the days of the Covenant,
Seven are the days of the week,
Six are the orders of the Mishnah,
Five are the books of the Torah,
Four are the matriarchs,
Three are the patriarchs,
Two are the tablets of the Law,

One is our God in heaven and on earth.

שְׁנֵים עָשָׂר מִי יוֹדֵעַ שְׁנֵים עָשָׂר אֲנִי יוֹדֵעַ
שְׁנֵים עָשָׂר שִׁבְטַיָּא
אַחַד עָשָׂר כּוֹכְבַיָּא
עֲשָׂרָה דִבְּרַיָּא
תִּשְׁעָה יַרְחֵי לֵידָה
שְׁמוֹנָה יְמֵי מִילָה
שִׁבְעָה יְמֵי שַׁבְּתָא
שִׁשָּׁה סִדְרֵי מִשְׁנָה
חֲמִשָּׁה חֻמְשֵׁי תוֹרָה
אַרְבַּע אִמָּהוֹת
שְׁלוֹשָׁה אָבוֹת
שְׁנֵי לוּחוֹת הַבְּרִית

Who knows *twelve*?
I know twelve!
Twelve are the tribes,
Eleven are the stars in Joseph's dream,
Ten are the commandments,
Nine are the months of bearing,
Eight are the days of the Covenant,
Seven are the days of the week,
Six are the orders of the Mishnah,
Five are the books of the Torah,
Four are the matriarchs,
Three are the patriarchs,
Two are the tablets of the Law,

One is our God in heaven and on earth.

שְׁמוֹנָה מִי יוֹדֵעַ שְׁמוֹנָה אֲנִי יוֹדֵעַ
שְׁמוֹנָה יְמֵי מִילָה
שִׁבְעָה יְמֵי שַׁבְּתָא
שִׁשָּׁה סִדְרֵי מִשְׁנָה
חֲמִשָּׁה חֻמְשֵׁי תוֹרָה
אַרְבַּע אִמָּהוֹת
שְׁלוֹשָׁה אָבוֹת
שְׁנֵי לוּחוֹת הַבְּרִית

Who knows *eight*?
I know eight!
Eight are the days of the Covenant,
Seven are the days of the week,
Six are the orders of the Mishnah,
Five are the books of the Torah,
Four are the matriarchs,
Three are the patriarchs,
Two are the tablets of the Law,

One is our God in heaven and on earth.

תִּשְׁעָה מִי יוֹדֵעַ תִּשְׁעָה אֲנִי יוֹדֵעַ
תִּשְׁעָה יַרְחֵי לֵידָה
שְׁמוֹנָה יְמֵי מִילָה
שִׁבְעָה יְמֵי שַׁבְּתָא
שִׁשָּׁה סִדְרֵי מִשְׁנָה
חֲמִשָּׁה חֻמְשֵׁי תוֹרָה
אַרְבַּע אִמָּהוֹת
שְׁלוֹשָׁה אָבוֹת
שְׁנֵי לוּחוֹת הַבְּרִית

Who knows *nine*? I know nine!
Nine are the months of bearing,
Eight are the days of the Covenant,
Seven are the days of the week,
Six are the orders of the Mishnah,
Five are the books of the Torah,
Four are the matriarchs,
Three are the patriarchs,
Two are the tablets of the Law,

One is our God in heaven and on earth.

עֲשָׂרָה מִי יוֹדֵעַ עֲשָׂרָה אֲנִי יוֹדֵעַ
עֲשָׂרָה דִבְּרַיָּא
תִּשְׁעָה יַרְחֵי לֵידָה
שְׁמוֹנָה יְמֵי מִילָה
שִׁבְעָה יְמֵי שַׁבְּתָא
שִׁשָּׁה סִדְרֵי מִשְׁנָה
חֲמִשָּׁה חֻמְשֵׁי תוֹרָה
אַרְבַּע אִמָּהוֹת
שְׁלוֹשָׁה אָבוֹת
שְׁנֵי לוּחוֹת הַבְּרִית

Who knows *ten*? I know ten!
Ten are the commandments,
Nine are the months of bearing,
Eight are the days of the Covenant,
Seven are the days of the week,
Six are the orders of the Mishnah,
Five are the books of the Torah,
Four are the matriarchs,
Three are the patriarchs,
Two are the tablets of the Law,

One is our God in heaven and on earth.

Who knows **thirteen**? I know thirteen!	שְׁלוֹשָׁה עָשָׂר מִי יוֹדֵעַ שְׁלוֹשָׁה עָשָׂר אֲנִי יוֹדֵעַ
Thirteen are the attributes of God,	שְׁלוֹשָׁה עָשָׂר מִדַּיָּא
Twelve are the tribes,	שְׁנֵים עָשָׂר שִׁבְטַיָּא
Eleven are the stars in Joseph's dream,	אַחַד עָשָׂר כּוֹכְבַיָּא
Ten are the commandments,	עֲשָׂרָה דִבְּרַיָּא
Nine are the months of bearing,	תִּשְׁעָה יַרְחֵי לֵידָה
Eight are the days of the Covenant,	שְׁמוֹנָה יְמֵי מִילָה
Seven are the days of the week,	שִׁבְעָה יְמֵי שַׁבְּתָא
Six are the orders of the Mishnah,	שִׁשָּׁה סִדְרֵי מִשְׁנָה
Five are the books of the Torah,	חֲמִשָּׁה חֻמְשֵׁי תּוֹרָה
Four are the matriarchs,	אַרְבַּע אִמָּהוֹת
Three are the patriarchs,	שְׁלוֹשָׁה אָבוֹת
Two are the tablets of the Law,	שְׁנֵי לוּחוֹת הַבְּרִית

One is our God in heaven and on earth.

Only One Kid, Only One Kid

דְּזַבִּן אַבָּא בִּתְרֵי זוּזֵי
חַד גַּדְיָא
חַד גַּדְיָא

That father bought for two *zuzim*.
Only one kid, only one kid!

וְאָתָא שׁוּנְרָא
וְאָכְלָה לְגַדְיָא
דְּזַבִּן אַבָּא בִּתְרֵי זוּזֵי

Then came a **cat** and ate the kid that father bought for two *zuzim*.
Only one kid, only one kid!

חַד גַּדְיָא
חַד גַּדְיָא

Had Gadya—"Only One Kid"

A Song in Praise of Israel—the Eternal People

The famed hymn *Had Gadya* is a topic of debate and discussion amongst the commentators and researchers of the *Haggadah*. Some claim that it was authored at a much later date, and others have even suggested that it was written as an imitation of sacred songs sung by various non-Jewish elements in Europe. But Rabbi Kasher, writing in his monumental *Haggadah Shleimah* (page 190), has already proven that the *Had Gadya*'s roots are indeed ancient, for we find a similar listing of topics in the words of our sages in the Midrash (Genesis Rabbah—conclusion of Noah) as part of a debate between Abraham and Nimrod.

We also find a similar passage in the Talmud (Bava Batra 10:A): "Ten hard things were created in this world: a hard mountain—metal cuts it; hard metal—fire can diffuse it; harsh fire—water extinguishes it; fierce water—clouds bear it. But death is the hardest of all." This rabbinic passage bears two similarities to the *Had Gadya* song. Firstly, the topics themselves—water, fire, and death—which conclude this statement, parallel the "angel of death" in the song. And the second thing: the rabbis mention *ten* difficult things, each being nullified by that which follows it. So too, in the *Had Gadya*, each of the ascending ten items has the power to nullify that which preceded it.

Thus, the song's subject matter and basic format already existed in ancient Jewish sources. This finding should certainly preclude any necessity to search for "imitations" taken from non-Jewish sources. However, we must nonetheless endeavor to understand the *Had Gadya*'s content in the light of the *Haggadah*, for the song was adopted as the conclusion of the Exodus story, and the hope for the future redemption.

"My Father Bought a Kid for Two *Zuzim*"

In truth, *Had Gadya* is a song of praise to the people of Israel, who, after leaving Egypt, were beset with crises, both in their own land and in exile, but ultimately will experience their true and eternal deliverance when God returns His presence to Jerusalem. The poet utilizes the kid as the object of his metaphor—for after all, the lamb is the central theme on this night, the night of the Passover sacrifice, which was brought from a lamb or a sheep, and this provides the poet with a tangible starting point for his song. The "father" in the song is of course the head of the household, master of the Seder, who purchased the kid for use as the Passover sacrifice.

All this is obvious, but what is the parable? It would appear likely that the author of this song was also referring to the "father" in a spiritual sense, and his intention was toward our master Moses, who bore Israel in the desert "like a nursing mother carried her suckling infant," in the words of the rabbis. Even though it was Moses who led the people of Israel out of the desert, he did not merit to be mentioned by name in the *Haggadah*—but at the conclusion of the recitation, this poet devised an allegory wherein he is mentioned.

There is a well-known midrashic passage which refers to Moses, tending his father-in-law's sheep in the desert (Exodus Rabbah 2:2): "When Moses tended Yitro's flock of sheep, one kid bolted, and Moses ran after it. Reaching water, the kid paused to drink. Said Moses: 'I had no idea you were so thirsty and tired!' He picked him up and carried him back on his shoulders. The Holy One, blessed be He, said: 'Since you possess the quality of mercy which enables you to look after the flocks of men, I want you to tend My own flock, Israel.'"

Thus we see that in the earlier rabbinic literature, Israel is likened to the "kid," and the "father" who buys, acquires, and takes responsibility on behalf of the Holy One is Moses, the man of God. Additionally, the concept of the "father" carries a higher spiritual connotation as well—our Father in Heaven, the Holy One, who has "acquired" Israel to Himself as a people. Indeed, Israel is one of the five acquisitions of God which He has taken to Himself in this world, as the verse states: "You have acquired this nation" (Exodus 15, Pirkei Avot 6).

This acquisition was begun at the Exodus from Egypt, when the Red Sea split into sections, allowing Israel to pass through unharmed. At this special moment the relationship between Israel and its Creator began to take shape, and about this singular moment the verse states: "Till Your people pass over, O Lord; till this people pass over, whom You have acquired" (Exodus 15:16). But it was only when Israel stood at the foot of Mount Sinai and received the two Tablets of the Covenant that this relationship was fully sealed and consummated—for God then acquired Israel to Himself in the fullest sense of the word, and from that moment, this nation belonged only to Him. An eternal covenant was established between God and the people of Israel throughout every generation; and with what did the Holy One "purchase" His people Israel? With "two *zuzim*"—the two stone Tablets of the Law.

"Then Came a Cat and Ate the Kid"

The "cat" symbolizes the deep-seated hatred which the nations of the world have for Israel. For the cat hates the mouse, even though the mouse has done it no harm. The cat has grounds to suspect the mouse or to hate it; nonetheless, if he merely spots a mouse from a great distance, he will take off after it in hot pursuit until he catches the mouse and kills it. Can this be anything more than blind hatred? This "cat" analogy represents the hatred of the nations toward Israel throughout the course of history, for throughout an endless succession of generations, Israel has been the object of baseless persecution.

In the *Haggadah*, our rabbis point out the example of Laban's hatred for Jacob: "Go and learn what Laban the Aramean wanted to do to Jacob." The great Maharal of Prague explains that Laban's hatred for Jacob was without cause, for after all, he was his relative; Jacob's children were his own, his flocks—his own. Yet despite this the *Haggadah* states: "Laban wanted to destroy everything."

In this manner the "cat" appears, symbolizing Laban's burning hatred, and that of all those who have persecuted Israel throughout the generations—"and ate the kid"—"for they have *eaten* Jacob, and laid his dwelling place to waste" (Psalm 79:7). Israel's spiritual nature and their simple faith in God is unbearable to the nations—their simplicity in serving God is like the kid who follows after its master, and this is the very reason why "the cat comes and eats the kid."

Then came a **dog**
and bit the cat
that ate the kid
that father bought for two zuzim.

וְאָתָא כַלְבָּא
דְּנָשַׁךְ לְשׁוּנְרָא
דְּאָכְלָה לְגַדְיָא
דְּזַבַּן אַבָּא בִּתְרֵי זוּזֵי

Only one kid, only one kid!

חַד גַּדְיָא
חַד גַּדְיָא

Then came a **fire**
and burned up the stick
that beat the dog
that bit the cat
that ate the kid
that father bought for two zuzim.

וְאָתָא נוּרָא
וְשָׂרַף לְחֻטְרָא
דְּהִכָּה לְכַלְבָּא
דְּנָשַׁךְ לְשׁוּנְרָא
דְּאָכְלָה לְגַדְיָא
דְּזַבַּן אַבָּא בִּתְרֵי זוּזֵי

Only one kid, only one kid!

חַד גַּדְיָא
חַד גַּדְיָא

Then came a **stick**
and beat the dog
that bit the cat
that ate the kid
that father bought for two zuzim.

וְאָתָא חֻטְרָא
וְהִכָּה לְכַלְבָּא
דְּנָשַׁךְ לְשׁוּנְרָא
דְּאָכְלָה לְגַדְיָא
דְּזַבַּן אַבָּא בִּתְרֵי זוּזֵי

Only one kid, only one kid!

חַד גַּדְיָא
חַד גַּדְיָא

Then came **water**
and put out the fire
that burned up the stick
that beat the dog
that bit the cat
that ate the kid
that father bought for two zuzim.

וְאָתָא מַיָּא
וְכָבָה לְנוּרָא
דְּשָׂרַף לְחֻטְרָא
דְּהִכָּה לְכַלְבָּא
דְּנָשַׁךְ לְשׁוּנְרָא
דְּאָכְלָה לְגַדְיָא
דְּזַבַּן אַבָּא בִּתְרֵי זוּזֵי

Only one kid, only one kid!

חַד גַּדְיָא
חַד גַּדְיָא

than the Torah and its study, for "the Torah is compared to water" (BT Bava Kama 17). This is why Rabbi Yohanan ben Zakkai, on the eve of the destruction, made one request of the Roman Emperor Vespasian: "Give me Yavneh and its scholars." For he knew that through Torah scholarship the people would be renewed; the Sanctuary of God will be rebuilt on new foundations. Thus Torah study was reintroduced into Israel en masse, and scholars of Israel bloomed out of the devastation of destruction: the *tannaim* who authored the Mishnah, and the *amoraim* of the Talmud, as well as the *savoraim*, the *geonim*, and on to the *rishonim* and *aharonim*, the earlier and later authorities—all the subsequent generations of Torah scholarship and leadership that emerged to guide the nation along its path in the service of God.

Thus, "water came"—the water of Torah—and extinguished the fire of destruction and Divine wrath. The Torah center which was established in Kerem B'Yavneh was planned by Rabbi Yohanan ben Zakkai to act as a way station along the route which would take the Jewish people back to the Temple. And it was there that Rabbi Yohanan ben Zakkai enacted the custom of "remembrances of the Temple" in the hope that, as we pray daily, "the Temple will be rebuilt speedily." But "an ox came and drank the water. . . ."

"Then Came an Ox and Drank the Water"
The ox is the symbol of wealth. In the words of the prophet Amos (4:1): "Hear this word, you cows of Bashan, that are on the mountain of Samaria, who oppress the poor, who crush the needy. . . ." The "cows of Bashan" are the rich—the "ox"—whom the prophet rebukes for amassing wealth at the expense of others (see

Targum on this verse). Kerem B'Yavneh and the Torah center which had been set up in the Jewish world are classic examples of the source of strength by which the people could renew itself based on the proper foundations. These academies are likened by the rabbis to "miniature temples," which were to serve as a temporary refuge and way station along the route to the rebuilt Holy Temple. So what is the element which prolongs the exile and causes the people to cloister themselves within these "miniature temples," preventing them from thinking about returning to Jerusalem and the Temple?

This is wealth! Already when the Second Temple was erected, some Jews refrained from heeding Cyrus' call to return to the Land to rebuild the Temple, for they clung on to the homes they built for themselves in Babylon, and the wealth they had amassed. Since then, and even prior to this, it was always the dangers of wealth—the "ox"—which retarded the return of the Jewish people to the Land of Israel, and the rebuilding of the Holy Temple in Jerusalem. The talmudic sage Simeon ben Lakish ("Resh Lakish") gave expression to the frustration he felt at this syndrome, when the Babylonian sage Rabbah Bar Bar Hana, crossing the Jordan, extended his hand to him and Resh Lakish called out to him in the language of an oath: "How hated you are to us!"

Resh Lakish poured out all the grievances that he and his colleagues, the sages of the Land of Israel, had against their contemporaries, the rabbis of Babylon, on Rabbah Bar Bar Hana. They held these Babylonian sages in contempt because they held on to their wealth and positions in exile and did not return to the Holy Land in the days of Ezra, and in this manner they prevented the *Shechina*—the Divine

Then came an **ox** and drank up the water that put out the fire that burned up the stick that beat the dog that bit the cat that ate the kid that father bought for two zuzim.	וְאָתָא תוֹרָא וְשָׁתָא לְמַיָּא דְּכָבָה לְנוּרָא דְּשָׂרַף לְחֻטְרָא דְּהִכָּה לְכַלְבָּא דְּנָשַׁךְ לְשׁוּנְרָא דְּאָכְלָה לְגַדְיָא דְּזַבִּן אַבָּא בִּתְרֵי זוּזֵי

Only one kid, only one kid!

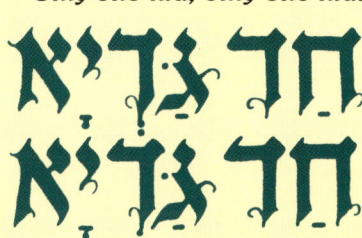

Then came a **butcher** and slaughtered the ox that drank up the water that put out the fire that burned up the stick that beat the dog that bit the cat that ate the kid that father bought for two zuzim.	וְאָתָא הַשּׁוֹחֵט וְשָׁחַט לְתוֹרָא דְּשָׁתָא לְמַיָּא דְּכָבָה לְנוּרָא דְּשָׂרַף לְחֻטְרָא דְּהִכָּה לְכַלְבָּא דְּנָשַׁךְ לְשׁוּנְרָא דְּאָכְלָה לְגַדְיָא דְּזַבִּן אַבָּא בִּתְרֵי זוּזֵי

Only one kid, only one kid!

"Then Came a Dog and Bit the Cat"

Like the cat, the dog also possesses the capacity to hate—but as opposed to the cat, the dog does not tear its enemies asunder to eat them. The dog's animosity to his surroundings will manifest itself through biting anything which crosses its path. When an animal attacks another in order to satisfy its hunger, its behavior can still be justified to some extent—but an animal who bites just for the sake of biting? He has nothing to gain; his intention is just to cause harm (Bava Batra, ch. 1), and this harm itself has value to him, and becomes his goal and purpose in life. This is a wicked quality indeed.

This describes the behavior of the Egyptians, and the treatment they gave Israel while the latter were in Egypt. The Egyptians enslaved Israel, but their objective was not only to use Israel's labor and thus take advantage of them; they derived particular enjoyment out of torturing Israel and afflicting them, and this became an objective in itself. This is inferred from the Torah's description of the Egyptian man whom Moses saw "hitting one of his Israelite brothers." What was it that Moses saw that angered him to the extent that he killed the Egyptian? He saw the great satisfaction and enjoyment that this taskmaster derived from his sport, whipping the innocent with no thought but to satisfy the full measure of his own cruelty. Confronted with this type of evil—cruelty for its own sake—Moses rose up and killed the Egyptian. The Torah states that the Egyptians enslaved Israel "with rigor," and according to the insight of the rabbis this means that "they would make the men do women's work, and the women to perform men's work." This was for no other reason than simply "to *afflict* them in their burdens." This *affliction*—the torture, physical abuse, and mental anguish which they caused the Jews to suffer—became its own goal for the Egyptians.

This was also the basis of Pharaoh's command to drown all the male children in the river. These children would have become the slaves who would build his empire and serve his nation—and yet he himself destroyed them. What sense does that make? But this is the nature of cruelty for its own sake—drowning these children was a source of pleasure for Pharaoh; it was this pleasure that drove him insane and led to his downfall. This is the face of the "dog"—the one who hates Israel and enjoys "biting."

The hatred of the dog comes on the heels of the "cat's" blind hatred. These are the original roots of anti-Semitism, the "wolves" who surround the "sheep and kid" to attack them. In the midst of this world of hatred, the kid goes the solitary way of his arduous journey—to fulfill the mission entrusted to him by his "father."

"Then Came a Stick and Beat the Dog"

This "stick" is none other than the plagues which God wrought in Egypt—for in every instance wherein Moses and Aaron stood before Pharaoh, they took with them the "rod of God." Of course, it was not the stick itself which brought about the Divine miracles, but the One who dwells on high, who sent Moses, the true servant of God, to bring punishment upon the evildoers. This messenger himself is the "rod of God" who visits punishment upon Pharaoh for his wickedness. The sea, too, parted before Israel when Moses raised his stick aloft, as it is written: "Raise your stick and spread your hand over the water, and divide it" (Exodus 14:17).

And it is this mission—to be the collective "rod of God" in this world—which was given by the Creator of heaven and earth to the Jewish people. When Israel fulfills the word of God, they are in effect His "rod," accomplishing His will on earth. Through them, reward and punishment are meted out to humanity, each according to the measure of his deeds. In this manner, "the stick came and beat the dog"—thus, the rod of Divine fury struck Egypt, punishing them for their evil with the ten plagues, and drowning them in the sea.

In this way the "rod" can be seen as Divine power. As long as Israel is filled with moral force and they faithfully perform the commandments of God, then they become His messengers in this world to execute charity and justice, as reflected by the verse, "I have formed this people for Myself; they shall relate My praise" (Isaiah 43:21). When the peoples of Canaan deserved to be punished for their multitude of sins and abhorrent ways, it was Israel who was chosen to be the messenger, the "rod" to obliterate these evil nations from the Land and take their place. "For the Lord your God goes before you in the midst of your camp, to deliver your enemies before you."

This is only the case as long as Israel holds high the banner of morality-based adherence to the Torah's Divine commandments and ethics, and thus embodies the principle of "and your camp shall be holy." But if, Heaven forbid, Israel abandons or neglects these ways of holiness—they will not be found worthy of being the "rod," the vehicle by which justice is accomplished in the world.

"Then Came a Fire and Burned Up the Stick"

The element of fire is at opposites with wood, the "rod"—and destroys it. Therefore when the angel of God appears before Moses to show him the power of Israel, he is revealed in a flame of fire in the midst of a bush—and Moses stands and wonders, "Why is the bush not consumed?" For when Israel performs the will of the Holy One and is found worthy, and they merit to act as the "rod of God" in His world, they are impervious to fire—just as fire had no power over the bush.

However, when Israel sins, Heaven forbid, the "rod of God" is transformed to a bit of dry wood, and is consumed by fire. Thus the Holy Temple, place of the Divine Presence, was destroyed by fire, and as the sages comment, "the enemy burned a Temple that was already burned" (BT Sanhedrin 96:B). For as soon as the rod loses its moisture, it burns and is transformed to dust and ashes. This is just what befell Israel and the Temple, when "the fire came and burned the stick."

"Then Came Water and Extinguished the Fire"

What has the power to put out this "fire," and assuage the Divine wrath that was poured out over Israel in the destruction? Only water—and "water" is none other

וַאֲתָא מַלְאַךְ הַמָּוֶת
וְשָׁחַט לְשׁוֹחֵט
דְּשָׁחַט לְתוֹרָא
דְּשָׁתָא לְמַיָּא
דְּכָבָה לְנוּרָא
דְּשָׂרַף לְחֻטְרָא
דְּהִכָּה לְכַלְבָּא
דְּנָשַׁךְ לְשׁוּנְרָא
דְּאָכְלָה לְגַדְיָא
דְּזַבִּן אַבָּא בִּתְרֵי זוּזֵי

Then came the **angel of death**
and slew the butcher
that slaughtered the ox
that drank up the water
that put out the fire
that burned up the stick
that beat the dog
that bit the cat
that ate the kid
that father bought for two *zuzim*.

וַאֲתָא הַקָּדוֹשׁ בָּרוּךְ הוּא
וְשָׁחַט לְמַלְאַךְ הַמָּוֶת
דְּשָׁחַט לְשׁוֹחֵט
דְּשָׁחַט לְתוֹרָא
דְּשָׁתָא לְמַיָּא
דְּכָבָה לְנוּרָא
דְּשָׂרַף לְחֻטְרָא
דְּהִכָּה לְכַלְבָּא
דְּנָשַׁךְ לְשׁוּנְרָא
דְּאָכְלָה לְגַדְיָא
דְּזַבִּן אַבָּא בִּתְרֵי זוּזֵי

Then came **the Holy One**,
blessed be He,
and slew the angel of death
that slew the butcher
that slaughtered the ox
that drank up the water
that put out the fire
that burned up the stick
that beat the dog
that bit the cat
that ate the kid
that father bought for two *zuzim*.

Only one kid, only one kid!

concept. Everything evil which takes place in this world can be said to be an aspect of "death." The sages enigmatically stressed (BT Bava Batra 16:A), "There are many guises, but they are all one and the same entity—whether he is called the Satan, the Evil Inclination (within each person), or the Angel of Death." Whenever any individual succumbs to the temptations of his own internal evil inclination—the side of evil, in potential, which is present in each one of us, and he commits an act of evil—whenever this happens, he is killing something in this world, whether this "something" is a part of himself, of his personality that is being destroyed, or whether it is a part of someone else's life. This itself is the evil inclination, the angel of death which the Holy One allows to excercise a limited amount of authority, temporarily, within the framework of our existence. The danger of this "element" is that his influence is not limited only to those who possess a natural tendency toward accepting his "advice"—for the true objective of this evil is to gain control and reign over the world of holiness.

One source in the rabbinic literature which illustrates this point in an exceptionally lucid—and chilling—fashion can be found in the Talmud (BT Yoma 69:B). There, it is written that the evil inclination is hidden, and can be found in the Temple's own Holy of Holies—the most sublime, lofty and holy location on earth. The rabbis describe an incredible scene which took place in the early days of the Second Temple era, in the days of Ezra. The people of Israel stood in the court of the Holy Temple and cried out "to the Lord God with a great voice" (Nehemiah 9). In their prayer, Israel bemoaned the presence of the Evil Inclination in this world, blaming it as the cause for the destruction of the Temple, the burning of the Sanctuary and the death of the righteous—"and still he dances amongst us"; they wept, meaning, his danger is still very much a constant part of our lives.

The Talmud continues to relate that upon that occasion, Israel's prayer was partially accepted—"and the evil inclination appeared, in the form of a lion cub made of fire—and exited from the Holy of Holies." This is an allusion to the reality of the human condition: the evil inclination within each human being, flaming like a fire, clings to the holiest things of all—to the veritable Holy of Holies. Thus we learn that in the days of the Temple, there were times when jealousy reigned among the High Priests, hatred was rampant in the ranks of Israel's kings—and even civil war—and all this in the courtyards of the Holy Temple itself.

Again, the evil inclination's run of this world is temporary; eventually, it will be destroyed—as will evil itself. Thus King David, himself the champion in the war against the powers of evil, writes (Psalm 92:7): "When the wicked sprout like grass, and when all the workers of iniquity flourish, it is because they will be destroyed forever." This threatening phenomenon need not terrify us, for though it may flourish, it is only temporary—and the end which awaits evildoers is that "they will be destroyed forever," for in the end God will vanquish all evil from His world. As opposed to the wicked, David describes that the destiny of the righteous is to flourish "as a palm tree" and "as a cedar tree"—for in the future they will be "planted in the House of God, in the Courtyards of our God shall they flourish."

"Then Came the Holy One, Blessed Be He, and Slew the Angel of Death"

The climax of this song is this, its tenth stanza—for "the tenth shall be holy" (Leviticus 27:32). And so in the tenth stanza, the author of the hymn depicts how the Holy One will ultimately put His world in order—and on "that great and awesome day," all of these manifestations of evil—the Satan, the Evil Inclination and the Angel of Death—shall be "slaughtered," and disappear forever.

In this light our sages have taught (BT Sukkah 52:A): "In the future, the Holy One will bring out the evil inclination, and slaughter him." In that lesson, the rabbis list the objectives which the evil inclination had strived for as his goals: "He gazed upon the First Temple . . . and it was destroyed! He gazed upon the Second Temple . . . and it too was destroyed!" The evil inclination—the angel of death—set his gaze upon these two previous Temples, and he succeeded in "dancing amongst Israel," amongst their sages and in the midst of the world of holiness. By causing Israel to stumble and sin, he aroused jealousy and hatred among them, and caused both Temples to be destroyed. But here, the author of *Had Gadya* informs us that in the future, the Holy One Himself will come and "slaughter" the Evil Inclination/Angel of Death. The tender "kid," which began the long and arduous journey of its life's mission at the Exodus from Egypt, and in the course of the generations, saw Solomon's Temple built, and destroyed; and saw the Second Temple built, and destroyed. This "kid," which experienced the travails of exile and learned of its suffering on its own flesh, in the end, it will return home, inviolate and unbroken. Not weak or tired; not helpless; the "kid" will return home, to Jerusalem, full of strength and vigor—and the knowledge gained from the experiences of the past.

This is how the Jewish people will build the Third Temple, directly from the ruins of its prolonged destruction—on holy and pure foundations. "And this House shall be the highest," the "eternal House,"—for the *Shechina*, the Divine Presence of God, shall dwell in Israel—and in Jerusalem—forever.

חַד גַּדְיָא, חַד גַּדְיָא

Only One Kid, Only One Kid!

Presence of God—from returning to dwell within the Second Temple, and thereby they ultimately contributed to the Temple's destruction (Yoma 9:2—Rashi; see also *Midrash Rabbah* on the Song of Songs, where a number of references are made to the wealthy who remained in Babylon, and thus led to the destruction of the Second Temple).

Even today, in our own generation—when multitudes of Israel have returned to their land from all corners of the globe—many others still continue to enjoy living the life of exile, clinging to their fine homes, wealth and material possessions. Their desire for higher "lifestyles" and "standards of living" drags them down and roots them deeply into the impurity of the foreign nations that they have grown fond of. The Sanctuary of God is indeed far from the hearts of these. But the *Shechina* itself waits for them from the site of the Holy Temple, and asks: "When will the Temple be rebuilt? When will the children awaken, and return to their own borders, to raise up the Temple of God from its ruins?"

"Then Came a Butcher and Slaughtered the Ox"

"An animal's end is to be slaughtered," says the Talmud (Berakhot 17:A), and this "ox" is destined to be slaughtered as well. The Torah itself assures us that Israel will never find respite amongst the nations, and that even if they find wealth, a storm wind will come and confound everything, bringing Israel back to their own land. Thus the rabbis teach (Genesis Rabbah 33:6): "What is meant by the verse 'And the dove could not find a resting-place for the sole of her foot?' If Israel, who is compared to a dove, would have found a 'resting-place' amongst the nations, she would not have returned to 'Noah's ark'—to Jerusalem." To this, the rabbis add the words of the prophet Jeremiah in the Book of Lamentations (1:3): ". . .she dwells amongst the nations; she finds no rest."

In his words of rebuke to Israel (Deuteronomy 28:65), Moses bears witness to the very same point and states: "And among those nations you shall find no ease, neither shall the sole of your foot find rest." Why? Because it is impossible to flee from the Divine Presence, to avoid the mission of returning to Jerusalem—and the Temple. As Rabbi Jacob Emden (in the introduction to his prayerbook, *Beit Jacob*) and the *Meshekh Hokhmah* commentary (in his explanation of Leviticus 26:44) have emphatically written, when a Jew begins to think "that Berlin is Jerusalem . . . a storm wind will come and pull him up by the roots." These were prophetic words indeed, since it was Berlin, the center of "culture," that declared war against the Jewish people and "Jerusalem"—yes, "the butcher came and slaughtered the ox," and Israel's wealth in the exile turned to dust and ashes.

"Then Came the Angel of Death and Slew the Butcher"

The "butcher," representing the forces of evil in this world, slaughtered the "ox," Israel and the wealth it amassed. But ultimately the butcher will also perish, for in the midst of evil itself, the "angel of death" lurks, poised to destroy evil and drive it from this world.

The "angel of death" is the Heavenly appointed executioner—but it is a broad

the Great to Rabbi Simeon: "This is just how Israel's redemption will come about: in the beginnning, it progresses very slowly . . . but as it continues, it grows brighter and brighter."

(Jerusalem Talmud, Berakhot 1:1)

אַיֶּלֶת הַשַּׁחַר ר׳ חייא הגדול ור׳ שמעון בן חלפתא היו מהלכים בדרך וראו איילת השחר שבקע אורה. אמר ר׳ חייא הגדול לר׳ שמעון: כך היא גאולתן של ישראל — בתחילה קימעא קימעא, כל מה שהיא הולכת — היא רבה והולכת.

[עפ״י ירושלמי ברכות א, א]

The Morning Dawn Rabbi Hiyya the Great and Rabbi Simeon ben Halafta were on a journey when they perceived the first rays of the dawn's light breaking. Said Rabbi Hiyya

isolated acts of individual Romans, or with chance happenings; this was a full-fledged campaign to eradicate Judaism.

It is in this light that the students' declaration before their masters can be understood: "Masters! The time to recite the *Shma* has arrived!" Their true meaning was, "the time to sanctify the Name of God is at hand!" (Because these students suspected that perhaps there were Roman "plants" amongst the other disciples who could be listening, they added the last words of the sentence, "...of the morning service.")

Bar Kokhba's Rebellion to Save the Torah and Liberate Israel: A Result of the Sages' Meeting

It was this atmosphere that gave birth to Bar Kokhba's rebellion. Rabbi Akiva, who hosted the Seder in which the other sages participated, comforted his colleagues as they gazed upon the city of Rome, telling them that Rome's grandeur was only temporary. Later, it was Rabbi Akiva who was able to comfort them as they stood opposite the site of the Holy of Holies on the Temple Mount, assuring them that Jerusalem is destined to be rebuilt. And it was this same Rabbi Akiva who beheld Bar Kokhba and proclaimed aloud: "This is the king, the Messiah!" (JT Ta'anit 4:5). Rabbi Akiva's conclusion was a logical imperative: at a time like this, with Judaism poised at the brink of destruction, the appearance of a redeemer is an intrinsic necessity.

Thus Rabbi Simeon bar Yohai, Rabbi Akiva's student, repeated that his own master had applied the verse "A star shall shoot forth from Jacob" (Numbers 24:17) to Bar Kokhba. For according to tradition, this verse refers to the Messiah (Targum ibid.).

Bar Kokhba's rebellion grew as a result of the general atmosphere of oppression, but it was made possible when viewed against the backdrop of that meeting in Bnei Brak, where the main agenda had been the desire to return and raise up Jerusalem. Bar Kokhba encouraged this goal by minting a coin of rebellion. One side of this coin depicted the facade of the Temple in Jerusalem, thus establishing the main goal of his rebellion—to reach the city and rebuild the Temple. The other side of this coin carried the image of the *lulav* and the other four species taken up on the Festival of Succoth, thus to demonstrate that the rebellion's aim was to liberate the Jewish people from foreign oppression, thereby enabling them to fulfill the Torah's commandments as free men. To this he added on the coin the words "In the First Year of Israel's Freedom," to emphasize that the performance of the Divine commandments is not complete unless there is total freedom in the Land of Israel.

In this light, it is instructive to note that Maimonides, in the section of his codes where he describes the attributes of the anticipated king, the Messiah, cites the example of Bar Kokhba, Rabbi Akiva and the scholars of that generation as an illustration. Their objective was to throw off the yoke of Roman rule in order to freely perform the Torah's commandments, and to facilitate the rebuilding of the Holy Temple in Jerusalem and the offering of sacrifices.

Maimonides states: "In the future, the Messiah King will arise and return the Davidic kingdom to its pristine state. He will rebuild the Temple . . . sacrifices will be resumed, as will the Sabbatical and Jubilee years, according to all of the Torah's requirements . . . and consider that Rabbi Akiva, who was one of the greatest sages of Israel and a scholar of the Mishnah, was himself the armsbearer of 'the King Ben Koziba,' and the former proclaimed him to be the Messiah. Rabbi Akiva and all the sages of his generation were under the impression that he was, in fact, the anticipated Messiah King—until, as a result of sin, he was killed" (Maimonides, Laws of Kings, ch. 11).

Bar Kokhba's Rebellion Ends in the Sanctification of God: As a Result, the Era of the Mishnah and Talmud Emerges

During the four years of insurrection, a small measure of temporary independence was gained. The rebels, clinging to Jerusalem and standing in the courtyards of God's Sanctuary, taught the Romans that even though they might succeed in crushing the body of the Jewish people, they cannot break her spirit. But the rebellion was savagely crushed, and the scholars and disciples gave their lives to sanctify the Name of God and His commandments, while reciting the *Shma*. But through the duration of the rebellion the Romans learned that the Jews clung fast and strong to their faith, and in the face of this inner faith—the true source of Jewish strength—no power on earth could overcome. The fact is that from that time on, their oppression was eased, and the study of Torah was legalized.

Our rabbis relate that on the very day Rabbi Akiva was martyred for the Name of God, Rabbi Judah the Prince was born (BT Kiddushin 72:B). In this context, the Tosafists cite an ancient Midrash which states that Rabbi Judah, known simply as "Rebbe," was born during the severest moments of the decrees against the Jews, when the Romans had outlawed circumcision. Even this infant's father, Rabban Simeon ben Gamliel, the President of Israel, was forbidden to circumcise his son Judah. When the Emperor learned that despite the edict, the President had circumcised his son anyway, he summoned the parents to appear before him together with their son. Arriving at the palace, Judah's mother exchanged him with a Gentile infant who was uncircumcised—and in this manner the parents and their child were saved (Tosefta, Avodah Zarah 10:B).

In reference to this episode, the rabbis cite the verse "The sun also rises, and the sun goes down" (Ecclesiastes 1:5) and explain the verse as signifying that even though Rabbi Akiva's generation was a dark time of relentless persecution, a time of "sunset," still, "the sun also rose"—the generation of Rabbi Judah the Prince. Rebbe's birth was marked by decrees of destruction, but he grew to become the man who merited to reestablish the world of Torah within Israel. In his era, the Torah flourished anew—in the Galilee, in Bet She'arim, Tzipori and in Tiberias—and the sages themselves testify that "Since the days of Moses, Torah and greatness were not found in one place—until Rebbe" (BT Gittin 59:A). This "sunrise" emerged in the merit of the great self-sacrifice, in the face of persecution, undergone by the previous generation. Those surviving students of Rabbi Akiva—Rabbi Meir, Rabbi Yose, Rabbi Simeon bar Yohai and others—they are the ones who transmitted Rabbi Akiva's teachings to the next generation (BT Eruvin 13:B, for example).

Even the Roman government learned to esteem Rabbi Judah the Prince; the Emperor Antoninus himself, realizing the value and holiness of Israel's Torah, posed many astute and far-reaching questions to Rebbe (see Tanhuma Miketz, 9; JT Sanhedrin 10:2; Genesis Rabbah 11:4). In his time, permission was granted allowing for public Torah study, and Rebbe's academy was flooded with students. It was in his study hall that the six orders of the Mishnah were arranged, and the foundation for the Talmud was laid. And it was along these lines that Rabbi Judah's successor, Rabbi Yohanan, composed the Jerusalem Talmud in his great academy at Tiberias (Maimonides, Introduction to his commentary on the Mishnah).

The Rebellion and Sparks of the Light of Redemption

This new "sunrise," following the temporary sunset during the dark days of Rabbi Akiva's era, guided Rabbi Yohanan to express his faith that from Tiberias, the Torah would also return to Jerusalem and the Holy Temple, as he stated in Tractate Rosh HaShanah (31:B): "Said Rabbi Yohanan: And from there (from the tenth station of the Sanhedrin's exile, in Tiberias) they are destined to be redeemed—as the verse states (Isaiah 52), 'Shake yourself from the dust; arise, and sit down, O Jerusalem.'"

Maimonides refers to this statement of Rabbi Yohanan in his Laws of the Sanhedrin (14:12), and writes: "At first, when the Holy Temple was built, the Supreme Court was stationed within, in the Chamber of Hewn Stone; afterwards they were exiled from place to place—a total of ten places. In the end they were located in Tiberias . . . and we have a tradition that in the future they will first return to Tiberias, and from there, they will relocate again to the Holy Temple."

In our exile, lasting almost 2,000 years since the destruction of the Second Temple, we also require encouragement and consolation—just as Israel did in the years of Egyptian bondage. The commandment to relate the story of the Exodus in the *Haggadah*, with which the sages of Israel in Bnei Brak occupied themselves that entire night, is precisely that which gave the sages and their disciples the strength to endure the terrors of persecution. And it is that which imparts to all the successive generations of exile their staying power and hope—and the power to survive through times of danger and the threat of extinction.

In this light, and bearing in mind the *Haggadah*'s opening—the episode of the sages who gathered together in Rabbi Akiva's city—the various segments woven together into the *Haggadah* can be understood properly. The *Haggadah* "opens with degradation and concludes with praise"—for it begins by relating that we were once slaves, and ends at the loftiest apex: ". . .that He did bring us to the Land of Israel, and He did build for us His Chosen House."

This was the aspiration of the generation of the Exodus; this is our same hope, the hope of the people of Israel in the generation of return.

others were prominent scholars of that generation, and their disciples.

Most of these sages were themselves students of Rabbi Eliezer, such as Rabbi Simeon ben Azzai, contemporary of Rabbi Akiva (Rabbenu Gershom on BT Bava Batra 158:B). Rabbi Hananiah ben Teradyon, who showed disregard for the Roman edict forbidding Torah study, committed the crime of teaching Torah in public and was burned to death together with his Torah scroll. He, too, was a student of Rabbi Eliezer (BT Yoma 78:B). Other talmudic references inform us that Rabbi Yeshevav the Scribe was a student of Rabbi Joshua, and Rabbi Hutzpit the Translator was Rabbi Joshua's colleague in Kerem B'Yavneh. Rabbi Hutzpit was also a colleague—and cousin—of Rabbi Akiva.

It was Rabbi Judah ben Bava, friend of Rabbi Akiva (BT Yevamot 122:A), who was alert to the danger, the distinct possibility, that due to these persecutions, perhaps the ordination of rabbis (*semikhah*) would be discontinued from the Jewish people—and it was he who ordained five disciples from amongst Rabbi Akiva's students: Rabbi Meir (BT Eruvin 13:A), Rabbi Judah (BT Eruvin 41:A), Rabbi Yose (BT Pesahim 18:A), Rabbi Simeon (JT Berakhot 6) and Rabbi Eleazar ben Shammua (BT Zevahim 93:A).

Rabbi Judah ben Bava perceived the great danger inherent in the cessation of the *semikhah* process: without the scholars to transmit knowledge from generation to generation, the Torah could be forgotten from Israel. Therefore he was even prepared to die for this. "Once, the government issued a decree against the Jews, that whoever ordains rabbis for the Sanhedrin will be put to death. Those who receive this ordination will likewise be killed, and the city in which it took place will be destroyed. Yet Rabbi Judah ben Bava went and positioned himself between two great mountains and two large cities—Usha and Shfaram. There he ordained five elders: Rabbi Meir, Rabbi Judah, etc. The enemy took notice of them, and he instructed his students to flee. But they said, Master! What will become of you? I will lie before them like an unturned stone, he answered. It was said that the Romans stood over him until he was pierced by 300 metal javelins. And if not for Rabbi Judah ben Bava—the Torah would have been forgotten from Israel." (BT Sanhedrin 13:B).

The Plowing of Jerusalem and the Decrees Against Torah: A Plan to Destroy Israel

The execution of these great scholars, and the circumstances of their deaths, reveals something of the danger which the Jews of the Land of Israel faced in that generation—the danger of destruction. Rabbi Nathan, himself a student of both Rabbi Eliezer (BT Sukkah 19:B) and Rabbi Tarfon (Tosefta Zevahim 10:6), provides vivid descriptions of events which transpired as part of this campaign, as quoted in the *Mechilta of Rabbi Ishmael* (Yitro 20:5; see also Leviticus Rabbah 32:1):

"Rabbi Nathan said: What is meant by the phrase 'for those who love Me and keep My commandments?' These are the people of Israel, who dwell in the Land of Israel and sacrifice their lives for the commandments. For why are they killed?

"Why are you being led out to death? 'I cirmcumcised my son!' Why are you to be burned? 'I read from the Torah!' Why are they taking you to be hanged? 'I ate matzah!' Why are you being whipped? 'I took the *lulav*! I kept the Sabbath! I built a *succah*! I donned *tefillin*! I wore a string of blue! In short: I did the will of my heavenly Father.'"

These edicts were decreed against the Jews as part of the Romans' plan to incorporate the Land of Israel, and the Jewish people, within the Roman Empire. The government sought to swallow them up into this huge empire, just as they had done to all the other peoples of that era. Those persecuted and beaten Jews of Israel who had survived the destruction became the test of the Romans' ability to achieve their goal.

Jerusalem was plowed over, all traces of reminders that it was once the city of the Holy Temple were erased, and it was transformed into a pagan center—this, together with the decrees against the Jews that limited their performance of the commandments. These were two parts of the plan to destroy the character and identity of Israel—the land, the people, and their God.

The Students Follow in Their Rabbis' Footsteps: The Pilgrimage to Jerusalem

The sages of Israel in that era, both masters and disciples, did not acquiesce. They did not diminish their Torah study activities or refrain from practicing their faith, but on the contrary, clung fast to the Divine commandments even more steadfastly—all of the commandments, including the pilgrimage to Jerusalem and the Temple.

Thus it is related (Tanna D'Vei Eliyahu, ch. 30) that Rabbi Zadok the Priest, disciple of Rabbi Joshua, went up to the Temple to bemoan the tragedy which befell his people. This action was in addition to Rabbi Zadok's fasts which he undertook at the time of the siege of Jerusalem, in an effort to prevent the Temple from being destroyed (BT Gittin 56:A). After the Temple had been destroyed, Rabbi Zadok returned to the site to intercede with Heaven on behalf of Israel's troubles, and to pray for the rebuilding of the Temple.

In the language of the Midrash: "On one occasion Rabbi Zadok entered into the Holy Temple and found it in ruins. He stood before the Holy One, blessed be He, and cried out: 'Master of the Universe! Father in Heaven! You have destroyed Your city and burned down your Sanctuary, and You sit quietly and peacefully?!' Rabbi Zadok immediately fell into a trance and saw a vision of the Holy One Himself, accompanied by the ministering angels, standing and eulogizing the Holy Temple."

Rabbi Nathan, Rabbi Eliezer's student (BT Pesahim 48:A), also traveled back to Jerusalem and the site of the Temple, to wail over the destruction and the decrees which came in its wake, as quoted in *Tanna D'Vei Eliyahu* (ch. 30): "Once Rabbi Nathan entered into the ruins of the Temple and found that one wall was still standing. He said, 'What is the nature of this wall?' Thereupon one of the wise men of Jerusalem told him, 'I will show you.' He took a ring and affixed it to that wall, and the ring shook (out of dread for the Divine Presence) until Rabbi Nathan experienced a vision. He saw the Holy One standing and wailing over the destruction of the Temple and Israel's exile."

Although these midrashic depictions portray something of the dedication that the Jews who dwelled in the Land of Israel demonstrated to uphold the Divine commandments—even when their lives were at risk on account of Hadrian's decrees—still, these descriptions are just a small portion of the testimony which has been passed down to us. Rabbi Judah the Prince and Rabbi Yohanan (as quoted in the Midrash Lamentations Rabbah 2:5 and JT Ta'anit 4:5) sat in the presence of their colleagues and students and recounted some of the horrible things which the Romans inflicted upon the Jews during Hadrian's time. These sources indicate that these two scholars alone related sixty incidents of brutality and torture in this sitting; more than once, the listeners could not bear what they heard, and wept so uncontrollably that they were forced to leave.

The Disciples Prove Their Intentions—Through Their Actions

Thus, only a proper understanding of the era we have been discussing, the era in which Rabbis Eliezer, Joshua, Elazar ben Azariah, Akiva, Tarfon and their students lived, can aid us in understanding those mysterious and cryptic words uttered by the students to their masters: "Masters! The time to recite the morning *Shma* has arrived!"

As we have already mentioned, it is difficult to believe that these students meant to instruct their teachers as to the proper time the *Shma* can be recited, since this very point was an issue of legal contention between the great men seated before them. But, the incidents of the students' self-sacrifice which follows, their willingness to die for the sake of the Divine commandments, and the story of Rabbi Akiva's recitation of the *Shma* in his students' presence as he was put to death, all bear witness and reveal to us the true intention of these disciples, hidden in their words "the time for the *Shma* has arrived!"

The deaths, torture, and all the evil dispensation described above which transpired in those days in the presence of the sages of Israel brought them to the conclusion that they must sacrifice themselves for the sake of the Torah's commandments. The Emperor's order, canceling permission for the Jews to rebuild the Holy Temple, was not coincidental. And when the sages of Israel journeyed to Rome to seek cancellation of the decrees which spelled destruction for the Jewish people, this was also a sure sign of the Romans' intentions.

The situation deteriorated to the point where it was even no longer possible to speak freely in the academy. As Rabbi Meir himself described: "Once we were all sitting before Rabbi Akiva in the study hall, and we were reciting the *Shma*, but we had to recite it under our breath because a quaestor stood by the door" (Tosefta Berakhot 2:13).

The order to plow Jerusalem into a field and transform the site of the Holy Temple into an idolatrous shrine served to fan the flames of rebellion in the Jewish people, which had started when the order canceling permission to rebuild the Temple arrived in the valley of Bet Rimon. This order proved beyond any doubt that they were not dealing here with the

The students' appearance and announcement before their masters is still more unusual when we reflect how the established custom amongst Torah scholars in the days of the rabbis was markedly different. If a student sought to raise a point to his teacher, he would use a specific expression, namely: "Our master, instruct us! Perhaps the time of reciting the *Shma* has arrived."

But in this instance we are simply told that the students arrived "and said to them!" without excusing themselves, and without giving the usual signal of respect. The incident is even more difficult to understand when we reflect upon the fact that this very topic which they are raising—the times for the reciting of the *Shma*—is a subject of controversy between these very sages sitting before the students in Bnei Brak, and as yet had not been decided upon! How could the students have involved themselves in a halakhic controversy between such intellectual giants, instructing them that the time had now arrived, when this very point had not yet been clarified between them!

The impression one gets from this story is that the sages of Israel were so totally involved in fulfilling the commandment of "telling the story of the Exodus" that they forgot themselves and simply lost track of the time. But this really seems highly unlikely—is it possible that the great and wise men of Israel, who were so preoccupied with studying the laws of *Shma* that they concerned themselves with minute details like "does the proper time begin when one can distinguish between blue and white, or between blue and green?" Is it then possible that these same sages would actually forget their own obligation altogether once the time finally arrived, and would not have fulfilled the commandment of *Shma* were it not for their students who came to remind them?

What better way to illustrate this point than to turn to the example of Rabbi Akiva himself! The Talmud relates that when the Romans were torturing him to death, scraping the flesh off his body with iron combs, "It was the time for reciting the *Shma*" (BT Berakhot 61:B). At that very moment, the Talmud continues, Rabbi Akiva said the *Shma* and accepted the "yoke of Heaven" upon himself. His students who stood around him asked, "Our Master! Until this point?" The students were incredulous to behold his attachment to God even in the midst of torture.

As we can see, the Talmud emphasizes the fact that this took place during the time of *Shma*, and despite Rabbi Akiva's difficult situation, he nonetheless made certain to carefully recite the *Shma* and fulfill the commandment in its proper time. From this we can certainly learn that the sages of Israel, the men of Rabbi Akiva's stature, were keenly aware of their own obligations for reading the *Shma* in its precise time, and if so, we must find an alternative explanation to understand the students' appearance before their teachers—and their enigmatic announcement, "The time for reading the morning *Shma* has arrived!"

Students and Masters Alike Sacrifice Their Lives in the Sanctification of Heaven

It would certainly appear that this lesson contains some profound hidden meaning. When we consider the fate of these sages and their disciples, we realize that the particular era during which this meeting in Bnei Brak took place was a time when terrible decrees of death and destruction were enacted against the Jewish people. It was in these very days that the Roman government embarked upon a program of eradicating the Torah from Israel.

We have already referred to a number of examples, culled from rabbinic sources, that are illustrative of the type of decrees the Romans enacted against the inhabitants of the Land of Israel. And if we but reflect upon the names of those who were executed by the Roman government, we can begin to understand just what really transpired in that troubled generation.

The rabbis of the Midrash (Lamentations Rabbah 2:5) provide a list of those sages who were executed by Hadrian's decree. In this midrashic passage, the verse "God consumed all the beauty of Jacob, and did not have compassion" is applied to these scholars whom the Romans put to death, meaning, all those who were beautiful in Jacob, who sanctified the name of Heaven with their deaths.

The standard version of this Midrash lists these sages as Rabbi Ishmael, Rabban Gamliel, Rabbi Yeshevav the Scribe, Rabbi Judah ben Bava, Rabbi Hutzpit the Translator, Rabbi Judah the Baker, Rabbi Hananiah ben Teradyon, Rabbi Akiva, Rabbi Simeon ben Azzai, and Rabbi Tarfon. Two of those mentioned in this list were amongst those sages who were gathered at the Seder in Bnei Brak—Rabbi Akiva and Rabbi Tarfon. The

one can tell between "a donkey and a wild ass," and still an anonymous opinion holds "when one can recognize his friend from a distance of four cubits." Similarly, the Mishnah also records a controversy as to the conclusion of the "morning *Shma*" time zone. One opinion holds that dawn marks the end of the time the *Shma* can be said; and Rabbi Joshua holds that it is permissible to read the *Shma* "until the end of the third hour of the day, since that is the time when princes are accustomed to arise" (BT Berakhot 9:B).

Rows of Priests Stand with Silver and Gold Vessels in Their Hands As the Passover sacrifice is offered, the officiating priests of the Temple stand in rows while holding the special silver and gold containment vessels to gather the blood from the sacrifice. The vessels are passed up the line from one to the next, until reaching the priest standing closest to the altar. He then sprinkles from the blood of the Passover sacrifice upon the foundation of the altar.

A Controversy Amongst the Rabbis Gathered in Bnei Brak: What Is the Proper Time for the *Shma*?

On the whole, this entire episode makes strange reading indeed. For those rabbis who sat together that night in Bnei Brak are the very same who were divided as to the proper time when the morning *Shma* can be begun, and by what time it must be concluded.

Various opinions were stated in this regard. As far as the beginning of the time for the *Shma* is concerned, the Mishnah records an opinion that this time begins "when one can distinguish between the colors blue and white." But Rabbi Eliezer opines that the time begins when one can distinguish "between blue and green," and Rabbi Meir states "between a wolf and a dog." Rabbi Akiva argues and maintains that the time is when

names of the students who were in attendance. But we can derive this information through the lessons discussed that evening which the *Haggadah* records—for sections of their own works are quoted verbatim in the text of the *Haggadah*.

The Style of Each Lesson Can Identify Its Author

Since each sage taught according to his own particular, unique style, some portions of the *Haggadah* can be identified by their style. For example, the fifteen "steps," or "benefits" which are listed in the *Dayenu* song each end with the word "*dayenu*" as its refrain—"it would have been enough for us." This word does not appear frequently in rabbinic literature, but it is a typical expression of Rabbi Joshua, one of the Seder participants in Bnei Brak.

As mentioned above, it was Rabbi Joshua who is quoted as saying "*Dayenu*—it is enough that we got involved (literally, that we came in) with this nation with no harm befalling us, and we also got away from them without harm." In fact, for that matter, we can even compare the opening words of *Dayenu* with this previous statement of Rabbi Joshua, and see the similarity: "If He would have only taken us out of Egypt . . . that would be enough." Later, as we explore the text of the *Haggadah* itself in our commentary, we cite a number of sources for this song, and it appears from these that the *Dayenu* song is in fact rooted in the time of the Temple itself, and was recited by the festival pilgrims themselves.

In any event, a survey of the names of those Tannaitic sages whose teachings are recorded in the *Haggadah* brings us to the conclusion that the text of our own *Haggadah* was in fact arranged by the sages of the generation of the Temple's destruction and Hadrian's decrees. The various sections which make up the contents of the *Haggadah* are the fruits of discussions on biblical verses held by the great rabbis of that generation, in the presence of their students.

The "Haggadah of Exile" Version: Composed in the Academy of Rabbi Akiva in Bnei Brak

This conclusion explains the structure of our present *Haggadah*, which differs from the text of the *Haggadah* that was recited when the Holy Temple stood. Even if the fundamental points included in the original *Haggadah* also form the basis of the post-destruction version, the additions which were added by the *tannaim* after the destruction were done so in the face of the new reality; this was the "*Haggadah* of Exile." This *Haggadah* placed the emphasis on the story of the Exodus from Egypt. At the time of its editing, attention was also directed toward those sections which are meant to strengthen and encourage faith during the darkness of the long exile; for the "exile of Edom (Rome) is nothing but an extension of the Egyptian bondage."

Thus, faith forms the very basis of the *Haggadah*, for the Exodus from Egypt must indeed be mentioned at "night," during the dark night of exile, and the faith that the time of our redemption will ultimately arrive "as an outstretched arm" as in the time of Egypt must be deepened. The power of this faith is that which will bring the redemption closer, and begin the process which will lead to the rebuilding of the Holy Temple.

Bnei Brak: A Way Station for the Sanhedrin's Exile to Usha

Why were the sages of Israel gathered in Bnei Brak, in the portion belonging to the tribe of Dan—in the center of the Land—and not in the usual place of their assembly, the academy in Kerem B'Yavneh? It can be assumed that this gathering took place during the time the Sanhedrin was exiled from Kerem B'Yavneh to Usha, in the northern part of the country. The presence of the sages in Bnei Brak—Rabbi Akiva's city—is telling, for it was Rabbi Akiva who projected faith and hope. Bnei Brak was an important way station for the Sanhedrin when it moved to the north, and these rabbis and students were themselves the exiles of Kerem B'Yavneh en route to Usha—the next stop for the Sanhedrin.

It would certainly appear that it was during their stay in Bnei Brak, on that fateful Seder night, that the new version of the *Haggadah* was composed, including changes necessitated by the harsh reality of the Temple's destruction—the "*Haggadah* of Exile."

The Authors of the "Haggadah of Exile"

The following is a list of lessons which were added by the rabbis as additions to the "*Haggadah* of the Holy Temple," together with their sources in rabbinic literature. Our intention here is not to establish this as absolute fact, but rather, to offer these conjectures as likely possibility, while in a number of instances, it appears nearly certain.

1. "It is related that Rabbi Eliezer, Rabbi Joshua, Rabbi Elazar ben Azariah, and Rabbi Tarfon were all gathered in Bnei Brak." **SOURCE:** Rabbi Akiva's academy in Bnei Brak (BT Berakhot 12:B).

2. "Rabbi Elazar ben Azariah said, 'Behold, I am like a man of seventy.'" **SOURCE:** ibid.

3. "Until Ben Zoma explained it." **SOURCE:** ibid.

4. "One might think . . . from the first day of the month." **SOURCE:** Rabbi Ishmael, *Mechilta* on Exodus.

5. "Go and learn what Laban the Aramean sought to do." **SOURCE:** Rabbi Simeon bar Yohai. This is the introduction to the *Sifre* on Deuteronomy, which is attributed to Rabbi Simeon (Sanhedrin 6:A). However, these passages have been omitted from the *Sifre* since they now appear in the *Haggadah*, but are mentioned in the *Yalkut Shimoni* on Deuteronomy.

6. "My father was a homeless Aramean." **SOURCE:** ancient. Latest version by Rabbi Ishmael, *Mechilta* on Exodus.

7. "And I will pass through the land of Egypt." **SOURCE:** ibid.

8. "'With a mighty hand' that is the pestilence." **SOURCE:** Rabbi Simeon bar Yohai, *Sifre* on Numbers.

9. "Rabbi Judah arranged them into mnemonic forms." **SOURCE:** Rabbi Judah, student of Rabbi Akiva (BT Eruvin 41:A).

10. "Rabbi Yose the Galilean said, 'How do we deduce that the Egyptians. . .'" **SOURCE:** Rabbi Yose the Galilean, student and colleague of Rabbi Akiva (BT Avodah Zarah 45:A; see Tosafot "Rabbi Akiva said").

11. "Rabbi Eliezer said, 'How do we deduce that every plague. . .'" **SOURCE:** Rabbi Eliezer.

12. "How can we deduce that every plague . . . was equivalent to five?" **SOURCE:** Rabbi Akiva.

13. "How many benefits!" **SOURCE:** ancient. Latest version by Rabbi Joshua (based on Genesis Rabbah 64).

14. "Blessed are You . . . who has redeemed." **SOURCE:** ancient. Latest version by Rabbi Tarfon (Pesahim 10:6).

15. "Our God and God of our fathers, may we live to celebrate . . . other festivals." **SOURCE:** Rabbi Akiva (ibid.).

16. Conclusion: to relate the story of the Exodus from Egypt all night long. **SOURCE:** *takkanah* (regulation) enacted by the sages gathered in Bnei Brak.

IX. "Our Masters! It Is Time to Recite the *Shma*!"

The anecdote of the students who enter and interrupt their teachers to inform them that the time has come to recite the morning prayer of *Shma Yisrael* is both perplexing and strange. We have already mentioned the words of the Tosefta referring to the gathering of Rabban Gamliel and the elders in the home of Baytus ben Zonin in Lod, when they stayed awake the entire night studying the laws of Passover until the rooster's crow at the break of dawn. In that instance, "the table was lifted away from them, and they proceeded to the academy."

From that previous incident, we can derive two things. Firstly, that it was enough for the sages to merely hear the rooster's crow outside for them to realize that the night was over and the time to say the *Shma* had arrived. And secondly, the Seder table was cleared away; this in itself was enough to remind them that the Seder night had been concluded!

It would certainly seem completely unnecessary for the sages' students to remind these great luminaries of the time for the prayer service, as if to nudge them not to forget their own halakhic obligations! Furthermore, according to the rabbis' descriptions, Rabbi Akiva was accustomed to take a rooster with him whenever he traveled, so that its cry would wake him at dawn (see BT Berakhot 60:B). If this were so, when the rabbis sat together in Bnei Brak, the voice of the rooster emanating from the courtyard should certainly have been enough; they were not in need of a special announcement that the hour of *Shma* had arrived.

believed just as fervently as Rabbi Akiva that these prophecies would be fulfilled in the future. Yet Rabbi Akiva succeeded in comforting his colleagues by reminding them of these words: "For his true meaning was that even if the Romans build a new city in Jerusalem, with streets, and balconies, and all the architectural splendor their cities are famous for—in the end, those streets will be filled with the elders of Israel, and they will ring out with the joyous sound of children playing, without fear. Thus, the 'curse' of the Romans will be transformed into a blessing."

Rabbi Akiva's attitude was always one of eternal optimism—for he learned this trait from his own master, Nahum of Gamzu (BT Hagigah 14:A), who was wont to say, "This, too, is for the best," even when tragedy struck. Rabbi Akiva followed in his footsteps and would say: "Whatever the Merciful One does, He only does for the good" (BT Berakhot 60:B). As we stated, the Romans sought to prevent unrest, and therefore sought to execute Rabban Gamliel, who was forced to flee for his life.

Now we can understand the incident which is recorded at the beginning of the *Haggadah*—why is it that when the holiday of Passover arrived, all the sages of Israel, from all over the land, converged at the home of Rabbi Akiva? For it was Rabbi Akiva who comforted them during the difficult moments of the decree. When they traveled to Rome, they saw that he had been correct; there was no reason to be despondent, for the edict had been canceled. And when they stood together facing the plowed field that had been the ruins of Jerusalem, there, too, it was Rabbi Akiva who comforted them and told them that Jerusalem will again return to its pristine glory. In an atmosphere of persecution, fear and hopelessness, the Seder at Rabbi Akiva's academy was only natural.

Thus the rabbis and their disciples gathered together on the night of the Festival of Redemption under the roof of the man who knew how to bring them life and hope in the most difficult moments. In the face of the oppression which grew progressively worse, this Seder brought hope and instilled faith that the nation of Israel will once again celebrate Passover in Jerusalem.

VIII. The Students and Their Masters in Bnei Brak

Rabbinic Teachings from the Mishnah and Midrashim Implanted Within the Haggadah

From this incident recorded in the *Haggadah*, we can derive that not only were these five sages mentioned by name in the *Haggadah* assembled in Bnei Brak, but so were their students as well. Even though the editor of the *Haggadah* did not record the names of these students, we are nonetheless familiar with some of the sages of Israel of that generation through talmudic references, and thus we can recognize them as being students of those who are mentioned in the *Haggadah*.

Based on this understanding of the master-student relationships of the rabbis, we can list some of these students who were likely to have been present at that gathering in Bnei Brak, for some of them are mentioned explicitly in the *Haggadah*, while the teachings of others are recorded in the *Haggadah* anonymously.

Ben Zoma's Connection to the Holy Temple

Rabbi Simeon ben Zoma was a student of Rabbi Joshua (see the Jerusalem Talmud, Tractate Nazir 8:1) and a colleague of Rabbi Akiva (BT Hagigah 14:B). His teaching is quoted in the *Haggadah* by Rabbi Elazar ben Azariah, who supported the former's position that the concept of the Exodus from Egypt must be mentioned at night.

Like the other five sages gathered in Bnei Brak, Ben Zoma had been an eye-witness to the beauty and glory of the Holy Temple. The Talmud records (BT Berakhot 58:A) the excitement Ben Zoma felt when watching special occasions in the Holy Temple, such as the arrival of the festival pilgrims. According to this same source, on one occasion when Ben Zoma saw "the multitudes of Israel, while standing atop a high point on the Temple Mount," he recited the special blessing "Blessed are You, Lord our God . . . Who is wise in secrets."

The Talmud goes on to explain that the particular blessing which Ben Zoma uttered is a rather unusual one, in that it can only be recited when one has the opportunity to gaze upon at least 600,000 Jews at once (the Talmud thus explains the reason for this blessing: upon seeing such an impressive number of people, one sees in wonder that no two look alike; the greatness of their Creator can be appreciated even more upon realizing that just as their faces differ, so, too, their internal qualities—their thoughts and intellects—all differ as well).

The opportunity to view so many of Israel at one time on the Temple Mount was indeed a rare one, but nonetheless there were such occasions, such as during the three festival pilgrimages. The description of Ben Zoma who stood "atop a high point on the Temple Mount" and recited the blessing of "wise in secrets" is telling of the deep impression this sight made on him, and the deep emotional response which the sight of the mulititudes streaming to the Temple in Jerusalem evoked in him. Presumably, this occurred when all of Israel arrived in Jerusalem to celebrate in the hallowed courtyards of the House of God.

Rabbi Simeon bar Yohai

Rabbi Simeon bar Yohai was one of the major students of Rabbi Akiva, and studied under him for 13 years (Leviticus Rabbah 21:8). Rabbi Simeon even received halakhic teachings from his master Rabbi Akiva when the latter was imprisoned (BT Pesahim 112:B).

It was Rabbi Simeon who authored the *Sifre*, the halakhic Midrash on the Book of Deuteronomy. This principle is established in Tractate Sanhedrin (6:A) of the Mishnah, where it is stated that "unless otherwise indicated, the *Sifre* is the teaching of Rabbi Simeon, according to Rabbi Akiva." This means that the contents and exegesis of the *Sifre* were studied and expounded in Rabbi Akiva's academy. In the same manner, Rabbi Simeon bar Yohai wrote the *Mechilta of Rashbi*, a commentary on the Book of Exodus.

In fact, one of the most central parts of the *Haggadah* is taken from the *Sifre*. The Mishnah states (Pesahim 10): ". . .and one should recite the entire section beginning with 'My father was a homeless Aramean.'" This section, included in the *Haggadah* in its entirety, is taken from the *Sifre* where it appears in the same language, and is based on the teachings of Rabbi Akiva, as stated above.

It would appear that during the course of that evening in Bnei Brak, Rabbi Akiva and his students discussed this lesson in detail. Rabbi Simeon bar Yohai expressed his objections to the Roman rule, for he bore personal witness to the decrees Rome enacted in that generation which were designed to uproot the Torah's commandments. In fact, on one occasion Rabbi Simeon was even dispatched to nullify such a decree, as recorded in Tractate Me'ilah (17:A): "Once the rulers issued a decree that the Sabbath could not be observed and children could not be circumcised. The sages said, 'Who will go and nullify this?' They said: 'Let Rabbi Simeon bar Yohai go, for he is experienced in miracles.'" This incident testifies to the general atmosphere of spiritual depression which served as life's backdrop for the sages of the Land of Israel and their students during that era.

Rabbi Ishmael

Rabbi Ishmael was a student of both Rabbi Eliezer and Rabbi Joshua (see Sifra on Leviticus 13). He was also a colleague of Rabbi Akiva. His teaching is quoted in the *Haggadah*, even if he is not mentioned by name, for Rabbi Ishmael is the author of the *Mechilta* on the Book of Exodus, and entire sections of the *Haggadah* are taken from this work.

Two examples are the parts "The Torah speaks of four sons" and that of "One might think that one is obliged . . . from the first day of the month of Nisan." It would seem that these two topics were also amongst the lessons discussed and considered by the students and their masters during that Seder in Bnei Brak.

Rabbi Ishmael was himself a *cohen*, of priestly descent, and in the course of the war and the Temple's destruction, he was captured and held in prison in Rome. He therefore understood exactly what the results of the destruction were, having experienced it personally, and he knew firsthand what Roman captivity was like. It was Rabbi Joshua who redeemed Rabbi Ishmael from captivity. The Talmud (BT Gittin 58:A) relates that Rabbi Joshua paid a huge sum to ransom Rabbi Ishmael, and a short time later Rabbi Ishmael was back teaching and guiding Israel. Rabbi Ishmael saw the Holy Temple and the priestly service with his own eyes, and from his earliest years he heard details about it from his father and brothers, as he grew up at home.

These are just several attempts to identify the students of these five sages who gathered in Bnei Brak, since the *Haggadah* does not specify the

"Five tragedies occurred on the Ninth of Av" (BT Ta'anit 26:B), and one of them was the plowing of Jerusalem. The rabbis add (ibid. 29:A) that "when the wicked Tinneius Rufus plowed over the Sanctuary, Rabban Gamliel was condemned to die." The connection between these two things is unclear. Furthermore, the Talmud continues to relate that Rabban Gamliel received a secret message from a member of the Roman Legion, and thereupon was forced to flee from his academy, and hide from the government. What was the reason?

As we have illustrated, the rabbis interpreted the plowing of Jerusalem and the Sanctuary on the Ninth of Av as a great catastrophe, which deserved to be bemoaned as much as the destruction itself. Rashi explains the significance of the plowing of the city (ibid.): "Zion shall be plowed into a field": "it was made completely into a plowed field." Maimonides also counts this event as a tragedy (Laws of Fasts 5:3): "...and on that same day which had been marked for retribution (Ninth of Av), the evil Tinneius Rufus, one of the Roman kings, plowed over the Sanctuary and its surroundings—to fulfill the verse, 'Zion shall be plowed into a field.'"

The Sages of Israel Weep As Hope for Rebuilding the Temple Is Lost—But Rabbi Akiva Laughs

As far as it is known, the plowing over of the city came about as the result of Hadrian's march through the Land of Israel and neighboring lands. When he reached Jerusalem, he ordered that the city be transformed into a Roman city, complete with a pagan temple in its center—on the site of the Holy Temple. He also changed Jerusalem's name to "Aelia Capitolina" in honor of the gods of Rome.

When the Romans planned the construction of a new city, their custom was to begin by the official act of publicly plowing over the land within the planned borders. This itself is why the sages of Israel made their way to Jerusalem, and explains why they wept and rent their garments: in front of their very eyes, the prophecy that "Zion will be plowed into a field" was fulfilled, and they wept to see it.

The sages interpreted this act of plowing, and the construction of the new city with a pagan temple on the spot of the Jewish Sanctuary, as the end of all hope that the Holy Temple of the God of Israel would ever be rebuilt in Jerusalem. Not only did the sages of that generation weep in despair, they also established that future generations throughout the exile should likewise weep over these events.

In light of these things, it is understandable why the Romans decreed that Rabban Gamliel must be killed—for the plowing of Jerusalem was done in preparation for the erection of a pagan temple, and the Romans could rightly suspect that Rabban Gamliel, as President of the Sanhedrin, would try to arouse his people against these actions.

And thus, at the end of Tractate Makkot, we are told that Rabban Gamliel arose and went up to Jerusalem, together with Rabbis Elazar ben Azariah, Joshua and Akiva, and there, confronted with this sight, they wept and tore their garments—and recited the verse "Zion will be plowed into a field" over that which their eyes beheld. But we can understand that when faced with this reality—the plowing over of Jerusalem—Rabban Gamliel had to react.

But in the face of such despair and anxiety, it is unclear as to why the sages took comfort in the words of the particular verse which Rabbi Akiva cited: "Old men and women will yet dwell in the broad places of Jerusalem . . . and children will play in its streets." After all, the other sages certainly

The Sanhedrin and the Sages of Israel in Exile This map depicts the final hours of Jerusalem and the Holy Temple. In the upper right corner, the walls of Jerusalem are defended against the onslaught of the Roman legions. Rabbi Yohanan ben Zakkai leaves the city gates in a coffin, and requests Vespasian to spare the city of Yavneh and its scholars. The sages of Israel move to Yavneh, where the new center of Torah study is established. Some of the great scholars resided in other cities: Rabbi Eliezer and Rabbi Tarfon dwelled in Lod; Rabbi Joshua in Peki'in; Rabbi Elazar ben Azariah in Kerem B'Yavneh; and Rabbi Akiva in Bnei Brak. Each one was a living witness to both the splendor and the destruction of the Second Temple. After the destruction, these sages gathered together on the Seder night in Bnei Brak, and established the post-destruction version of the *Haggadah*—the "*Haggadah* of Exile."

attempts to return and rebuild the Temple. This event occurred only a few years after the destruction, in the generation of the sages who celebrated the Seder together in Bnei Brak.

Here is a description of what actually happened, based on the Midrash (Genesis Rabbah 64:8): "In the time of Rabbi Joshua ben Hananiah (the same Rabbi Joshua who appears in the *Haggadah*), the evil empire (the Roman government led by the Emperor Hadrian) decreed that the Holy Temple may be rebuilt. Papus and Lulianus were appointed to finance the project; they set up counters all the way from Acre to Antioch, and supplied the exiles with silver, gold, and all their needs.

"Meanwhile, the Samaritans went to the Emperor and lied. They said, 'Know, O King, that the Jews are planning to rebel against you! Once they rebuild their seditious Temple, they will cease to pay the royal taxes!' Hadrian replied, 'But what can I do? I have already authorized the decree!' They responded, 'All you need to do is to send a message to them saying, change the location of the Temple just a bit, or, add on another five cubits to the site. Then they will withdraw of their own accord!'

"The whole nation had gathered in the valley of Bet Rimon when the Emperor's message arrived. They began to wail and cry; some considered rebelling against Hadrian. The people said, 'Bring a wise man before us, who can assuage the people's anger!' The rabbis said, 'Let Joshua ben Hananiah step forward, for he knows how to give beautiful explanations of the Torah.'

"Rabbi Joshua began to speak. 'A lion devoured his prey, and a bone lodged in his throat. The lion declared, "I shall pay the reward for whoever can remove this bone from my throat." An Egyptian heron came to the rescue and stuck his head into the lion's mouth. He removed the bone and told the lion, "Pay me my reward!" The lion told the bird, "Go from me, and everyone will praise you, for you entered into the lion's jaws in peace, and you left in peace." So it is with us,' continued Rabbi Joshua. 'It is enough that we have escaped from these people with our lives.'"

The Fire of Rebellion Is Ignited as a Result of Roman Abrogation

This chance to rebuild the Temple, officially sanctioned by the Roman government, breathed new hope into the collective soul of the Jewish people, which had been devastated by the destruction. They saw the Emperor's original announcement as a ray of hope in their darkened world. From the Midrash's description it appears that many even returned to live in Israel in preparation for the rebuilding, even though they lacked means of support. Furthermore, they certainly did not possess the materials required for building the Temple, but nevertheless, they heeded the call and came—young and old, some simple and others learned; there were even scholars of Rabbi Joshua's caliber amongst them. For him, and many others like him, the memory of the destruction was still quite vivid. The multitudes that began this trek back to Jerusalem were filled with the hope and expectation of renewing Jerusalem and the Temple at its heart.

In confronting this vast wave of enthusiasm, Rabbi Joshua had to choose his words carefully, and restrain the young generation—and all those who had come thinking that their objective was within reach. For now they were bitterly disappointed. It should be no surprise that under these conditions some called openly for rebellion—for the fire of rebellion had been sparked. This development was not hidden from the eyes of the Roman government, however, and so the situation for the Jewish population in the land, already intolerable, began to steadily decline.

The Sages' Mission to Rome: An Attempt to Cancel the Decree of Destruction

In the face of new decrees of destruction issued against the Jews, the leaders of the Sanhedrin now took the hardships of a long journey upon themselves and traveled to Rome, leaving behind their important task of establishing the foundations for Torah, in Kerem B'Yavneh.

The Talmud, in Tractate Makkot (24:A), describes the incident: "Rabban Gamliel, Rabbi Elazar ben Azariah, Rabbi Joshua and Rabbi Akiva were on a journey, when they heard the sounds of the Roman hordes in Puteoli, 125 miles away. The other sages began to cry, but Rabbi Akiva laughed. They said, 'Akiva, why do you laugh?' But he only responded, 'Why do you cry?' 'Because these Romans, who worship idols, sit in snug comfort . . . but us? The House of our God smolders with fire, and we should not cry?!' But Rabbi Akiva said, 'This is why I am laughing. If He provides for those who transgress His will, how much moreso will He see to those who perform His will!'"

The sages were not only crying because they heard the thunderous noise of the Roman camp; they cried out of dread for the decrees which they had been sent to cancel. The continuation of this incident, and its results, are told in another source (Deuteronomy Rabbah 2:15): "It occurred when our sages were in Rome that the King's counselor decreed, 'In thirty days from now, there shall not be one Jew left in all the world!'"

But this particular counselor was a person who feared God. He had himself circumcised as a Jew, and in order to save the Jewish people, he committed suicide. For according to Roman law, when a national figure dies, all the legislation which was due to take effect during the next month is canceled, as was this edict against the Jews.

Spies and Government Informers in the Academy

This edict, which was thankfully rescinded, came about as a result of the seditious spirit which took hold of the nation. So too, it would seem that this was the reason for the Sanhedrin's repeated relocations. Even in Usha, we find that the government persecuted Rabban Gamliel, the Sanhedrin's president. The Midrash tells us (Sifre on Deuteronomy 33:4) that "the government sent two Roman officers to Usha with instructions that they were to convert, in order to investigate the Torah. They came to Rabban Gamliel and studied with him in Usha, and learned their fill of the entire Torah. When they died, they told the Jews, 'All of your Torah is pleasant and praiseworthy, except for two things.'"

The government succeeded in implanting spies in all the Jewish centers. This tells us something of the danger which confronted the sages of Israel, and the Torah itself—for these informers made it impossible to engage in Torah study freely. A leader of Rabban Gamliel's stature was certainly not at liberty to speak his mind in the presence of his students; neither could he properly instruct them.

We find similar misgivings recorded on behalf of Rabbi Simeon bar Yohai, himself a student of Rabbi Joshua and Rabbi Akiva. In a conversation with a colleague, he happened to speak derogatorily of Rome, saying that "whatever they did, they have done only with their own interests in mind. They built marketplaces—for prostitutes; bathhouses—for their own pleasure; bridges—to collect taxes." The government was informed of these remarks and sought to execute Rabbi Simeon. He was forced to escape, and hid in a cave in the mountains of Galilee for 13 years (Shabbat 33:B).

The Romans Decree That Jerusalem Be Plowed Over, and the Sages Travel There

In spite of the decrees and the general atmosphere of fear which the Roman government instilled, the sages never lost sight of Jerusalem, and never stopped hoping that the Temple would be rebuilt. Thus we are informed of an incident involving Rabbis Gamliel, Elazar ben Azariah, Joshua and Akiva (BT Makkot, conclusion):

"(These sages were) ascending to Jerusalem. When they reached Mount Scopus, they rent their garments. But when they reached the Temple Mount they saw a fox exit from the Holy of Holies. All the sages began to weep, except for Rabbi Akiva—Rabbi Akiva laughed. They asked him, how could you laugh? He told them, regarding Uriah it is written (Micah 3:12): 'On your account, Zion shall be plowed into a field.' But the prophet Zechariah (8:4) states that 'Old men and women shall yet dwell in the broad places of Jerusalem. . . .'

"Rabbi Akiva continued, now that Uriah's prophecy regarding the destruction has indeed come to pass, we can rest assured that Zechariah's prophecy of the rebuilding will be fulfilled! The sages declared aloud, 'Akiva, you have comforted us! Akiva, you have comforted us!'"

This story is much more than just a simple anecdote with words of inspiration. It plays a vital part in a broad picture, a movement whose objective was nothing less than the rebuilding of the Holy Temple. Even the bare facts of this story—the journey of these sages to Jerusalem in that particular period, and their stopping opposite the ruins of the Temple—are not devoid of meaning. For although Jerusalem had been laid to waste, the mighty Roman Legion remained in the city to ensure their rule over it and, always, carefully monitering the movements of the city's Jews. There were periods when the city was off limits to Jews, and entrance was even forbidden to them within a wide radius of the city limits. Therefore, the appearance of these great sages at the site of the Temple, with the President of the Sanhedrin amongst them, was certainly a mission with a specific purpose. And, their tears were for more than just the destruction. From various comments made by these sages at that time, we can be sure why they came to the site. This special pilgrimage was in response to the evil act of Tinneius Rufus to plow over Jerusalem and the Temple.

Preparing the Passover Offering Upon the "Pillars" In the courtyard, the offering is prepared for the sacrifice and offering. The Mishnah explains that metal hooks protruded from the walls and from special "pillars," which aided in skinning the offerings in preparation for sacrifice and roasting.

Skinning the Sacrifice Upon occasion, so many pilgrims arrived in the Temple for Passover that the offerings became too numerous to prepare in the conventional way. Under such circumstances, when the courtyard was especially crowded, additional methods were used: two priests would stand with a thin pole extended between them, resting on their shoulders, and in this manner they would skin the offering.

main thrust of the *Haggadah*, not only for lack of the Passover sacrifice but because it filled another important need of the new era. This story carries a message of consolation and courage for Israel in its exile, and it serves to strengthen the anticipation and hope for the Holy Temple to be rebuilt.

As they reclined at the Seder in Bnei Brak, Rabbi Elazar ben Azariah sat together with the other sages of Israel, including Rabbi Eliezer. The latter spent his time relating the story of the Exodus with his colleagues, despite the fact that his own opinion, as quoted above, called for studying about the sacrifices!

This is the reason for Rabbi Elazar's wonderment. "I am like a man of seventy . . . I have even been appointed President—but never before have I 'merited' to see the sages of Israel spend Passover night relating the story of the Exodus at such great length! But now, in the light of Ben Zoma's novel explanation, I understand . . . from this point on, one must 'be occupied with the story of the Exodus at night.'" It was Ben Zoma's opinion that the major event of this night must be the story of the Exodus, which was accepted and implemented by the sages at the Seder. Rabbi Elazar ben Azariah expressed his astonishment, but he accepted this opinion and supported it. For as the exile continued and seemed to be lasting longer than expected, and the wicked decrees against Israel were increasing in their intensity, relating this story took on new significance and importance: to strengthen Israel and give them faith and hope. These masters instructed their disciples, assembled together with them in Bnei Brak, that they must now understand the new style which the Passover *Haggadah* needs to face in the era of exile: in this time of darkness, "one desires to hear only words of blessing and consolation."

VII. The Seder Is Conducted in Rabbi Akiva's City

We have already stated that the very fact of the sages of Israel assembling in the home town of Rabbi Akiva on Passover night is an event that requires an explanation. According to the ideas we have discussed above, the version of the *Haggadah* for the exile was established during the course of the Seder in Bnei Brak. But if this is so, it serves to strengthen our question: why did the sages not gather together in Kerem B'Yavneh for this purpose? After all, that is precisely what they did when it came to establishing the accepted formula for prayer: "Simeon HaPakuli set the order of the 18 blessings in the presence of Rabban Gamliel in Yavneh" (BT Berakhot 28:B). The rabbis and their disciples would gather there regularly, to discuss *halakhah* and all the other important matters. The selection of this location for the sages' communal Seder would have been the natural choice; why should they have chosen Rabbi Akiva's home over the Sanhedrin's home to finalize the formula for the *Haggadah*?

To understand that gathering in Bnei Brak, we must first be aware of the crisis that ripped through Israel during the first few years that followed the destruction. This crisis resulted in the abandonment of Kerem B'Yavneh. The Sanhedrin was exiled and traveled from the south of the country to the north, to Galilee, where it was reestablished in Usha. At the same time, the nation of Israel suffered more retribution at the hands of the Roman government, including decrees aimed at the destruction of Judaism.

With regard to the Sanhedrin's exile from Kerem B'Yavneh, the Talmud (BT Rosh HaShanah 31:A) records that "the Sanhedrin was exiled to ten different locations: from the Chamber of Hewn Stone (in the Temple at Jerusalem) to Hanoth, from Hanoth to Jerusalem, from Jerusalem to Yavneh, from Yavneh to Usha, from Usha to Yavneh, from Yavneh to Usha, from Usha to Shfaram, from Shfaram to Bet She'arim, from Bet She'arim to Tzipori, and from Tzipori to Tiberias." Our sages refer to the Sanhedrin's wanderings as "exile," even though they were all within the Land of Israel, for they were brought on as a result of persecution. From its first stop in Yavneh, in the south, the Sanhedrin initially moved to Usha in the western Galilee, and on to other cities in the north, finally coming to a stop in the eastern Galilee city of Tiberias, far removed from the country's center of population.

The Roman Government Permits the Rebuilding of the Temple

The cause of these wanderings can be found in the spirit of rebellion which had begun to spark within the nation as a result of the failed

XXV

the Seder in Bnei Brak), were divided amongst themselves as to whether these 18 blessings should be committed to a fixed, standard text, or if they could remain more flexible. As the Talmud states (ibid. 4:3): "Rabban Gamliel taught: *every day a man should pray 18 blessings.* But Rabbi Joshua said, *similar to 18 blessings* (meaning, one may shorten the middle blessings). And Rabbi Akiva said, if he is fluent in his prayers, he should recite all 18. If he is not, let him pray 'similar to 18.'"

At this point in history, the standard text of our prayers had not yet been established. In this light we can realize that the *Haggadah*'s status in Temple times was no different, from the point of view of having a fixed text, than prayer itself. The short version of the *Haggadah* which is discussed in Mishnah Pesahim includes the main points relevant to the eating of the Passover sacrifice, matzah and *maror*, and the singing of the *Hallel* as well. But apart from these points, each man improvised according to his own inspiration, and the amount of time at his disposal.

Studying the Laws of the Passover Sacrifice Is a Part of the Haggadah

There is another differentiation between the post-destruction Seder and its counterpart, held in the shadow of Jerusalem and the Holy Temple. While the Temple still stood, the Seder members utilized the little time available to them for the study of *halakhah*—the laws of the Passover sacrifice. This according to the "wise son's" question, which we read of in the Torah: "What are the testimonies, statutes, and judgments which the Lord our God has commanded you?" And you shall tell your son: "We were slaves to Pharaoh in Egypt . . . and God took us out from there . . . and God commanded us to perform all these statutes, to fear the Lord our God, for we will be careful to perform all of this commandment" (Deuteronomy 6:2). In keeping with these verses, whose question revolves around the statutes and ordinances which we were commanded this night, each father is obligated to explain the commandments and laws of the Passover to his son.

This is the meaning of that which is said in the *Mechilta* (end of Parshat Bo): "What does the wise son ask? What are the testimonies, etc. In reply, you should teach him all of the ordinances of Passover . . . 'do not serve dessert after the Passover lamb.'" The meaning behind this statement is that since we are instructed to answer all of his questions about the laws of Passover, one should begin for him, starting from the most basic laws and ending with the last one—the *halakhah* of the *afikoman*. This *halakhah* requires that sweets not be served after the meal, so that the taste of the Passover remains.

Based upon this verse of "what are the testimonies, etc.," Rabbi Eliezer goes a step further and adds: "How do we deduce that if a group of scholars or disciples were celebrating the Passover in Jerusalem, that they must occupy themselves with the laws of Passover until midnight?" For this reason the verse specifies "what are the testimonies. . ." to inform us that these laws must be studied until the time for eating the sacrifice expires—that is, midnight.

When One Studies the Laws of the Sacrifice, It Is Considered As If He Offered It

The obligation to study the laws of the Passover on this night is also mentioned in the Tosefta. There, the time this can be done is expanded to include the entire night, until dawn, for it is written: "A person must be occupied with the laws of the Passover the entire night; it matters not if he sits with his students, or even if he is all by himself. It happened that Rabban Gamliel and the elders conducted their Seder in the home of Baytus ben Zonin in Lod, and they studied the laws of Passover until the rooster's crow. At dawn, the table was removed and they went off to the academy [to pray]."

Thus we see that on a practical level, it had been customary to study these laws during this night; Rabban Gamliel and the elders did so the entire night. It would also seem that they had a basis for extending their study until dawn, for theoretically, it is halakhically permissible to eat from the Passover sacrifice until dawn as well. And since this incident occurred after the destruction (which explains why their Seder was held in Lod, not in Jerusalem), the sages felt even more obligated to occupy themselves with these laws—for we are taught, "Whoever learns the laws of a sacrifice is considered (by God) as if he actually offered it" (BT Menahot 110).

Now obviously, studying the laws of the Passover sacrifice was an intrinsic part of the Seder while the Temple still stood. The host, by necessity, had to instruct his guests how they should conduct themselves. This applied not only to laws pertaining to matzah and bitter herbs, but to many other practices which were done in that time. In this light we can understand that at the Seder of Temple times, the Passover sacrifice and its laws took up the majority of the evening. Thus by default, the story of the Exodus, as well as the explanations of all the unusual commandments and customs in force this evening, had to be accomplished within a relatively short time frame. This being the case, Rabban Gamliel took pains to stress that these things must be given their adequate time as well: eating of the Passover sacrifice, matzah and *maror*.

The Haggadah of the Exile Emphasizes the Story of the Exodus

Following the destruction, the *Haggadah* underwent several changes:

1. Due to the lack of the two sacrifices which played such a central role in the Seder, an empty space remained; very little remained in the original *Haggadah* which could still be implemented or even recited.

2. The festive pilgrimage had also ceased, and the Passover sacrifice was no longer offered; the study of these laws therefore became superfluous.

3. The dispersion and exile of the Jewish people necessitated a standardized text for the *Haggadah*, which would emphasize the important points. A freestyle version would no longer work; when left for themselves, not everyone was capable of preserving the *Haggadah*'s integrity—some were so concerned with fulfilling the Divine commandment to partake of matzah that they inadvertently refrained from reciting most of the *Haggadah*.

In order to meet the needs of Israel that had been brought on by the reality of their new situation, the Torah center at Kerem B'Yavneh began a project of standardizing the yearly prayers and various blessings. So too when it came to the *Haggadah*; without the sacrifice, the emphasis was now shifted to the story of the Exodus. Thus the expression, "And even if we were all wise, all men of knowledge, we are still nonetheless commanded to relate the story of the Exodus from Egypt."

The *Haggadah* cites the incident of the sages who conducted their Seder in Bnei Brak—not in Jerusalem—and teaches by their example: for they sat up and told the story of the Exodus the entire night. This is a marked contrast to all that which had been accepted previously, for in the past the entire emphasis was placed on the laws of the Passover sacrifice.

This background can also serve to explain Rabbi Elazar ben Azariah's wonderment when he asks: "Behold, I am like a man of seventy, yet I was unable to prove why the story of the Exodus from Egypt should be recited at night." He was referring to the question of whether or not it is necessary to mention this concept in the prayers of the evening service throughout the year (Berakhot 12:B). Yet this Mishnah is here cited in the *Haggadah* precisely because it expresses astonishment that, unlike the days of the Temple, the *Haggadah* now emphasizes the story of the Exodus, and the laws of the sacrifice have become a minor issue.

Rabbi Elazar is wondering aloud about the Seder he now witnesses as well. For when the wise son asks "What are these testimonies. . ." we are commanded to "teach him all the ordinances of the Passover. . . ." But instead, the sages in Bnei Brak dwell only on the story, practically ignoring the laws. Rabbi Elazar's opinion is that it is wrong for the commandment of relating the story of the Exodus to take the place of studying the laws of the sacrifice.

Of course, Maimonides writes (Laws of Hametz and Matzah 7:1) that "it is a positive Divine commandment to relate the miracles and wonders which were performed for our fathers in Egypt on the 15th day of Nisan, as it is written: 'Remember this day on which you left Egypt.'" But he did not intend that this requirement should supersede a man's duty to teach his children and guests the laws of the Passover sacrifice, as was obligatory in the era of the Holy Temple.

The Need for Words of Comfort and Consolation in Exile

It was the suffering brought on by the exile that was responsible for the major change in the post-destruction *Haggadah*—the shift to the story of the Exodus. "In the past, when livelihood was abundant," said Rabbi Levi (BT Soferim 15), "A man was inspired, and had a desire to hear teachings of Mishnah, *halakhah*, and Talmud. But now, when we lack livelihood, and even worse, we are faint from our exile—one desires to hear only words of blessing and consolation."

As we shall explain at length, the sages' Seder in Bnei Brak took place at a time of heightened sanctions made by the Roman oppressors. The Jews that remained in the land, as well as those in the Diaspora, were impoverished and destitute. The story of the Exodus was replaced as the

VI. The "Haggadah of the Holy Temple" and the "Haggadah of Exile"

Before we consider the question of the Seder's location, it would be worthwhile to examine some of the changes which the *Haggadah* underwent in the course of time. Following the destruction of the Temple, an updated version replaced that which had been in use when the Holy Temple stood. By all indications, these changes in version were put into place during the Seder which Rabbi Akiva hosted that Passover night in Bnei Brak.

In the Temple Era, a Shorter Version of the Haggadah Was Used

The differences between the two versions, that of the Temple era and that of the post-destruction edition, are easily distinguishable. These differences can be placed into two categories:

During the time of the Holy Temple, the *Haggadah* which Israel used at the Seder was considerably shorter—since the central themes which occupied those gathered around the table were the *hagigah* festival offering and the commandment to partake of the Passover sacrifice. Everything revolved around the sacrifices; preparations for the Seder lasted well into the evening on account of the need to roast the *hagigah* offering for all the participants in the band (and perhaps more than one, if there were many participants). The same was true for the Passover sacrifice. Sometimes, the 14th of Nisan—the eve of the festival—would fall on a Sabbath, and the roasting of the kid or lamb for the Passover could not begin until the conclusion of the Sabbath, at dark. This roasting would take a considerably long time, since it is prohibited to eat the Passover sacrifice only partially roasted. Since those gathered for the Seder could not even begin until the sacrifice was properly roasted, this did not leave them much time for protracting the story of the Exodus, for the *halakhah* requires that the *afikoman*, eaten at the conclusion of the Seder, must be eaten before midnight. Ample space was probably a problematic issue for those in the time of the Temple as well; it may be that the Seder was held throughout homes in Jerusalem in shifts, with each band waiting its turn for a spot to conduct the Seder. This is because the Passover sacrifice was required to be eaten by the entire congregation of Israel—within the walls of Jerusalem.

An examination of the version of the *Haggadah* which is cited in the last chapter of Mishnah Pesahim (and also quoted by Maimonides, Laws of Hametz and Matzah, ch. 8) reveals that it is that which is actually the original *Haggadah*, recited by Israel in the days of the Temple. The Mishnah describes the scene of the Seder; the four food items which the Torah commands to be eaten on this night were brought before the host. Following the *Kiddush* which marks the Seder's commencement, "they brought matzah, bitter herbs and haroseth before him. In the Temple, they also brought the Passover sacrifice." This was in addition to the *hagigah*.

The four questions that the son poses to his father are all based on the food-related commandments which are practiced on this night, such as: "On this night, why do we matzah and *maror*?" and "Why do we eat meat roasted, boiled or cooked on every other night, but tonight only roasted?" His question is actually directed to both the *hagigah* and the Passover offerings—why are both served roasted?

This particular question is based on the custom which was prevalent in Israel, that the *hagigah* offering should also be served only roasted—like the Passover one. This is the opinion of the sage Ben Teimah (BT Pesahim 70:A), and although it was not established as law, as we indicated, it was nonetheless accepted at the time. This can be inferred from Maimonides, who writes (Laws of Hametz and Matzah, ch. 8:4) that in the Temple era the question was phrased in this manner: "On this night, why do we eat exclusively roasted?" It appears that the pilgrims adopted the custom of roasting all the meat which was to be eaten this evening, since this was the quickest and most efficient way to prepare the food in a "hasty" manner—as our forefathers ate the night of the Exodus (see *Sefer HaHinukh*, Commandment 13).

It Is Obligatory to Recall the Reason We Are Commanded to Partake of the Passover Sacrifice

Throughout Jewish history, a number of important personalities bore the same name. However, they lived in altogether different generations. One of the central figures of our *Haggadah* is that of Rabban Gamliel. The commentators and expositors of the *Haggadah* are all in agreement that the "Rabban Gamliel" who is mentioned in Pesahim of the Mishnah and in the *Haggadah* is the one who lived at the close of the Second Temple era, who witnessed the destruction and who lived a number of years thereafter. As the "Rashbatz" (Rabbi Simeon ben Tzemah Duran) writes in his commentary:

"The 'Rabban Gamliel' who spoke of the three important concepts in the *Haggadah* is not that Rabban Gamliel the Elder, who lived earlier in the Temple era. When Rabban Yohanan ben Zakkai appeared to make his requests before the Roman General Vespasian, he beseeched the latter to ensure that Rabban Gamliel's princely lineage not be interrupted" (BT Gittin 56:B). This is certainly the "Rabban Gamliel" who saw the Temple in its glory, and in whose days the Passover sacrifice was offered. As Rabbi Zadok stated (BT Pesahim 74:A): "An incident occurred in which Rabban Gamliel instructed his servant Tavi to go and roast the Passover sacrifice. And this Rabbi Zadok who related this anecdote, he, too, witnessed the destruction."

The statement made by Rabban Gamliel which appears in the *Haggadah* reads: "Whoever does not mention these three things on Passover has not fulfilled his obligation." It is obvious from his words that he does not mean to say that one must mention these concepts during the entire duration of the seven-day festival. For in Hebrew, the word we have translated here as "on Passover" is "*b'pesach*," which actually indicated the Passover sacrifice. In other words, Rabban Gamliel states that these three concepts must be mentioned while eating the Passover sacrifice; otherwise, one does not fulfill his religious obligation. For the verse states, "And you shall *say*, it is a Passover sacrifice to the Lord." The "saying" itself, the declaration, is a necessary part of the eating. This exhortation of Rabban Gamliel was said when the Temple yet stood, and it was meant as an instruction to those who brought the Passover offerings.

Maimonides agrees with this understanding of Rabban Gamliel's words, and quotes him as saying, "This Passover sacrifice which *we are eating*—what is its meaning? It is because the Holy One, blessed be He, passed over the houses of our fathers in Egypt." From this Mishnah of Rabban Gamliel, it is clear that this original text of the *Haggadah* was later edited in the time of the exile; we do not recognize the language of the version as it appears before us now, for the changes that we are familiar with were not yet effected. With the exception of those points that were already set down in the Mishnah, such as the questions, the mentioning of the "three things," and the blessing of "who has redeemed us," everything else was given over to the leader of each Seder, to shorten or lengthen the recitation of the *Haggadah* at his own discretion, however time allowed. This is the very reason why Rabban Gamliel found it necessary to mandate that if these three important things are not mentioned, one's duty has not been fulfilled!

The reality of the situation was that sometimes the Seder participants had very little time to work with. If there is not enough time to recite the entire *Haggadah* and dwell for hours on the miracles of the Exodus, Rabban Gamliel was concerned with educating the people that they accustom themselves to the minimal declaration of these three concepts.

Whoever draws out the story of the Exodus from Egypt on this night is considered praiseworthy. The fact is, there is no greater story than this— the simple fact that the Jewish people, as free men in Jerusalem, could sit reclined around the Passover sacrifice just as their ancestors did as slaves in Egypt; this is a living story of Exodus. But nevertheless, Rabban Gamliel added that eating from the Passover sacrifice without informing and reminding the participants of the objective—that God passed over the houses of Israel when he smote Egypt—such "eating" would be meaningless. It would be as if the commandment had not been performed at all.

In the Temple Era, the Haggadah Was Recited Freestyle

As we have learned, from the Mishnah's description we can see that the other parts of the *Haggadah* were freely improvised by those present at each Seder. This was like a communal study session, with general guidelines that had been provided by the sages of Israel as to which subjects to discuss.

We would do well to remember that in those days, even the activity of prayer itself was conducted in much the same way. There was a "general guideline" for an individual to pray "18 blessings" each morning, afternoon, and evening. The rabbis of the Mishnah, as recorded in Tractate Berakhot (these are the same rabbis who assembled together for

He has already proven himself to be a master of Torah; moreover, his lineage was also weighed in his favor.

If so, Rabbi Elazar was not as old as the other sages, but he was not as young as 18, either—he was an adult, and in his youth, he had the privilege of seeing the Holy Temple standing in all its glory. It would therefore follow, since he was a priest—and a priest with a pedigree, at that, being a direct descendant of Ezra—that as a youth he had participated in the Temple service, including the Passover sacrifice.

It would also appear that Maimonides' view can be substantiated from a passage in the *Mechilta* (Parshat Bo, 17). Although this passage is not actually related to the person of Rabbi Elazar, it indicates that Rabbi Elazar could in fact have been much older than 18, and that the Talmud's description of his sudden age could be an anecdotal expression and not a literal fact. For there, we read that Rabbi Joshua also utilized this very same expression: in an entirely different context, he declared, "Behold, I am like a man of seventy, and I have not merited this until today." As we find no tradition of Rabbi Joshua's beard turning white, or anything of the sort, we discover that this particular expression was simply accepted form, taken for what it stood for and understood by the Torah scholars of that time.

Rabbi Eliezer ben Hyrcanus—of the Tribe of Levi

Rabbi Eliezer had also beheld the sight of the Holy Temple, and had even been in charge of the Levites. This is detailed in the beginning of the work *Pirkei D'Rabbi Eliezer HaGadol* (as well as in *Avot D'Rabbi Nathan*). There, we learn that Rabbi Eliezer arrived in Jerusalem as a young man, and studied in the academy of Rabbi Yohanan ben Zakkai. Rabbi Yohanan became very close to him; once, Rabbi Joshua and Rabbi Yose the Priest inspected Rabbi Eliezer's lodgings and discovered that the latter had nothing to eat. Rabbi Yohanan then arranged for all his provisions.

In Jerusalem, Rabbi Eliezer rose to become a great scholar. As Rabbi Yohanan ben Zakkai testified (Pirkei Avot 2:5): "If all the sages of Israel were placed on one side of a scale, and Eliezer ben Hyrcanus was placed alone on the other side—he would outweigh them all." During the course of his years in Jerusalem, he had many opportunities to observe the service in the Holy Temple.

As we have stated, Rabbi Eliezer was placed in charge of the Levites. We glean this information from a midrashic account (Tanhuma, Hukat 8) wherein Moses ascended into the heavens and heard the voice of the Holy One Himself, who was occupied with the laws of the red heifer. Moses heard God quoting these laws in the name of Rabbi Eliezer, and he heard God saying, "In the future, one righteous man is destined to appear in My world, and he will teach these very laws about the red heifer." Said Moses before the Holy One: "Master of the universe! May it be Your will that such a man as this be one of my descendants!" And God responded: "As you live, I promise that he will be your descendant."

Now as we know, Moses was from the tribe of Levi, so obviously, if Rabbi Eliezer is Moses' descendant, he is also a Levite. Additionally, another reference—this one from the Jerusalem Talmud (Sotah 3:4)—refers to Rabbi Eliezer's son Hyrcanus as receiving the levitical tithe.

And so Rabbi Eliezer, close disciple of Rabbi Yohanan ben Zakkai, undoubtedly witnessed life in the Temple and participated as well. As one who was responsible for the other Levites, he himself must have served in the capacity of a singer, or possibly that of gatekeeper, like his colleague and fellow Levite, Rabbi Joshua.

Thus, we have clearly established that out of that group of great scholars who gathered together in Bnei Brak, two were *cohanim*, priests descended from Aaron, and two were Levites—and all four served in the Holy Temple in the years immediately prior to its destruction. These men, numbered amongst the greatest sages of their generation, chose Rabbi Akiva's home as the location for their Seder—though the latter was neither a priest nor a Levite.

Rabbi Akiva

Rabbi Akiva, the host of that Seder in Bnei Brak, is singled out from all the great men who sat around his table—for as an Israelite, he alone did not serve in the Holy Temple.

But yet Rabbi Akiva, who observed the functions and details of Temple life from the side, from the outsider's view of an ordinary Israelite, was aware of important details about the Temple which even his colleagues who served there had already forgotten. It would seem that Rabbi Akiva had ample opportunity to closely observe the service in the Holy Temple in simple anonymity, during the many years which preceded his rise to fame as one of the great luminaries of Israel—for he began his career relatively late in life. Rabbi Akiva only embarked upon the course of Torah study at the age of forty, upon marrying Rachel, the daughter of Kalba Savua, one of Jerusalem's wealthiest men.

Kalba Savua strongly objected to his daughter's decision to marry an ignoramus. He was so incensed that he swore an oath of disownment, preventing his son-in-law from deriving any benefit from any of his possessions. But when Rabbi Akiva returned 24 years later as an accomplished scholar, Kalba Savua realized his son-in-law's true greatness. He requested from the sages to release him from his vow, and once freed, he presented Rabbi Akiva with half of his estate as a gift (BT Ketubbot 62–63).

Thus while the Holy Temple yet stood, Rabbi Akiva was a man of substantial wealth, and in keeping with the Torah's requirement, he brought the finest sacrifices to the Temple when he arrived there as a pilgrim on the three festivals. For the verse requires such conduct of those who have the means at their disposal, as it is written: ". . .each man according to his means, and according to the level of blessing which the Lord has given him." Perhaps this itself is the reason why, although Rabbi Akiva was not a *cohen*, he nevertheless remembered minute details pertaining to the Temple service which even Rabbi Tarfon forgot—though the latter, as a priest, personally performed the service.

Furthermore, in the Jerusalem Talmud (Yoma 1:5; see also *Sifre* on Numbers 10) there is a lengthy disputation between Rabbi Akiva and Rabbi Tarfon as to the question of whether or not a *cohen* who is disqualified from regular service because of a blemish is allowed to perform the service of blowing the trumpets in the Temple. In the course of their discussion, it is Rabbi Akiva's opinion which prevails, based on his interpretation of the verses. And although Rabbi Tarfon had served in the Temple as a young man, he did not witness the details which they were discussing. But Rabbi Akiva, who frequented the Temple as one of Jerusalem's citizens, experienced many details of Temple life when he was already mature, and was thus able to recall precise details.

Still, it remains a puzzle as to why these sages—some of whom were Rabbi Akiva's own masters—should all leave their own respective communities in order to spend Passover night with their student. What motivated Rabbis Eliezer and Joshua to leave Lod and Peki'in on the eve of the festival? Rabbi Tarfon, too, left his own academy in Lod to be with Rabbi Akiva; and Rabbi Elazar ben Azariah left his position as dean of the Kerem B'Yavneh academy and President of the Sanhedrin. All these men, each together with his entourage of students, came to the Seder in Bnei Brak.

Now obviously, a Seder of this nature, peopled by the greatest sages of Israel—who also happen to be priests and Levites who served in the Holy Temple—is in itself a great learning experience. For in the course of the evening, they doubtless related the Exodus from Egypt and recounted details of the Passover sacrifice for their students; certainly original Temple melodies and songs were heard as well. Who would not have desired to be present at such an event? Doubtless too, many tears were shed by disciples and masters alike, as the verse states: ". . .there we sat and wept, when we remembered Zion" (Psalm 137:1). But the great question still remains: why was this gathering held at Rabbi Akiva's table?

A Priest Stands Atop the Altar A priest takes up the portions of the sacrifice and offers them on the fires of the altar.

waiting for the gates to be closed as a signal for them to begin singing the *Hallel*, might leave the platform occasionally in order to assist their fellow Levites with the doors, and in order to hasten the beginning of the sacrifice.

Rabbi Joshua, who was a member of the Sanhedrin during the era of the Temple, is also known for another Temple connection, for he figured in a dispute in the Sanhedrin regarding bones that had been discovered in the Chamber of Wood. Many of the Sanhedrin's members were inclined to decree a state of ritual impurity on the entire city of Jerusalem, but Rabbi Joshua maintained that ritual impurity should not be declared on the city or the Temple. The Talmud describes the incident:

"On one occasion, bones were discovered in the Chamber of Wood (within the Women's Court) and the rabbis sought to declare the city of Jerusalem impure. Rabbi Joshua stood up and declared: 'Would it not be a shame and a disgrace for us to decree the city of our forefathers impure?'" (BT Zevahim 113).

The stand that Rabbi Joshua took on behalf of Jerusalem's honor was accepted by the members of the Sanhedrin, and they refrained from declaring the city impure. As a member of the Sanhedrin and a levitical singer, it is highly probable that during the course of the Seder in Bnei Brak, Rabbi Joshua brought up some of the laws and customs pertaining to Temple life—as well as his own personal recollections—before his colleagues. And who else would have sung the festive *Hallel* in that assemblage other than Rabbi Joshua, an accomplished member of the Temple's own choir, who sang these very songs a few short years before, when the Passover sacrifice was offered in Jerusalem.

Rabbi Tarfon: A "*Cohen*" Who Stood Next to the High Priest

Another participant in the Bnei Brak Seder was Rabbi Tarfon. This sage was also of priestly descent, a "*cohen*" who had served in the Holy Temple and who had been able to see it in all its glory. The Talmud (BT Kiddushin 71:A) mentions that Rabbi Tarfon had the honor of hearing the High Priest utter the Ineffable Name on the Day of Atonement. This name was only revealed to a select number of individuals in every generation. The Talmud explains: "Originally, the Name consisting of 12 letters was taught to everyone. But when immodesty became rampant, this name was only passed on to members of the priesthood who retained their proper modesty. These would quietly pronounce this sacred Name against the background noise of their fellow priests' humming (so that it would not be discerned). We learned that Rabbi Tarfon said: 'Once I followed my uncle up to the platform and I leaned my ear next to the High Priest, and heard how he quietly uttered this Name while the other priests were humming.'"

Rashi comments that this passage is referring to the 12-letter Name; the Name consisting of 42 letters was not explained to us. He further states that the "modest amongst the priesthood" would bless the people in the Temple after the offering of the congregation's daily sacrifice in the morning.

Rabbi Tarfon had been worthy of standing atop the steps to the Sanctuary gate, where the Priestly blessing took place. Himself a priest, he merited an experience that was afforded to few others—he actually stood next to the High Priest and heard the Ineffable Name of God. Following the destruction, when Kerem B'Yavneh became a center of Torah study, Rabbi Tarfon was amongst the principal spokesmen (Gittin 83:A; Yoma 76:A).

When the question was posed before all the elders, "Which is greater—study or action?" it was Rabbi Tarfon who answered with a resounding "Action is greater!" This response is instructive as to Rabbi Tarfon's world view, and his general approach to life, for some have a tendency, upon occasion, to substitute certain types of study—such as the analytical method—for action. But Rabbi Tarfon here declares that the very essence of study is the abililty to translate what has been learned into action.

Rabbi Tarfon was a priest who was not only expert at expounding the Torah, he was expert in fulfilling it. He used his priestly positon, and his own personal wealth, to dispense charity to many during their hour of need. One example is cited by the Tosefta (Ketubbot 5:1): "Once during a time of famine, Rabbi Tarfon married 300 women—only so that he would be enabled to give them *terumah* (the sacred priestly tithe) to eat." In the years following the destruction, many men had either been killed or taken captive, and women were left abandoned and without means of sustenance. Rabbi Tarfon went and married 300 women, thus allowing them—as the wives of a *cohen*—to eat *terumah*.

As a priest who served in the Holy Temple and assisted his colleagues with the Passover sacrifice, its memory was still fresh for him. We can easily imagine that when he sat together with Rabbi Joshua ben Hananiah, the Levite who sang in the Temple, and the other sages who carried vivid memories of the Temple, Rabbi Tarfon must have conjured up images from his own recollections of the Passover sacrifice in the Temple courts, to share with his colleagues.

Rabbi Elazar ben Azariah the Priest: A Descendant of Ezra the Scribe

Another *cohen* who was present at the Bnei Brak Seder was Rabbi Elazar ben Azariah. As mentioned above, he, too, was chosen to be President of the Sanhedrin at Kerem B'Yavneh, and one of the major qualifications he possessed which influenced his fellow sages in this decision was his lineage—for he was a direct descendant of the prophet and priest, Ezra the Scribe. At first glance, Rabbi Elazar's participation in this Seder might seem rather unusual. After all, it certainly was not common practice for the President of the Sanhedrin—who was also head of the academy at Kerem B'Yavneh—to leave his own home for the festival, and undertake to journey to the home of Rabbi Akiva for the Seder night, for Rabbi Elazar was the President, and Rabbi Akiva would have been considered like his student. But the Talmud's rendition of the events as recorded in Tractate Berakhot reveal to us that Rabbi Elazar ben Azariah was extremely young at the time he received his appointment. Since the other rabbis were substantially older than Rabbi Elazar in years, it would seem that his inconvenience of traveling to be with them was not considered as disrespectful to his position.

In this context it is interesting to note that Maimonides interprets Rabbi Elazar ben Azariah's famed statement of "I am like a man of seventy" in a completely different light than that which we cited from the Talmud in Tractate Berakhot. There it states that when Rabbi Elazar received his presidential appointment at the age of 18, a miracle occurred and his hair turned white. But is it not surprising that the sages of Israel would have preferred such a young man, wise as he might be, over Rabbi Eliezer, or Rabbi Joshua, or Rabbi Akiva—or for that matter, over any of the other great scholars of that generation? These had already proven their own greatness, and it was a matter of public record—there was no doubt as to their character or accomplishments. In Rabbi Elazar ben Azariah's case, however, the criteria upon which the rabbis had based their decision were all secondary considerations—his lineage, wealth, etc. After all, to assume the mantle of leadership for an entire generation is an awesome task, and this would be true in any era—how much moreso, in that particular generation, immediately following the Temple's destruction. How could they have appointed an office of such great responsibility to an inexperienced young man, when there were other scholars who were far greater than him in both wisdom and years?

Maimonides' alternative approach takes all this into consideration. He writes: "Now Rabbi Elazar ben Azariah's statement was 'Behold, I am like a man of seventy' and not 'I *am* a man of seventy,' because he was not seventy, but much younger than this. But he was very diligent in Torah study, and would engage in study day and night, until he became physically weakened to the extent that the process of aging was actually accelerated to the point that his body became like that of a seventy-year-old man. But he brought this process upon himself, of his own volition, as the Talmud explains" (Maimonides, Commentary on the Mishnah, Berakhot 1:9). Obviously, according to Maimonides' view, the Talmud's description of Rabbi Elazar's beard turning white does not refer to a miraculous event in which his hair changed color in one day; rather, the lifestyle of great physical duress, which the relatively young rabbi had elected to live over the course of many years, had the effect of advancing the scholar's aging process—and his hair turned prematurely white.

To take this a step further: Maimonides does not take the Talmud's statement that Rabbi Elazar ben Azariah was 18 years old as a literal fact. Rather, he maintains that this expression is merely anecdotal, an expression of example. It merely intends to differentiate between the ages of Rabbi Elazar and the other sages, in that the former was comparatively younger than the latter. Thus the Talmud intends to provide some context of Rabbi Elazar's physical appearance, in order to point out that he appeared older than his actual age.

Now, according to this interpretation, there is no longer any question as to why Rabbi Elazar ben Azariah was chosen for the role of President over the other sages, even though he was not as aged or experienced as they.

THE HAGGADAH OF EXILE

V. The "Incident of Rabbi Eliezer": The Introduction to the Haggadah

"It is related that Rabbi Eliezer, Rabbi Joshua, Rabbi Elazar ben Azariah, Rabbi Akiva and Rabbi Tarfon once met for the Seder in Bnei Brak and spoke about the Exodus from Egypt all night long." Interestingly, the *Haggadah* is the exclusive source for this incident, and it receives no mention elsewhere in all the annals of rabbinic literature. All of the other sections of the *Haggadah* are lessons which are taken from sources such as the *Sifre*, *Mechilta*, and the Mishnah, as well as the Babylonian and Jerusalem Talmuds.

This incident can be properly viewed as the *Haggadah*'s "introduction," an accepted literary device extant in various midrashic literature—such as *Esther Rabbah* (on the Book of Esther), *Lamentations Rabbah* (on Lamentations), and others. This introduction has great significance toward an overall understanding of the *Haggadah* as a whole.

This simple anecdote contains two ingredients:

Firstly, it provides a list of those who taught the *Haggadah*'s content and edited its format; and *secondly*, the incident points out the men who laid the foundations for the spiritual survival of the Jewish people following the destruction of Jerusalem and the Holy Temple, at the beginning of the long exile.

As we shall explain, this incident is not recorded merely to give the *Haggadah* a colorful start by relating some sort of "tale"; its significance is central, and is culled from the "valley of tears"—Israel's experience in exile. In all probability, the *Haggadah* which we have today was arranged in Rabbi Akiva's academy in Bnei Brak (with the exception of several lone paragraphs, and the hymns found at the conclusion). This *Haggadah*, our extant version, differs from the one which was recited during the time that the Holy Temple stood. Maimonides substantiates this fact. At the end of his Laws of Hametz and Matzah, after citing the version of the *Haggadah* which was in use at the time of the Temple in chapter 8, he writes: "The version of the *Haggadah* which Israel practices in the era of exile is as follows. . ."—and Maimonides cites our contemporary version.

The Group Which Gathered in Bnei Brak Lays the Foundations for the New Torah Center at Yavneh

In order to understand the nature of this gathering of the great scholars of Israel in Bnei Brak, just several years after the destruction, we must follow the chain of events which transpired in the Land of Israel following the destruction. According to an account in the Talmud (BT Gittin 56:A), Rabban Yohanan ben Zakkai, the President of the Sanhedrin, turned to Abba Sikra, who was leader of all the warriors in Jerusalem, and appealed to him to save the city—or at least whatever could still be saved. But as the commander no longer had any influence over his men, he suggested an alternative idea to Rabban Yohanan: let the rabbi feign illness, and let rumors to this effect spread, so that his students would be allowed to carry him out of the city walls—in a coffin.

In this manner, Rabban Yohanan would reach the Roman encampment and endeavor to request the aid of Vespasian. And so it was; Rabbi Yohanan was borne from Jerusalem in a coffin, with Rabbi Eliezer carrying one side, and Rabbi Joshua, the other (both of these sages were amongst those present at the Seder in Bnei Brak).

Two of the requests which Rabban Yohanan made of Vespasian were concerned with the establishment of a new Torah center for the Jewish people. The first request was "give me Yavneh and its scholars," which Rashi explains to mean—do not destroy Yavneh and do not kill its scholars. And the second request: "Do not kill the family of the President (of the Sanhedrin)," so that the lineage of the Davidic dynasty would not disappear.

It did transpire that following the destruction of Jerusalem and the Temple, the yeshiva at Kerem B'Yavneh developed, and a number of the sages who participated in the Bnei Brak Seder—including Rabbis Eliezer and Joshua, who were rescued from hunger and the destruction of Jerusalem, were among those who established the new Torah center for the Jewish people.

It was these Torah scholars, in Kerem B'Yavneh, who established the order of the presidency. "Rabbi Simeon bar Yohai stood and asked a question in the academy," records the Talmud (BT Berakhot 27:B), and Rabbi Joshua answered. In the course of the discussions, Rabban Gamliel—the President—embarrassed Rabbi Joshua, who was chief justice. Because of this the elders of the academy decided to appoint Rabbi Elazar ben Azariah, who was "wise, and wealthy, and a tenth-generation descendant of Ezra the Scribe," to deliver a lecture to the students one Sabbath each month. Rabbi Elazar ben Azariah accepted this position, despite the drawback of his youth, and according to the Talmud's description, a miracle occurred and his beard became white, as befitting his role as head of the academy before the elders and great scholars.

Now, according to the Talmud's accounting of these events, Rabbi Akiva was not chosen for this position, despite his great wisdom, because he did not have "the merit of forefathers" as did Rabbi Elazar ben Azariah.

This particular group of scholars, appearing together, are mentioned a number of times throughout the rabbinic literature, in various contexts. For example, in an incident recorded in Tractate Sanhedrin (101:A), we read that "when Rabbi Eliezer fell ill, four elders came to visit him: Rabbi Tarfon, Rabbi Joshua, Rabbi Elazar ben Azariah, and Rabbi Akiva. Upon hearing Rabbi Akiva speak, Rabbi Eliezer said, 'Hold me up, so that I can hear the words of my student Akiva, who said that suffering is a precious thing.'"

These Sages Survived the Destruction—and Many Served in the Holy Temple

When we ponder the names of those particular scholars who were gathered together in Bnei Brak, as well as the names of those sages whose lessons are embodied in the *Haggadah*, we discover that each one of them had some connection to the Holy Temple—and to the offering of the Passover sacrifice. Only a short number of years had actually passed since the destruction, and vivid memories of the Holy Temple lived on in the heart of each man. They regarded the destruction as a temporary phenomenon, for the hope of rebuilding seemed so real and practical to them that they regarded it as being only a matter of days. In fact, four of the five sages who participated in that Bnei Brak Seder were priests or Levites who actually served in the Holy Temple, and the Talmud relates a number of anecdotes and laws relating to their service in the time of the Temple.

Rabbi Joshua ben Hananiah: A Singer in the Levitical Choir

"It once occurred that Rabbi Joshua ben Hananiah went to assist Rabbi Yohanan ben Gudgada with the doors of the Temple. But the latter instructed him: 'My son, turn aside! For you are a singer, and not a gatekeeper!'" (BT Arakhin 11:B). This incident indicates that Rabbi Joshua was numbered amongst the Levites who sang on the platform in the Holy Temple.

Even after the Temple was destroyed, the priestly and levitical families preserved their traditions regarding the various watches, and the official duties which they attended to when the Temple was standing were passed down in family tradition. This fact—that Rabbi Joshua was a member of one of the families that peopled that levitical choir—is mentioned in the Talmud in the context of a question that had been raised regarding one who left his position in the Temple. For example, the Talmud asks, what is the law regarding a Levite who was a singer, but went to assist with the doors? The Talmud's conclusion: "A singer who acted as gatekeeper is punishable with death."

The logistic circumstances which could create this problem are only possible on one occasion during the year—on the 14th day of Nisan, when the Passover sacrifice is brought to the Temple. Every other day of the year, the gates of the Temple are closed at the conclusion of the day's service, and the Levite gatekeepers would pass from gate to gate, bolting the doors. But when the Passover sacrifice is offered, and within a very short period of time, three different groups were necessitated to open and close the gates, in addition to their task of keeping order in the courtyard between those entering the Sanctuary and those leaving it through the courtyard's thirteen gates—on this day, they had a great deal of work to do. It was natural that many extra Levites were required for the doors. It would certainly be possible that those Levites who stood atop the platform,

The First Passover Sacrifice, in Egypt When the Children of Israel left Egypt, the Passover lamb was hurriedly sacrificed, for the Egyptians pressed them to leave immediately. In the picture, a household member uses a hyssop branch to place some of the blood on the doorposts and lintel of the house, as God commanded. The other family members can be seen eating of the Passover sacrifice, and in the center we discern one participant who eats with his belt girded about him; he wears his shoes on his feet and holds his walking stick in his hand—ready to depart Egypt. The wife is busy kneading dough to prepare the *matzot* that they will take with them on their trek. Some family members are dressed in traditional Israelite garb—for we are taught that the Jews retained their own style of dress while in Egypt—but others here have donned the Egyptian style of dress, for the verse states: "And a woman shall ask from her neighbor. . . silver and gold utensils, and garments; and you shall place them upon your sons and daughters" (Exodus 3:22).

XVIII

The Passover Sacrifice The Passover lamb could be slaughtered either by the priests, or the Israelite who brings the offering. Special rings which were set into the floor of the courtyard facilitated this process, and enabled the sacrificial service to proceed with greater speed and ease.

The Blood of the Sacrifice is Sprinkled The priest standing closest to the altar takes the blood of the Passover lamb and sprinkles it on the foundation of the altar.

two more; "and with wonders"—another two. These are the Ten Plagues which the Holy One, blessed be He, brought upon the Egyptians in Egypt, and here they are: Blood, Frogs, Vermin, Beasts, Pestilence, Boils, Hail, Locusts, Darkness, the Slaying of the Firstborn.

And He brought us out from there, as it states: "And the Lord brought us forth out of Egypt."

PESACH, MATZAH, and MAROR

Rabban Gamliel used to say, Whoever does not mention these three things on Passover has not fulfilled his obligation, and they are: the Passover sacrifice, matzah, and bitter herbs.

The Passover sacrifice—because the Holy One, blessed be He, "passed over" our fathers' houses in Egypt, as it is said: "And you shall say, it is the sacrifice of the Lord's Passover, who passed over the houses of the Children of Israel in Egypt, when he smote the Egyptians, and delivered our houses. And the people bowed the head and worshipped" (Exodus 12:27).

This matzah—because we have been redeemed, as it is written: "And they baked unleavened cakes of the dough which they had brought forth out of Egypt, for it was not leavened; because they were thrust out of Egypt, and could not tarry, neither had they prepared for themselves any victuals" (Exodus 12:39).

This bitter herb—because the Egyptians embittered our fathers' lives in Egypt, as it is said: "And they made their lives bitter with hard bondage, in mortar and in brick, and in all manner of labor in the field; all their labor was imposed on them with rigor" (Exodus 1:14).

The Exodus in Every Generation

In every generation, each person is obligated to regard himself as if he personally came out of Egypt, as it is said: "And you shall tell your son on that day, saying, this is because of what the Lord God did for me, when I came forth out of Egypt" (Exodus 13:8).

Giving Thanks

So let us thank, praise, laud, glorify, exalt, and honor Him who did all these miracles for our fathers and for ourselves, and who brought us out from slavery to freedom. And let us declare before Him, Hallelujah!

Hallel—Praise

Praise, O you servants of the Lord, praise the name of the Lord. Blessed be the name of the Lord from this time forth and for evermore. . . . Tremble, earth, at the presence of the Lord, at the presence of the God of Jacob; who turned the rock into standing water, the flint into a fountain of waters.

The Blessing of Redemption

Blessed are You, O Lord our God, King of the universe, who has redeemed us and our fathers from Egypt and has brought us to this night on which we eat [the Passover sacrifice,] matzah and bitter herbs. O Lord our God and God of our fathers, may we live to celebrate in peace other festivals and holy seasons, joyful in the building of Your city and happy in Your service. And there may we eat of the sacrifices and Passover offerings, whose blood shall be acceptably sprinkled on the side of Your altar; then we shall sing to You a new song for our redemption. Blessed are You, O Lord, who has redeemed Israel!

The Blessing for *Korekh*

Blessed are You, O Lord our God, King of the universe, who has sanctified us with His commandments, and commanded us to eat [the Passover sacrifice,] matzah and bitter herbs on this night, to recall the might of the King, the King of kings, Blessed be He, who performed miracles for our fathers in this time, for the sake of Abraham, Isaac and Jacob. Blessed are You, O Lord, who remembers the covenant.

Blessed are You, O Lord our God, King of the universe, who brings forth bread from the earth. Amen.

Eating of the Festival Sacrifice

[Blessed are You, O Lord our God, King of the universe, who has sanctified us with His commandments, and commanded us to eat the sacrifice. All partake of the meat from the sacrifice of the 14th of Nisan.]

Eating the Passover Sacrifice

[Blessed are You, O Lord our God, King of the universe, who has sanctified us with His commandments, and commanded us to eat the Passover sacrifice. All eat from the Passover sacrifice.]

This version of the *Haggadah*, found in the Cairo *Genizah*, appears to be the preserved text which was used in the Temple era, with some slight modifications.

IV. The "Haggadah of the Holy Temple"

As mentioned previously, throughout the era of the First and Second Temples, there was no established or fixed version of the Passover *Haggadah*. Rather, the main points of the text were transmitted orally, and everyone was free to recite it in any manner they felt comfortable with. In this way, the leader of the Seder could adapt the *Haggadah* to suit his family's level of understanding. This is reflected by the language of the rabbis of the Mishnah, who stated, "a father should teach his son according to the latter's understanding" (Pesahim 10:4). Thus, the *Haggadah* was like an informal lesson or talk which a father delivered to all the family members.

This can also be inferred from another statement recorded by the Mishnah—that "the *Haggadah* opens with words of degradation, and concludes with praise." These instructions seem to indicate that the sages saw fit to establish the main points of the Seder only, but left the actual presentation of the *Haggadah*'s contents up to each man, to be recited in the manner he finds most natural. An open license of interpretation is even granted for the important portion of "my father was a homeless Aramean," and each person is required to recite these passages according to the ability of his own understanding—again, an idea substantiated by the Mishnah: "a man should expound (which literally means a freestyle type of presentation) from the beginning of 'my father. . .' until he finishes the entire section."

The actual version of the "Haggadah of Exile" only received its format after the Temple was destroyed—and in all probability, this transpired at the Seder in Bnei Brak, under the auspices of Rabbi Akiva, when all the varied interpretations were gathered together, and a standardized redaction was edited and approved.

The Haggadah from the Temple Era

The rendition of the *Haggadah* presented below is an ancient one, and was found in manuscript form in the famed Cairo *Genizah* (collection of hidden books). By all indications, this was the *Haggadah* which was recited in the time of the Holy Temple, but with slight alterations that were added following the Temple's destruction, that were necessitated by the new reality of exile. This *Haggadah* is reprinted here as it was published by Daniel Goldshmidt in his book, *The Development of the Passover Haggadah*. This also conforms with the manuscript extant at Dropsie College, Philadelphia.

The text is certainly quite ancient. However, for some inexplicable reason, Mr. Goldshmidt attributes the text's authorship to the Karaites. From its contents, it is clear that this *Haggadah*, despite its brevity, contains many instances of rabbinic interpretations and analysis—just as they appear in Midrashim of the Oral Tradition. Thus, there is no basis whatsover for attributing this abbreviated text to those suspected of Karaite tendencies.

In any event, this short text reflects the style of the *Haggadah* that Israel was accustomed to recite during the era of the Holy Temple. It also includes some changes which had been introduced as a result of the exile, and we have included these additions here in square brackets, in an attempt to provide a reasonable picture of the complete "Temple *Haggadah*." These additions are culled from the words of the sages, Maimonides, and the commentators of the *Haggadah*, and they are discussed in the course of this historical overview as well as in our own commentary. These things were apparently woven into the *Haggadah*'s recital during the era of the Temple.

We have also provided titles for the *Haggadah*'s various sections, and placed emphasis on those sentences which are unique to the text of the "Temple *Haggadah*." These are the sentences that deal with customs relating to eating the festival and Passover sacrifices which are eaten on the Seder night, and which must be mentioned when the Holy Temple is standing.

The inclusion of the post-destruction additions to the "Temple *Haggadah*" will be readily understood in view of the text's extremely concise format. In the following section, we shall present a list of these additions, and associate each with the particular sage who authored it. Together, these comprise the "*Haggadah* of Exile," while the remaining hymns, appearing at the *Haggadah*'s conclusion, are a much later addition, having been authored over the course of many generations.

A Restoration of "The Haggadah of the Holy Temple"

An Invitation to Partake of the Passover Sacrifice
[This is the bread of affliction which our fathers ate in the land of Egypt. Let all who are hungry enter and eat, and all who are needy come and celebrate the Passover!]

The Questions
Why is this night different from all other nights? On all other nights we do not dip even once, but on this night twice. On all other nights we eat either *hametz* or matzah, but on this night only matzah. On all other nights we eat meat either roasted, boiled or cooked, but tonight only roasted. A father teaches his son according to the latter's understanding.

And You Shall Tell Your Son
What does the wise son say? He asks: "What are the testimonies, statutes, and judgments which the Lord our God has commanded you?" In reply, you should teach him all the ordinances of the Passover [sacrifice], ending with "Do not serve *afikoman* (dessert) after the Passover lamb."

Now, one might think that it is possible to begin relating the story of the Exodus from the first day of the month of Nisan onward—"all of this" limits it to the time when [the Passover sacrifice,] the matzah and *maror* are laid out before you.

Open with Degradation
". . .Your fathers dwelled on the other side of the river (the Euphrates) in olden times, even Terah, the father of Abraham, and the father of Nachor, and they served other gods. And I took your father Abraham from the other side of the river, and let him go throughout all the land of Canaan, and multiplied his seed, and gave him Isaac; and I gave to Isaac, Jacob and Esau; and I gave Mount Seir to Esau to possess it; but Jacob and his children went down into Egypt" (Joshua 24:2–4).

Blessed be He who fulfills His promise to Israel! Blessed be He! For the Holy One [For the Holy One, blessed be He,] determined the end of the captivity so that He could fulfill what He had said to Abraham our forefather in the "Covenant between the Portions": "And He said to Abram, Know of a surety that your seed shall be a stranger in a land which is not theirs, and shall serve them, and they shall afflict them four hundred years."

And this same promise has stood by our fathers and ourselves. For not only one man has risen up against us; but in every generation there are those who have risen up against us to destroy us. But the Holy One, blessed be He, has delivered us out of their hands!

"My Father Was a Homeless Aramean"
Go and learn what Laban the Aramean sought to do to our father Jacob! For Pharaoh ordered the destruction of the male children only, while Laban intended to uproot everything! As it is said: "The Aramean sought to destroy my father; and he went down into Egypt, and sojourned there, few in number, and there he became a nation, great and mighty, and numerous" (Deuteronomy 26:5). "And he went down into Egypt," impelled by the word of God, "and sojourned there, few in number, and there he became a nation, great and mighty, and numerous. And the Egyptians ill-treated us, and afflicted us, and laid hard bondage upon us. Then we cried to the Lord God of our fathers, and the Lord heard our voice, and saw our affliction, our sorrow and our oppression."

Conclude with Praise
"And the Lord brought us forth out of Egypt with a mighty hand and with an outstretched arm; with great terror and with signs and with wonders" (Deuteronomy 26:8)—not through an angel, not through a seraph and not through a messenger, but the Holy One, blessed be He, alone and in His glory. "With a mighty hand"—this is two; "and with an outstretched arm"—another two; "with great terror"—another two; "and with signs"—

The Passover Lamb and Slaughtering Knife are Brought to the Temple on the Holy Sabbath When the 14th of Nisan falls on the Sabbath, the knife cannot be carried about, and so the pilgrim weaves the knife into the lamb's wool, thus transporting the instrument to the Holy Temple.

Taking all this confusion and deliberate miscalculation into consideration, it is no wonder that some laws had been forgotten by the time the Pharisees finally regained control of the Sanhedrin a number of years after this era.

The Pharisees Reestablish the Sanhedrin, and the Day of Passover Is Fixed: A Day of Rejoicing Is Declared

Over a period of several years, Simeon ben Shetah was successful in gradually changing the Sanhedrin's character, until finally all of its members were once again Pharisees. The date is even recorded as cause for celebration (Megillat Ta'anit, ch. 10): on the 28th of the month of Tevet, the Sanhedrin ceased to be a group of simpletons and Sadducees, and was transformed into an assembly of great Torah scholars. "The day the Sanhedrin of Sadducees was disbanded and the true Sanhedrin once again sat in session . . . was established as a holiday" (ibid.).

The 28th of Tevet was celebrated not only on account of the Sanhedrin's reinstatement—it was the Torah's honor that had been reinstated as well. And this day was not the only holiday that was observed, for the date of the Festival of Passover, which had been a point of contention between the Sadducees and Pharisees, could now be kept as well. This in itself became a cause for public rejoicing.

(Right) **In the Courts of the Holy Temple—When the 14th of Nisan Falls on the Sabbath** When the 14th day of Nisan (the eve of Passover) falls on the Sabbath, three groups must remain within the Temple precincts throughout the day. The pilgrims sit alongside their sacrifice within the courtyard for the duration of the day, in order to prevent them from carrying it within the city (carrying is prohibited on the Sabbath day). Once the first group has brought their offering, they sit within the Temple Mount limits until the conclusion of the Sabbath. The second group sits within the *cheil* (the area of the stairs, beyond the *soreg* latticework fence). The third group stands within the court itself (at the top of the steps) until dark. At the conclusion of the Sabbath, all go their own way, off to roast the Passover sacrifice in the special ovens prepared throughout Jerusalem for this purpose.

III. In the Days of Hillel the Elder: When the Passover Sacrifice Was Offered on the Sabbath Day

All who are familiar with the Passover *Haggadah* know that the name of Hillel is inexorably bound up with the *Haggadah* itself, on account of his famous custom, re-enacted at the Seder to this very day, to make a "sandwich" of a portion of the Passover sacrifice together with matzah and bitter herb, and to eat them together in this manner.

Another great halakhic (legal) innovation which was enacted by Hillel concerned what is done if the 14th day of Nisan falls on Shabbat, the holy Sabbath. The sages of Hillel's day had been unclear as to what the proper conduct should be in these circumstances—indeed, the Great Sanhedrin, the High Court of the Jewish people, had forgotten the details of the necessary procedure as mandated by biblical law for this particular scenario. The leaders had no idea whether or not the Passover sacrifice should be offered on the Sabbath—for perhaps the laws of the Sabbath superseded the requirement to bring the Passover offering to the Temple?

How did it occur that the entire body of leadership forgot what to do if the festival of Passover falls on the Sabbath? The Talmud (BT Pesahim 61:A) relates the details of this story:

"The presidency of the Sanhedrin forgot this law. Then, it once occurred that the 14th of Nisan (the day prescribed by Scripture to offer the Passover sacrifice) did indeed fall on a Sabbath. They simply did not recall whether or not the sacrifice could be offered on the Sabbath. They said: 'Isn't there anyone who knows what to do?'

"The sages were informed that one man who returned from Babylon, Hillel the Babylonian, had been the attendant of the two great luminaries of that generation, Shemaiah and Avtalyon—and it was said that he knew the answer. They sent for him, and asked him, 'Do you know if the laws of Passover overpower those of the Sabbath?'

"Hillel replied: 'Is it only the Passover sacrifice which takes precedence over the Sabbath?! After all, there are several hundred holiday sacrifices which are brought during the year, on days which sometime fall on Shabbat, and yet they are offered nonetheless. . . .'

"They asked him: 'How can you prove that you are correct?' And so he proved through biblical exegesis and logic that his position was indeed correct; that the Passover sacrifice should be offered on the Sabbath. He sat and expounded on the laws of Passover all that day, while all the sages sat spellbound. They immediately appointed him president of the Sanhedrin.

"The other sages further asked Hillel, 'Our Master! If one forgot to bring the knife to the Temple before the onset of the Sabbath, how should he then conduct himself?' (Since it is forbidden to carry objects from one domain to another on the holy Sabbath.) He told them that he recalled having once heard a ruling on this very question, but he forgot it because of an instant of pride. But, Hillel continued, since all of Israel are considered as the sons of prophets, he instructed them as follows: 'Tomorrow, he whose Passover offering is a lamb, let him set the knife in its wool (and thus the animal would carry it by itself). He who has chosen a kid as his offering (which has no wool), let him set the knife between its horns.' The next day, when Hillel saw the scene spread before him—Israel having followed his intuitive instructions—he recalled, 'Now I remember! This is exactly what I heard from my masters, Shemaiah and Avtalyon!'"

The meaning of this entire story is extremely elusive. For Passover to fall on the Sabbath is not such a rare occurrence—indeed, it repeats itself once every few years, and the Jerusalem Talmud (Pesahim 6:A) emphatically states that it is absolutely impossible for this configuration not to occur at least once in fourteen years—as a minimum. There was never an instance wherein the Passover offering was not brought to the Holy Temple because it coincided with the Sabbath. What then is the meaning of these statements—that all the leaders, and the heads of the Sanhedrin, forgot the law? Obviously, there is a deeper message behind this teaching—and we must endeavor to understand the backdrop of this historical period in order to penetrate the mystery.

The Sect of Sadducees Establish a Sanhedrin

From various talmudic references we learn that twice during an approximate 100-year period toward the close of the Second Temple, the kings who ruled over Israel during those times had all the sages of the Sanhedrin executed—once during the reign of Alexander Yannai, and once again in the days of Herod.

It is recorded that "King Yannai had all of the Sanhedrin's wise men killed; the world was in great shock, until finally the sage Simeon ben Shetah came and restored the knowledge of the Torah" (BT Kiddushin 66:A). And: "King Herod extinguished the light of the world" by killing off all of the great sages, except for one, Bava ben Buta, whom he blinded (BT Bava Batra 3:B).

It is obvious that the killing of the spiritual leaders of Israel on two separate occasions, within such a short period of time, had a most detrimental effect on the spiritual life and development of the nation as a whole. This action would be enough to bring the study of Torah and the observance of its commandments to a virtual halt, on both a national and individual level, out of fear of governmental reprisal. And we must not forget that the method of teaching and transmission of Jewish knowledge and tradition during this period was entirely oral in nature—information was repeated and passed down from master to student. Even under the best of circumstances, this method could potentially leave a great deal open to errors in communication, confusion, forgetting or misunderstandings—and now, with the sudden severance of the entire echelon which possessed this knowledge, such breakdown was inevitable. It was more than inevitable: *it was the very result desired by the rulers.*

Although this very period in question—dominated by corrupt rulers such as Yannai, Hyrcanus, Aristobulus and Herod—also saw great spiritual leaders such as Simeon ben Shetah, Shemaiah and Avtalyon, and Hillel and Shammai, we can easily understand how the interruption of the authentic transmission of knowledge and dismantling of the authentic Sanhedrin for several decades could easily wreak havoc on the nation's spiritual life. This is enough to explain how it was possible for the law pertaining to Passover falling on the Sabbath to have been even temporarily forgotten from the body of Israel.

It should also be noted that during this period, the king chose men from the sects of Sadducees and Boethusians who would remain loyal to him, and with these he peopled the "Sanhedrin." These men deliberately enacted legislation that changed the accepted customs which had been practiced for generations.

The Saducean and Boethusian Sanhedrin Celebrates the Passover Sacrifice on Friday

After Alexander Yannai put all the members of the original Sanhedrin to death, the sages Simeon ben Shetah and Judah ben Tabbai succeeded in escaping from the Holy Land, and by so doing saved their lives. Only after some years passed, King Yannai allowed himself to be somewhat appeased—this thanks to his wife, Queen Salome Alexandra (Simeon ben Shetah's sister)—and only then, Simeon ben Shetah returned from his exile (Genesis Rabbah 91).

But the Sanhedrin, under Saducean domination, continued to issue their own legal rulings for years—rulings which contradicted the original and authentic teachings of the Torah as revealed to Moses on Mount Sinai, and safeguarded in the traditions of the Pharisees. During this period, the Sadducees arranged the calendar so that the 14th of Nisan, Passover eve—when the offering must be brought—*would always fall on a Friday.* They did this because of the way in which the Sadducees and Boethusians interpreted the Scripture (Leviticus 23:15), "And you shall count for yourselves *from the morrow after the Sabbath*, from the day that you brought the *omer* of the wave offering, seven complete sabbaths shall there be. . . ." Since these groups did not accept as valid the traditional Pharasaic interpretation of the Torah, they believed that the intention of this Scripture by the words "from the morrow after the Sabbath" is to teach that the first day of the week—Sunday—is "the morrow after the Sabbath."

There were two factors that led up to this situation, wherein the straightforward and clear *halakhah*—that the Passover sacrifice can be offered any day of the week, including the Sabbath—was forgotten. Firstly, during the years of Israel's domination by cruel and vicious kings, the Torah world had been virtually destroyed. This caused many laws and traditions to be forgotten. Secondly, the Sadducees' administration of the Sanhedrin created new "facts"—they arranged the calendar so that the first day of Passover would always fall on a date that would enable the first day of *hol ha-mo'ed* (the intermediate festival days) to fall on Sunday.

in the bringing of the firstfruits, together with the entire nation—showed his disinterest in the service.

In summary, the Second Temple era was filled with ups and downs. The Jewish people did know greatness and spiritual supremacy during these days as well. Generally, the Passover sacrifice was attended by great High Priests and the revered scholars of Israel. But occasionally, as we have seen, the leaders were not fit for their positions, and this unfortunate situation had a direct effect on what transpired in the Holy Temple on festivals, as well as the year round.

The Great Sage Hillel the Elder Enigmatically Stated: "If I Am Here, Everyone Is Here"

In truth, though there were periods of spiritual morass wherein the kings and High Priests were unworthy, even during these trying times the people of Israel rose above the loathsome mediocrity of the ruling class and clung steadfastly to their scholars and sages. Great rabbis such as Shemaiah and Avtalyon, and Hillel and Shammai, were towering spiritual giants, and served as the example and inspiration for Israel. Thus, the nation flowed en masse to the Temple, and celebrated the festivals in the company of the truly great. The Passover sacrifice, the firstfruits on Shavuot, and the Festival of the Water Libation on Succoth, were all experienced in the company of the great sages of Israel.

In this light, a cryptic statement made by the great Hillel yearly at the joyous gathering of the Water Libation in the Temple courts can finally be understood. At that famous celebration, in the presence of all of Israel, with the great sages and pious saints looking on, Hillel was wont to say: "As long as *I* am here—everyone is here!" (BT Sukkah 53:A).

This was not what it might appear to be—pride or self-flattery. For Hillel the Elder was the paragon of humility, to such an extent that the rabbis even stated: "Let a man forever strive to be as modest as Hillel!" (BT Shabbat 30:B).

Rather, Hillel's statement had an inner meaning. He was speaking in the name of God Himself, as if to say, "As long as the only true 'I' is here—'I Will Be.' As long as the fear of Heaven will be felt in this house; and the High Priests will tend to their holy duties as befitting the descendants of Aaron; and the kings of Israel will conduct themselves here with honor and a feeling of reverance—then, the entire nation of Israel collectively, as one man: 'everyone is here!'" But he would continue: "If *I* am not here . . . if the God of Israel is not here . . . if there is no fear of Heaven in this place—then who is here?"

This is how the greatest Bible commentator, Rashi, interprets Hillel's words. He explains that Hillel would preach to the crowds in the Holy

The Passover Ovens Special ovens were prepared in Jerusalem to roast the Passover sacrifice. One oven could accommodate the roasting of several sacrifices in succession. In this picture, a father and son adjust the fire of the oven, and supervise the roasting of the sacrifice.

Silver and Gold Vessels These were sacred vessels especially designed to gather the blood of the Passover sacrifice, in order to bring it to the altar, in keeping with the commandment. These vessels were constructed in a special manner, without a base, in order to keep the blood inside from hardening—a biblical requirement. Additionally, the vessel has a long handle which allows it to be passed quickly up the line of priests, from one to the other, until reaching the altar.

Temple in this manner, exhorting the people not to sin, and to uphold the honor of God's sacred Name. This is what he meant by "If I am here, everyone is here": (God says:) "As long as I desire this House, and My presence rests in it, its honor will be upheld, and 'everyone'—all of Israel—will be here for the festivals. But if Israel sins and I am forced to remove My presence, 'Who will be here?'—this House will be empty of the festival pilgrims."

Hillel Senses the Upcoming Destruction—and Is Fearful

Hillel was not insensitive to the reality around him. He saw the shape of things to come and realized that the people were bringing inevitable destruction upon themselves. The Talmud records an incident which once occurred on Passover in the Holy Temple during Hillel's time. Although this may appear to be minor, it is in no way insignificant, for Hillel himself surely saw it as a portent which bode ill for all Israel. Despite the general rule that all had ample space in the Temple, as we have learned, that particular year an old man was trampled to death by the rush of pilgrims. The people were in such a hurry to beat each other and complete the service that they did not pay attention to the needs of the elderly to keep a slower pace. Hillel interpreted this as the result of a general negative trend amongst the people; the strong and powerful would now push and shove their way into that most holy of places, without consideration for those who are weak. An incident which was similar in spirit occurred as well, wherein a priest who ran along the altar to do his duties saw that another priest was "gaining on him"—and the former took out a knife and stabbed him in the heart (BT Yoma 23).

This type of conduct, together with a general spiritual decline, causes the *Shechina*—the Divine Presence of God—to depart from Israel. The constant miracles we have mentioned took place in the Holy Temple only during a time that all Israel showed honor and respect for each other; but when individuals sought out their own honor above that of their Creator, and thought only of themselves, without considering the next one, this behavior can cause the *Shechina* to depart.

With his own eyes, the great Hillel witnessed the spiritual bankruptcy of the priesthood continue to plummet in an ever lower progression, as they purchased their office with money. In the realm of the kingship, too, their strife, bickering and civil wars (like that between Hyrcanus and Aristobulus in Jerusalem) caused Hillel grave concern for the future. He began to suspect that the days of the Second Temple were numbered.

For this reason, when all of Israel gathered together in the Temple on Succoth to celebrate the Festival of the Water Libation, the great sage took the opportunity to rebuke the nation as a whole, and remind them that "If *I* am here"—as long as you will all fear the Lord—"Everyone is here." But if the "*I*," the fear of God, is not here, and you battle amongst each other, and the sanctity of the priesthood and kingdom is profaned—who is here, for what is it worth?

living up to the power and promise of our own lives.

The festivals of the Lord are not mere commemorations replete with symbolism and ritual; they present us with the opportunity to reap God's blessing *by connecting with their message.* Thus, it is not enough for Jews to believe that God created the world in six days, a long time ago, and rested on the seventh, and therefore we are obliged to rest on the seventh as well. *Rather, we believe that this process is constant*—that God actually renews the creation every six days. Therefore when we rest on the Sabbath, we bear witness to God's constant sovereignty and power.

The challenge of the festival of Passover is to achieve the level of spiritual birth—by becoming free. On Passover, we do not merely remember the Exodus; we must take the challenge to once again be liberated from Egyptian bondage, from modern Egyptian bondage. For the ancient Pharaoh of Egypt represents the evil inclination which lurks within the heart of every man, and attempts to keep him from serving God, just as the Pharaoh of old tried to keep our ancestors from worshiping the One true God, *and it is that aspect of our lives which we must purge and leave behind.*

On the first Passover, with the Exodus from Egypt, the Jews received their emancipation—in a sense, it was then that they became a nation. It was on that first Passover that they collectively began their life's mission— to spiritually ascend to a level where they could be servants of God, not of man. Thus at the Seder, in the *Haggadah*, we recite that "whoever does not see himself as if he personally left Egypt on this night, has not fulfilled his Passover obligation."

Spiritual Decline in the Days of the Second Temple

In spite of the picture of Jerusalem's spiritual heyday which we have painted, not all of the Second Temple era was a Golden Age of Jewish scholarship and spiritual devotion. There were also difficult periods marked by spiritual decline. Amongst the priestly ranks who served in the Temple, a change took place, too. Some High Priests did not live out their term of office, for these were not men who deserved their position, but corrupt individuals who purchased their title with money and influence.

The rabbis of the Talmud (BT Yoma 9:A) utilized a verse from the Book of Proverbs (10:27) to illustrate the contrast between the First and Second Temple eras: *"The fear of the Lord prolongs days, but the years of the wicked shall be shortened."* The first part of this verse, "The fear of the Lord prolongs days," refers to the pristine days of the First Temple. Although it stood for a total of 410 years, it was overseen by a succession of only twelve High Priests—so great was their righteousness, that they enjoyed great longevity. But the second half of this verse, which reads "but the years of the wicked shall be shortened," is an allusion to the Second Temple, for it stood for 420 years but was presided over by more than 300 High Priests!

Similarly, a spiritual decline was manifest in the kingship of Israel as well. Some kings, such as the allegedly illegitimate, priestly Hasmonean King Alexander Yannai, were not satisfied with the kingdom but tried to gain control over the High Priesthood as well. His audacity knew no bounds, for though it was rumored that he was born out of wedlock, he sought to place the High Priest's crown upon his own head. Finally, the sage Judah ben Gedidyah exhorted him: "Be satisfied with your royal crown! Enough! Leave the Priestly crown for the rightful descendants of Aaron!" (BT Kiddushin 66:B).

Unseemly behavior which does not befit a king is also reported in connection with the Passover sacrifice. Although biblical law specifically instructs that each individual should participate in only one Passover sacrifice, we find the following anecdote recorded in Tractate Pesahim (88:2): "A certain king and queen instructed their servants: 'Go out and slaughter the Passover sacrifice for us.'" The servants brought *two* Passover offerings on their behalf (a kid and a lamb). They then appeared before the king and asked him, "Which would His Majesty prefer to eat from?" He answered, "Go and ask the queen." The queen told them, "Go and ask Rabban Gamliel (the greatest sage) which we should eat." Rabban Gamliel responded, "The king and queen—who are lightheaded—should eat of the first sacrifice. But *we*—we will not eat from the first *or* from the second sacrifice" (for such is the rule established in Jewish law; one is forbidden from participating in, or partaking of more than one Passover sacrifice).

Maimonides, in his commentary to the Mishnah (Pesahim 5:2), explains the background: "Only a king and queen are permitted to eat from the first of two Passover sacrifices. Normally, only one sacrifice may be slaughtered, but these two told their servants to go out and do it for them, *and this ruling is on account of the fact that the rulers are lightheaded and do not adequately humble themselves before the commandments."*

Maimonides' ruling requires clarification. After all, we know that there were also kings and rulers during the time of the Second Temple who were exceedingly just and righteous, and dedicated to God's commandments. For example, the Mishnah informs us that on Shavuot, the Festival of the Bringing of Firstfruits, King Agrippa himself entered into the Temple with a basket of fruits on his shoulder, in the same humble manner which is required of every other man (Bikkurim 3:4). If so, we must but wonder: why did Maimonides interpret the question which was posed to Rabban Gamliel as to which sacrifice should be eaten, as a cynical and haughty question?

A Sign of the Times: The Immature Behavior of Kings and High Priests

But the strange incident of the king and queen, in which they instruct their servants to slaughter the Passover sacrifice on their behalf, can only be understood in the context of the equally enigmatic lesson which precedes it (BT Pesahim 57:A): "The Rabbis taught: . . .the Temple courtyard cried out, 'Issachar of the village of Barkai (the presiding High Priest), get out of here! For he honors himself greatly but profanes God's sacrifices . . . he wraps his hands in silk, and officiates in the Temple.'" (Through his actions he demonstrated his contempt for the Temple service.)

The Talmud gives us the background to this story: there sat a certain Hasmonean king and queen. They argued over which meat is more tasty. The king said, "The kid makes for a delicious meal!" And the queen said, "The lamb is more desirable than that!" They argued and said, "Who will settle this for us?" Finally it hit upon them—"Let the High Priest decide! He must be a culinary expert! After all, he offers up sacrifices from both types every day!"

The High Priest was summoned before the king, and the "important" question was posed to him. He answered the king by first making a haughty and sarcastic gesture with his hand, and then he said, "If the king is correct—that the kid is more delicious—then the Torah would command that the kid should be offered up on the altar every day! But instead, the Torah commands that a sheep should be the daily Temple sacrifice—proving the king is wrong!" (The High Priest Issachar was so arrogant that he was not cautious with his words; he revealed that he actually thought *God* prefers that a more tasty type of meat be offered on the altar!)

The king decided that the Priest must be punished, since he showed contempt for the former's authority, through his gesture and word. He decreed that the Priest's right hand be severed, but Issachar bribed the officer in charge, and the latter severed his left hand instead. When the king found out, he commanded that his right hand be cut off as well.

From this unseemly, bizarre episode we can certainly ascertain that both the kings and High Priests of this particular Second Temple era had sunk to a record low. From their hedonism, arrogance and immaturity, we can see that their morals had decayed to the extent that they functioned in a virtual spiritual vacuum: the High Priest himself, required to be the spiritual conduit for the entire Jewish nation, did not execute his duties faithfully, but showed scorn and disdain for them. And the King of Israel cruelly commanded that the man's hands should be cut off—not because the Temple service was not important to him, and not to serve as a warning to other priests to show respect for the Holy Temple, but because he did not like his answer!

So the subject matter which dominated the palaces of these kings was—which meat is more tasty, kid or lamb? And to substantiate their opinions, they called for none other than the High Priest. The incredible level to which they sank in their foolishness shows us where the kingship lay—in veritable ruin.

In this light, we can understand the previous incident: why the royal servants slaughtered *two* Passover offerings, in contradiction to biblical law, for they knew that they would be executed by the king or queen simply for bringing the one which was not their preference to feast on. Instead the servants chose to violate the commandment and bring two Passover offerings, and thereby get away with their lives.

Additionally, the very fact that the King of Israel commanded a proxy to prepare his Passover offering, rather then tend to it himself together with the rest of his people—like the example of King Agrippa, who participated

II. The Offering of the Passover Sacrifice

The ceremony of offering the Passover sacrifice was one of the most important events in the yearly calendar of Jerusalem's Holy Temple. This was true to such an extent that long after the destruction, its deep and indelible impression was still carried in the hearts of all who were privileged to witness it. The Talmud contains many accounts of both the pilgrimage and the sacrificial ceremony in Second Temple days: the sight of the huge Temple gates opening, and the vast multitudes of joyous celebrants, divided into three groups, streaming into the beautiful and majestic Holy Temple courtyard; blasts are sounded from the trumpets, the Levite choir sings; the Passover sacrifice itself is eaten by everyone together, with a deep feeling of joyous religious freedom; song and *Hallel* prayers of thanksgiving within the walls of Jerusalem—all this helped to transform the Passover experience into the climax of the Jewish year.

"Passover of Density"

Many descriptions are extant which depict all that transpired in the Temple. For example, the sages recorded vivid depictions of the great throngs which pressed into the Temple complex, and of the rows of officiating priests who passed amongst their ranks the special silver and gold containment vessels for gathering the blood of the sacrifice, to sprinkle it upon the altar. These reports give us some idea of the large number of sacrifices that were offered up in the Temple of the One God on this holy day.

While the entire nation of Israel made the pilgrimage to the Holy Temple on each of the sacred festivals, it would seem that the record for participants was set on Passover, with more people arriving in Jerusalem for that festival than any other. One very basic reason for this is the simple fact that the Passover sacrifice is a holy obligation, which by biblical law is incumbent upon both men and women alike. This differs from the other festival offerings, which are only obligatory upon the men of the community. Furthermore, those who do not participate in the Passover offering face a most severe penalty: the biblical penalty of *karet*, literally, "to be cut off," which is interpreted by some to mean premature death, and by others to be an indication of a spiritual demotion in the future world. Clearly, all who had the ability made certain to be among those who arrived in Jerusalem for Passover.

The Talmud offers an example which can serve to illustrate the incredible numbers which converged upon Jerusalem for this holy occasion. It seems that one year, King Agrippa wanted to determine the exact number of pilgrims who arrived to celebrate the Passover, so he hit upon a unique idea for conducting a census. He instructed the High Priest who was officiating in the Temple: "Pay attention to the exact amount of offerings that are brought." And so the Priest set aside the offerings and numbered them . . . until the figure reached a staggering 1,200,000, which is twice the number of the Jews who participated in the Exodus from Egypt. And this figure is still excluding those who were impure, and those who had not arrived in time! Because of these great numbers, each year they would refer to the holiday as "Passover of density" (based on BT Pesahim 64:B).

Despite Their Great Numbers, the Multitudes of Israel Miraculously Enter the Temple Courts Simultaneously

Obviously, in order to successfully absorb the sudden influx of such a huge number of people, it was necessary to make many technical and logistical arrangements—for the preparation of the city of Jerusalem in general and the Holy Temple complex in particular. As we mentioned, one of the most important innovations on a municipal level was the introduction of many Passover ovens in many locations, to enable everyone to promptly roast the Passover sacrifice after it was offered in the Temple, in preparation for the Seder later that evening.

Imagine the atmosphere of the Holy City during this most special season! Small wonder that the famed "Chapters of the Fathers" (Pirkei Avot, ch. 5) lists Jerusalem's transformed holiday state as one of the ten miracles which occurred during the great era of the Holy Temple: "No man ever had reason to complain, 'Jerusalem is too crowded for me to find lodgings overnight.'" All found a place within the confines of the ancient walled city—for indeed, the biblical commandment requires that all of Israel eat of the Passover sacrifice within Jerusalem's walls; it is forbidden to partake of the Passover outside. Another miracle was the conditions within the Temple itself, for it is recorded (ibid.) that "while standing in the courtyard of the Holy Temple, all would be pressed close together . . . but yet when it came time to bow prostrate, all would have ample room." It seems that the very physicality of Jerusalem itself was transformed into the stuff of raw spiritual experience, catapulting all its inhabitants into another, more rarified dimension. No person ever found Jerusalem to be crowded, even under the circumstances we have described—when those who descended upon Jerusalem reached one million and more, with all their very real needs of lodging and space—for the city itself transcended the physical and achieved an all-encompassing ethereal, universal theme.

The Temple Half-Shekel In the Holy Temple era, each member of the community of Israel brings a contribution of one half-shekel to the Temple. This is required once a year, and these funds are used to purchase the congregational sacrifices for the coming year. On the first day of the month of Adar, a proclamation was issued that the time to bring this contribution had arrived. Stations for receiving this donation were established in the Temple as well as in all the cities throughout the land. The festival pilgrims then collected all the funds from their countrymen, and brought the money with them up to the Temple.

The Passover sacrifice differed from all others that were brought to the Temple throughout the year, in that the ordinary Israelites who brought them participated in the preparation of the animal for sacrifice. Although a delegation of Israelites stood in the Temple and accompanied every service, generally only the priests had an active role in the sacrificial service itself. Thus the Passover offering was particularly special in that it provided one of the few occasions when the ordinary people could enter the Temple's inner court, where the altar stood.

It was necessary to conduct the service with great precision and zeal in order to ensure that all the festive offerings were accommodated within the prescribed time. In the Mishnah, the rabbis describe the speed and efficiency with which the sacrifices were carried out.

The Joyous Feeling in Jerusalem

The overwhelming sense of joy and elation in Jerusalem itself knew no bounds. It permeated every street, every courtyard, every house. . . ; the homes were filled to capacity with family and guests from far and wide, an unparalleled feeling of belonging and brotherhood encompassed all the participants, and their great sentiment of freedom and redemption was the unsurpassed height of true religious experience. Jerusalem veritably rang out with song and the holy, intense celebration of life lived in religious freedom and Divine purpose. Indeed, a popular expression in the Talmud coined by the rabbis recalls that the very walls of Jerusalem shook and "the roofs were shattered" from the sounds of joy as the Passover sacrifice was eaten and songs of *Hallel* thanksgiving burst forth from every house and courtyard at midnight.

The Jewish Concept of Time

Let us reflect for a moment on the Jewish concept of time and festival commemoration, which differs drastically from people's general notion of time. For when the Jewish people are entrusted to commemorate the biblical festivals, it is not a question of remembering something that happened once upon a time, long ago; on the contrary, it is happening again right now, and we are exhorted—and challenged—to relive it! Thus the blessing which is recited on these sacred seasons of the Lord reads, "In those days, *in this time*. . ."—for the challenge of life is for us to latch on to the potential for spiritual growth inherent in these days, and sanctify God,

Preparing these ovens was a huge project which took months of effort and coordination. A well-known passage in the Mishnah (Tractate Ta'anit 3:8) describes what transpired during one year of dearth: "They told Honi the Circlemaker (a saint of great renown): 'We beseech you, pray for rain!' He told them, 'Go and bring all the Passover ovens indoors, so they will not be ruined.' He then prayed for rain—and the rains fell in such plenty that all of Jerusalem's population hurried to the Temple Mount to seek shelter under its awnings and balconies." This was toward the end of the winter, and many of the clay ovens had already been set in their places in anticipation of the upcoming festival.

Maimonides (1135 – 1204), great codifier of Jewish law, sums up in his ever-lucid fashion the acceptable reasons for postponing Passover and declaring a leap year: "The court could see fit to declare a leap year out of necessity caused by certain circumstances. If the state of the roads is so damaged that the pilgrims do not have proper access, the extra month is instituted until the rains cease and the roads can be repaired. Likewise, if bridges are out and the rivers prevent passage, endangering the travelers, time must be granted until they can be set to right. The same action is warranted, too, if the ovens have been ruined and the people do not have the facilities to roast the sacrifices. And if word comes that the exiles have left their homes and are in transit—but have not yet reached Jerusalem—a leap year will be declared to enable them to arrive" (Laws of the New Month, 4:5).

"Arise, and Let Us Go Up to Zion!"

A vivid eye-witness description of the vast numbers of pilgrims making their way to Jerusalem from the far-flung corners of the Jewish exile is recorded by Philo of Alexandria (circa 20 BCE – 50 CE), a leader of the great Jewish community of Alexandria, Egypt, toward the end of the Second Temple era. He writes: "Multitudes of people *from a multitude of cities* flow in an endless stream to the Holy Temple for each festival . . . from the east and west, from the north and south" (On Laws 1:96).

Faced with the importance of the event and the amount of people involved, we can readily understand how no effort was spared to make certain that all would be ready for the arrival of the festival pilgrims in Jerusalem—on time. The great rabbis and leaders of Israel sought at all costs to avoid a situation wherein these travelers would find themselves stranded on the open roads on the 14th of Nisan—the day God commanded the Passover offering to be sacrificed.

An atmosphere of great joy and comraderie prevailed all along the way to Jerusalem, imbuing both the travelers and their co-religionists who waited for their arrival in the Holy City itself with a deep feeling of unity. The Mishnah (Tractate Bikkurim 3:2) provides a colorful description of the caravans of pilgrims in procession as they make their way to a way station in one of the field cities on the road to Jerusalem: "The populace who live in the vicinity of the Assembly Head (who is responsible for the priests and Levites, and also for the pilgrimage to Jerusalem) gather together in his home town, and everyone sleeps the night outdoors, in the town's streets. They do not enter into the houses (to circumvent becoming exposed to ritual impurity). Waking them in the morning, the overseer would cry out: 'Arise, and let us go up to Zion, to the House of the Lord our God!' (Jeremiah 31:5)."

Those Who Were Held Up in Modi'in and Could Not Arrive in Time

As the time of the festival drew closer, the great processions of pilgrims swelled in numbers. While a number of roads furnished access to Jerusalem in those days, the main route of the pilgrims from the Jordan Valley passed through the city of Modi'in and then continued past Beth Horon.

In the Mishnah (Tractate Pesahim 9:1 – 2) a legal question is deliberated by the sages—what should those travelers do who, on the morning of the 14th day of Nisan (the very day in which the Divine commandment to offer the Passover sacrifice in Jerusalem is binding), still find themselves out on the road, far from their destination?

From the discussion itself, we can surmise that this indeed was no small problem, that a great many people were still far from Jerusalem, out on the roads leading up to the city, on the morning of the 14th of Nisan. The Mishnah considers the plight of these people, those who are "far away," who had only now reached the outskirts of the city of Modi'in. Modi'in is located at a distance of "15 *mil*" (a biblical measurement—approximately 18 kilometers, or 11 miles) from Jerusalem. The sages considered this distance as being far enough to prohibit these unfortunate pilgrims from arriving on time to offer the sacrifice, and therefore they established the law as follows: "Whoever finds themselves at Modi'in or beyond at dawn on the morning of the 14th of Nisan—and is therefore prevented from offering up the Passover sacrifice on time, together with the rest of Israel—may offer it on the 'Second Passover,' one month later on the 14th of Iyar, as prescribed by the Torah (Numbers 9)."

The Talmud mentions several examples of situations whereby a man might find himself in the vicinity of Modi'in, or at some other locality whose distance is "15 *mil*" from Jerusalem. For example, a case is discussed pertaining to a man who was "*outside* of Modi'in, but could make it to Jerusalem by horse—what should he do?" And in another scenario: "He was already *past* Modi'in (closer to Jerusalem), but could not make it any further because the caravans of camels and wagons were blocking his way—what should he do?"

These examples give us some idea of the crowded conditions caused by the massive influx of so many pilgrims making their way to the city. Those locals who lived nearby, and did not make it to Jerusalem on time, had but to return to their homes, and to make the trip again next month—but what of those who had already traveled from great distances and yet were prevented for some reason from reaching their destination? They had to remain in the area for a full month, until the 14th of Iyar, when they could bring the offering of the "Second Passover"—only afterward did they return to their homes. Of course, most of the congregation *did* manage to arrive in Jerusalem in time, and these people were warmly welcomed with great honor by the citizens and elders of the city, who provided the weary pilgrims with lodgings in their homes and courtyards.

Cedar Wood, Hyssop and Crimson Wool Pictured in the hand of a priest, ready to be thrown into the flames, for the preparation of the red heifer's ashes.

Preparation of the Water for the Solution of the Ashes A priest mixes spring water—brought from the Shiloh Spring—into the ashes of the heifer. Together they comprise the biblical formula for reinstating ritual purity. The vessels used for this process are specially made of stone, since this is the only material impervious to the penetration of ritual impurity.

A Sprig of Hyssop This is used to sprinkle the ashes from a stone vessel.

HAGGADAH OF THE HOLY TEMPLE

I. Jerusalem Prepares for the Festival Pilgrims' Arrival

To be in Jerusalem for Passover! This was the one objective, as the entire Jewish nation converged on Jerusalem from all corners of the ancient world to celebrate in the Holy City. Those who had made their home in the Holy Land itself, these had a comparatively easy journey. Some came from neighboring lands, such as Egypt and Babylon, while others traveled great distances—from the east, Persia and Media; and from the west, Greece and Cyrene. Some even traveled from as far away as Rome to be in Jerusalem for the festival. The pilgrims came in caravans, numbering hundreds of participants—sometimes thousands. Each group brought the obligatory "half-shekel" donation to the Temple treasury, on behalf of their respective constituency.

The famed Jewish historian of the Temple era, Josephus Flavius, describes the danger these festival pilgrims faced as they made their way: highwaymen and robbers lay in wait to ambush them, for they knew of the money the caravans carried for the Temple in Jerusalem, and they sought to plunder it. Accordingly, the Jews traveled in large, armed groups whenever possible. The processions had to travel for weeks and sometimes months at a time—meanwhile, Jerusalem busied itself with the task of preparing for the massive arrival.

Access Roads to Jerusalem

Preparations in Jerusalem for the influx of such large numbers began early. On the first day of Adar, a full six weeks before the festival, special agents appointed by the rabbinical court went about the countryside "to repair the roads, squares, and *mikva'ot* (ritual baths), and to ensure that the gravesites were properly marked" (to protect the pilgrims from exposure to ritual impurity—Mishnah Shekalim 1:1). After the rainy winter, it was important to make sure that the roads were not washed out, and all the approaches to Jerusalem were traversable. Likewise, the city squares and public areas along the way were cleared, so that they could function as way stations where the pilgrims might spend the night and replenish their supplies along their arduous journey.

Special supervisors were appointed by the Temple to ensure that an adequate number of wells were prepared along the roads, and *mikva'ot* were set up to enable the pilgrims to immerse themselves in accordance with biblical law, and thereby arrive in the Holy City in a state of purity.

The Court Postpones Passover

Upon occasion, more time was required in order to complete these preparations. There were instances when the rabbinical court found it necessary to postpone the observance of Passover by one month in order to see to these arrangements. At these times, the worldwide Jewish community was informed by messengers that this would be a leap year.

Such is the testimony we find in the Tosefta (additions to the Mishnah by Rabbi Hiyya and Rabbi Oshia—circa 230 CE) on Tractate Sanhedrin (2:5): "It happened once in this very manner . . . Rabban Gamliel and the elders stood upon an elevation on the Temple Mount, while Yohanan the Scribe waited upon them. They dictated to him: 'Write the following missive to our Israelite brothers in Upper and Lower Galilee, and to our brothers in the south, and in the Bablyonian exile, and the Median exile, and in all the places of their dispersions—Peace unto you! We hereby inform you: the sacrificial pigeons are still tender, the sheep are too small, and springtime has not yet arrived . . . therefore my colleagues and I have deemed it proper and fitting to add another 30 days to this year.'"

Another talmudic source spells out the mitigating circumstances by which reason the sages of Israel have the obligation to declare a leap year in order to prepare for Passover: "Our Rabbis have taught, we do not declare a leap year unless such action is necessitated by the following: the roads were ruined by heavy rains, bridges have collapsed and have as yet to be repaired, the ovens for roasting the Passover sacrifice were likewise ruined by water and need additional time to dry, or—because the court has heard that Jews living in the Diaspora have left their homes and begun to make their way to Jerusalem, but obviously will not reach it in time" (BT Sanhedrin 11:A).

Special Passover Ovens Are Prepared in Jerusalem

With all of Israel in their multitudes converging at once to celebrate the Passover, we can imagine the huge throngs making ready to bring their sacrificial offering to the Holy Temple—as required by the God of Israel. Ovens for roasting the Passover sacrifices were set up throughout the city. After the sacrifice is offered, it is taken by each family and group, roasted in a special manner as prescribed by law, and eaten in the evening at the Seder.

Preparation of the Ashes of the Red Heifer In preparation for the festival pilgrimage to the Holy Temple on the holiday of Passover, each Jew must ready himself to arrive at the Temple in a state of purity. This illustration depicts the manner in which the ashes of the red heifer are produced. The priests proceed to the Mount of Anointment, located opposite the Temple Mount, and in that spot they erect a singular altar, on which the red heifer is placed. As one priest prepares to slaughter the heifer, we can see another who makes ready to ignite the fire of the altar, while a third priest stands with cedar wood, hyssop and crimson wool—to be included in the fire of the heifer, as prescribed in the Bible, Numbers 19. A large assembly, including the elders of Israel, looks on and supervises the proceedings.

Purifying with the Ashes A priest uses a sprig of hyssop to purify those who have become ritually unclean. He dips this branch into the solution of pure water and ashes, and sprinkles the solution onto a father and son who have become exposed to the impurity caused by death. This is done on the third and seventh days following the initial exposure, and afterward they must also immerse themselves in the *mikvah*—this concludes the process of purification. They may then offer the Passover sacrifice together with all of Israel.

HISTORICAL OVERVIEW

THE HAGGADAH FROM THE TEMPLE ERA TO THE PRESENT DAY

HAGGADAH OF THE HOLY TEMPLE

I. Jerusalem Prepares for the Festival Pilgrims' Arrival

II. The Offering of the Passover Sacrifice

III. In the Days of Hillel the Elder:
When the Passover Sacrifice Was Offered on the Sabbath Day

IV. The "Haggadah of the Holy Temple"

THE HAGGADAH OF EXILE

V. The "Incident" of Rabbi Eliezer:
The Introduction to the Haggadah

VI. The "Haggadah of the Holy Temple"—
and the "Haggadah of Exile"

VII. The Seder Is Conducted in Rabbi Akiva's City

VIII. The Students and Their Masters in Bnei Brak

IX. "Our Masters! It Is Time to Recite the *Shma*!"

To the Reader:

In keeping with the format of Hebrew books which read from right to left, the text of the Passover Haggadah begins on the other side of this book.

(*Overleaf*) **Three Groups in the Courtyard** Once within the Holy Temple, the festival pilgrims participating in the offering of the Passover sacrifice were divided into three groups. The first group entered, and the Levites locked the gates of the courtyard after them. Other Levites, standing atop the platform, sang the festive *Hallel*, accompanying the prayers with trumpet blasts. The first group of pilgrims concluded their sacrifice and left the courtyard, carrying the lamb on their backs. Thus would the second and third groups enter, attend to their offerings, and leave the Temple.

Co-published by:

The Temple Institute • Carta • Cana — All in Jerusalem

Copyright © 1996
Carta, The Israel Map and Publishing Company Ltd., Jerusalem

All rights reserved. No part of this book may be reprinted or reproduced or utilized in any form or by any electronic, mechanical, or other means now known or hereafter invented, including photocopying and recording, or in any information storage or retrieval system, without permission in writing from the publishers.

Translated from the Hebrew by Chaim Richman

Hebrew script: Ada Yardeni

Design: Eli Kellerman

Editor: Barbara Ball

All the drawings and photographs were prepared specially for this Haggadah by The Temple Institute.

Drawings: George Berdichevsky, Dmitry Baranovsky, Grigory Vechlis, and Michael Putilov

Artisans: Gadi Nataf and Chaim Odem (gold and silver vessels); S. Mishali "Y'dei Uman" (copper vessels); Harrari Family (musical instruments)

Photographs: Ya'acov Harlap

Color separations: Scanli, Tel Aviv

Plates: Printone, Jerusalem

ISBN 965 – 220 – 340 – 8

Printed in Israel

THE PASSOVER HAGGADAH

THE TEMPLE HAGGADAH

Israel Ariel

The Temple Institute
Carta • Cana

THE TEMPLE HAGGADAH